Praise for
Making Cell Grou

"Scott Boren has done an excellent job of laying out the
along each stage of their transition to cell-based m.
contained in this book will help both those churches starting the journey and those needing
mid-course corrections. I highly recommend it."

JOEL COMISKEY
Author, Professor, and Cell Group Consultant

"A traveler on the path to small group ministry needs a clear map, simple directions,
and a working compass. This book helps each traveler design an itinerary that is
appropriate for his or her geography, mode of travel, and desired destination. If you
are a Small Group or Cell Church 'traveler,' don't leave without your map and
compass: *Making Cell Groups Work*."

BILL BECKHAM
Director, TOUCH Global

"All the new creative cell church models that have evolved over the past 10 years have
created the need for a book that brings comparison and clarity. *Making Cell Groups
Work* is a compilation of the best thoughts about the cell church with fresh ideas that
link everything together. Re-learn how it works and glean from Scott's 8-Stage process
for success."

BILLY HORNSBY
Director of the Association of Related Churches

"Most churches implementing a cell vision have experienced short-term success and long-
term disappointment. Finally, we have a practical and comprehensive book that identifies
the critical factors and shows the path to success. Scott Boren gives us a road map that
shows us the potholes and points the way to establishing a vibrant small group system. I
strongly recommend this book to all pastors and leaders who want long-term success with
cells."

JIM EGLI, PH.D.
Author and Small Group Pastor, The Vineyard Church, Champaign, IL

"Wow! In *Making Cell Groups Work*, Scott Boren has developed the most
comprehensive resource for today's cell church that I have yet seen. He provides an
excellent outline of the values, practices, and strategies that have resulted in strong cell
group systems around our world, then suggests processes and steps that provide
workable guidelines for your church, too!"

KAREN HURSTON
Author, Consultant, Director of Hurston Ministries

"The hope for the church of the 21st century is not in buildings, programs, or
showmanship but rather deeply meaningful connections with others centered on Christ.
If this is your belief and a part of your calling, then *Making Cell Groups Work* by Scott
Boren is a must read. It is filled with thick meat to chew on, a balanced diet of
approaches and practical recipes for successful implementation. Bon Appetite!"

RANDY FRAZEE
Pastor, Pantego Bible Church

MAKING CELL GROUPS WORK

MAKING CELL GROUPS WORK

Navigating the Transformation
to a Cell-based Church

M. SCOTT BOREN
with Don Tillman

Cell Group Resources™, a division of TOUCH Outreach Ministries
Houston, Texas, U.S.A.

Published by Cell Group Resources™
10055 Regal Row, Suite 180
Houston, Texas, 77040, U.S.A.
(713) 896-7478 • Fax (713) 896-1874

Cover design by Don Bleyl
Text design by Brandy Egli
Editing by Brandy Egli

International Standard Book Number: 1-880828-43-X

Cell Group Resources™ is a book-publishing division
of TOUCH Outreach Ministries, a resource and
consulting ministry for churches with a vision for cell-
based local church structure.

Find us on the World Wide Web at
http://www.touchusa.org

CONTENTS

Foreword   9
Acknowledgments   11
Introduction   13
Navigational Hazards   27

Stage 1: Discover the Cell Group Vision
    1.1 Discover Cell Group Models   39
    1.2 Discover the Cell Group System   55
    1.3 Discover How Cell Groups Fit in Tomorrow's Church   67
    1.4 Discover How to Lead Change   83

Stage 2: Develop Vision and Strategy as a Team
    2.1 Develop a Vision Team   107
    2.2 Develop Vision and Strategy   119
    2.3 Develop a Cell Group Definition   127

Stage 3: Assess Your Current Reality
    3.1 Assess the Readiness for the Journey   147
    3.2 Assess the Current Small Group System   157
    3.3 Assess to Create Urgency   167

Stage 4: Prepare the Church Through Transformation
4.1 Prepare People Through Transformation   185
4.2 Prepare Individuals for Cell Group Life   199
4.3 Prepare the Corporate Life for Cell Groups   213

Stage 5: Launch the First Groups with Kingdom-seekers
5.1 Launching Strong   235
5.2 Launching Strategies   249

Stage 6: Generate Cell Group Momentum
6.1 Generate Momentum Through Spiritual Community 265
6.2 Strategies for Generating Spiritual Community   281
6.3 Generate Momentum by Developing Leaders   295
6.4 Generate Momentum by Coaching
and Supporting Leaders   311

Stage 7: Establish the Hidden Systems that Support Cells
7.1 Establish Critical Mass   325
7.2 Establish Pastoral Oversight   339
7.3 Establish a Cell Group System Including Children 363

Stage 8: Expand the Cell Groups to Reach the Unreached
8.1 Expand to Re-anchor the Culture   377
8.2 Expansion Strategies   389

Conclusion   409
Notes   411
Index   419

FOREWORD

According to Webster's Dictionary, to navigate is "to plan or compute the course of a vessel or vehicle." *Making Cell Groups Work* is intended to help a congregation sail through unfamiliar waters, moving from a traditional or innovative lifestyle to a New Testament structure. The journey can be fraught with unseen obstacles. Navigation is particularly difficult when there is no map to follow.

A couple of years ago, only a few churches had successfully made the journey to cell group ministry. Observers flocked to visit them. They witnessed the basic Christian communities in action. Upon returning to their traditional church cultures, they had a desire to restructure, to transform, to experience what they had seen elsewhere. But many found that getting from "here" to "there" was not an easy task. One church sailed too fast and lost numerous members. These people left to join a traditional church that had no intention of changing anything. The receiving church had to build a balcony to house the newcomers and jokingly called it, "the space built for us by the church down the road."

The larger the ship, the slower it must turn to head in a new destination. The author of this book has gleaned information from many different sources to provide you and your church with the proper navigational tools. Scott seeks to answer the question, "How does a church go from a traditional program-based structure to working cell groups at the heart of the church?" The eight stages defined in this handbook will guide you. They will also help churches that already have small groups but want to become completely cell-based.

In 1990, I wrote a book similar to this one. It was a "first generation" book that expressed all I knew about cell groups and how they worked. But I could not include what I did not know. The book you hold in your hands is not written by an old man, but a brilliant young man who has been in the cell church movement long enough to be able to blend all the learning he has received from others into a comprehensive and understandable process. He has also inserted his own life experiences and the experiences of countless others who have crossed over from "churchianity" to New Testament basic Christian community. He has done a splendid job!

The term "Bible" is now bandied about, particularly by those who write instructional manuals. Bookstores sell "The Macintosh Bible," "The Screenwriter's Bible," even "The Airbrush Bible!" I have a suspicion that, before you are halfway through with it, you will designate this book, "The Cell Church Bible." That's not really so profane. You see, this is one of the first books you can get your hands on that is going to explain the church as it was intended to be by Christ, who formed it to be inhabited by His presence. Of course, it does not have the inspiration of the Books of the Canon, but you will certainly find it inspiring!

So hoist the sails, cut the anchor, and let's head for the open sea!

Ralph W. Neighbour, Jr.
Houston, Texas

ACKNOWLEDGMENTS

The writing of a book is never a solo effort. This project started with long conversations with Jim Egli. Don Tillman joined the TOUCH staff, and we had deep, insightful discussions over coffee developing many of the ideas found on these pages. Then Don and I tested this material by consulting with numerous churches and teaching at TOUCH conferences.

Without the detailed editorial eye of Brandy Egli, reader comprehension would be immediately halved. The excellent editorial feedback by Michael Mack provided clear direction from the mind of a writer, editor, and pastor. My pastor, James Bell, gave insight from the point of a view of a pastor in the trenches. The gracious input of Karen Hurston helped to take parts of this book to new levels.

This book would have been impossible without the pastors across North America who volunteered hours to share their stories about how they developed cell groups. Their names are too many to list, but what they shared forms the backbone of this book.

Next I want to thank my patient wife, Shawna, who put up with my long hours of sitting behind a computer while I sought to make sense of the whirlwind of ideas and words. She continues to teach me how relational ministry through cell groups works, as her life is about relationships. To her I dedicate this book.

Finally, there are no words to express the impact God has had upon my life and the writing of this book. He has taken me on a journey in cell group community that is beyond description. I can only say that I am glad to be on this journey.

INTRODUCTION

One spring day over three years ago, Jim Egli, (a close friend and former Director of Training at TOUCH Outreach) and I held a walking meeting. As we wandered around the field of an old dairy farm that had been purchased by a church, one question dominated our discussion: why do so many churches struggle with making cell groups work? Many church leaders came to TOUCH conferences or went to conferences hosted by cell-based churches, but few were seeing the success with cell groups that they had been promised.

The church on whose grounds we were walking was a typical example. The senior pastor had a clear vision for multiplying cell groups. The church members had received training from cell group experts. The senior pastor started with one prototype group to model cell group life, exactly as the books and the experts said, but the church was stuck. The church tried and tried but could not get over the hump and take the few groups it had started and expand Christian community throughout the church and into the lives of relatives, neighbors, and friends.

George Barna reports that seventy percent of the senior pastors his organization surveyed stated that small-group ministry is "central to the overall success" of the church's ministry. Barna argues, "Since tens of thousands of Protestant churches have staked their future on the success of small groups to deliver effective ministry to their adherents...the triple zero decade will be a make-it-or-break-it period for small groups."[1] If Barna is right on these counts, and churches are struggling, then these pastors need something more. They need answers to questions that have rarely been asked. On that day, Jim and I asked a foundational question: "Why do some churches succeed in making cell groups work while others do not?" This question has spawned a series of subsequent questions that have consumed much of my job since that day. The answers to these questions formed the seedbed for the book that lies in your hands.

Do We Have the Vision Right?

As an employee of TOUCH Outreach Ministries, a ministry organization whose sole focus lies on helping churches establish effective cell groups, I was an admitted cell group diehard. I could not have kept my job otherwise. Even so, the only way to begin was to evaluate the cell group vision. If it was wrong, it must be changed regardless of my personal stake in the matter.

To answer this question, I began with the findings of statisticians. After surveying over 1000 churches around the world, Christian Schwarz found eight church health factors, one of which is holistic small groups. He concludes, "If we were to identify any one principle as the 'most important'—even though our research shows the interplay of all basic elements is important—then without a doubt it would be the multiplication of small groups..."[2] Pollster George Gallup said, "Nothing is more important for ministry today than small groups."[3] George Barna predicts the trend in the church that, "Tens of thousands of Sunday Schools will close down in favor of small group and Net-based ministry."[4]

Yet statistical evidence alone does not prove that the vision is correct. Popular Christian commentator Chuck Colson wrote, "No Christian can grow strong and stand the pressures of this life unless he is surrounded by a small group of people who minister to him and build him up in the faith."[5] My former professor, J.I. Packer, has stated, "How can God's one family, locally and denominationally separated, be enabled to look like one family?...by wisdom in structuring house-churches and small groups within congregations."[6]

Other theologians have made a similar point. Howard Snyder wrote, "It is my conviction that the *koinonia* of the Holy Spirit is most likely to be experienced when Christians meet together informally in small-group fellowships."[7] Deitrich Bonhoeffer understood the importance of life together in the church when he wrote, "But if there is so much blessing and joy even in a single encounter of brother with brother, how inexhaustible are the riches that open up for those who by God's will are privileged to live in the daily fellowship of life with other Christians."[8]

These arguments for life in Christian small groups seem to line up with life in the early church. The early Christians

> ...devoted themselves to the apostles' teaching and to fellowship, to the breaking of bread and to prayer...every day they continued to meet together in the temple courts. They broke bread in their homes and ate together with glad and sincere hearts, praising God and enjoying the favor of all the people. And the Lord added to their number daily those who were being saved (Acts 2:42-47).

The early church leaders were following Jesus' ministry model. Jesus focused most of His ministry on small group leadership, spending the majority of His time with the twelve apostles while never neglecting the crowds and other disciples. In fact, 51% of Jesus' words in Mark are addressed to the twelve apostles.[9] The Apostle Paul followed a similar model of ministry when he said, "You know that I have not hesitated to preach anything that would be helpful to you but have taught you publicly and from house to house" (Acts 20:20). Even Moses used a similar model of ministry when he organized the children of Israel into groups of 1000s, 100s, 50s, and small groups of 10s because he was being worn out trying to minister to the entire nation by himself.

Dr. Ralph Neighbour has been a pioneering voice for cell groups since the 1970s, stating, "We must recognize the activity of the Holy Spirit in the cell group movement and seek to use it for the harvest of precious souls. No other form of church life promises to harvest at the same rate the population is growing."[10] The church cannot continue to accomplish its God-ordained mission with traditional methods in a world population that is multiplying exponentially.

There is one final piece of evidence for the rightness of the cell group vision: my own experience. As a young Christian in college, God gripped my heart with the power of Christian community. I felt the touch of being loved by a small group of people and this love transformed me and revealed God to me. I developed as a leader in small groups and heard God's call on my life while praying with group members. I cannot imagine church without the people who have shared life with me in cell groups. On top of this, I cannot imagine church without the joy of seeing God touch others through me as I loved them in community. This vision must be shared with others no matter what the cost.

Do Cell Groups Work Today?

Alister McGrath, Anglican theologian and professor of theology at Oxford University, estimates in his book *The Future of Christianity* that as many as 75 million people are part of churches that base their lives on cell groups. Cell groups, when done well, produce great results. Churches around the globe are proving this.

Church Name	Country	# of Groups
Deeper Christian Life Ministry	Ghana	> 600
Elim Church	El Salvador	> 6,000
Faith Community Baptist	Singapore	> 1,000
Family of God	Indonesia	> 1,000
International Charismatic Mission	Colombia	> 20,000
Las Acacias	Venezuela	> 400
Living Water Church	Peru	> 1,000
Love Alive Church	Honduras	> 1,000
New Life Fellowship	India	> 1,200
Saint Patrick's Church	Malaysia	> 300
Shepherd Community Church	Hong Kong	> 170
Showers of Grace	Guatemala	> 1,000
The Christian Center	Ecuador	> 2,000
Works and Mission Baptist	Ivory Coast	> 15,000
Yoido Full Gospel Church	Korea	> 25,000

Though the numbers are astounding, these churches do not focus on growth simply for the sake of growth. They are growing not by transferring believers from other churches, but rather by reaching out to nonbelievers and demonstrating true Christian life. When Dr. Neighbour helped Faith Community Baptist Church develop cell groups, they reported five conversions every day. David Yonggi Cho sets a goal for every cell group to lead two families to the Lord per year. Such results speak for themselves.

Do Cell Groups Work in North America?

All of the churches above are located in non-Western cultures. This has led many pastors to conclude that cells will not work in the West. While the churches in Europe and North America do not boast of such astronomical numbers, they also began their cell group ministries more recently. The following churches have developed networks of expanding cell groups that have transformed their churches and are transforming their cities.

Church Name	City	# of Groups
Belmont Church	Nashville, TN	> 90
Bethany World Prayer Center	Baton Rouge, LA	> 900
Celebration Church	New Orleans, LA	> 100
Christian Fellowship Church	Benton, KY	> 75
Clearpoint Church	Houston, TX	> 90
Colonial Hills Baptist Church	Southaven, MS	> 160
Cornerstone Church	San Antonio, TX	> 400
Community Covenant Church	Santa Barbara, CA	> 30
Cypress Creek Church	Wimberley, TX	> 100
Door of Hope Church	Fairbanks, AK	> 60
Faith Promise Church	Knoxville, TN	> 90
Long Reach Church of God	Columbia, MD	> 80
New Life Community	Chicago, IL	> 80
Northwood Christian Center	Gulfport, MS	> 40
Pantego Bible Church	Fort Worth, TX	> 200
The Vineyard	Champaign, IL	> 60
Venice Bible Church	Venice, FL	> 50
Victory Christian Center	Tulsa, OK	> 1,000
Wenatchee Free Methodist	Wenatchee, WA	> 90

These churches are discovering how to make cell groups work. They are pioneers on the journey to prove that cell groups do work in North America. In addition, these churches come from many different denominations and traditions.

These churches are seeing success with cell groups because Americans are dying for community. People look for community in anonymous chatrooms, discussing ideas with faceless people who cannot judge them. Others look for it at work, helping the United States become one of the most overworked nations in the world. They use money to gain acceptance from others through fancy cars or oversized, empty houses and endless parties. Millions of other people sit in front of the television watching reruns of sitcoms like "Friends," "Seinfeld," "Cheers," "M.A.S.H.," and "I Love Lucy." They try to live vicariously through the television characters, hoping to get a taste of close friendship, to go to a place where "everybody knows your name," to understand what it feels like when people really know one another—all the troubles and victories, the attractive features and the warts—and they still accept and love one another.

The Apostle John wrote, "We proclaim to you what we have seen and heard, so that you also might have fellowship with us. And our fellowship is with the Father and with his Son, Jesus Christ" (1 John 1:3). The church must provide a context where lonely, searching people can find friends who not only know their names but also know their hearts. The gospel of Jesus Christ is a relational message. Truth without fellowship is a lie. The church no longer needs stories like this:

A faithful Christian man led a sales clerk to Christ while out buying pants. He told his pastor about this experience, but when the pastor asked him what the man's name was, the Christian responded, "I have no idea." The pastor asked if he was going to visit the man in the store again. The Christian responded, "I never thought about that."

Sermons about Christ preached at people who lack life together are "sounding gongs" and "clanging symbols." The church has the opportunity to share the content of the gospel while at the same time providing a place for people to truly experience the love of God.

Do We Have the Right Cell Group Model?

Cell group models abound: the 5x5, the pure Jethro, the Groups of 12, the J-12, the G-12.3, the D-4, the interest group model, the hybrid model, and others currently in development. Up until a few years ago, the focus lay upon the 5x5 model, which has been used to describe the model developed by Yonggi Cho in Seoul, Korea. Most have started with that model and then have developed new models from it. Many are asking if they have the right or best cell group model. We, at TOUCH, have had to ask ourselves if we were teaching the optimal cell model.

Michael Green performed research on the Anglican cell group churches found in Southeast Asia. In his book, he does not talk so much about models as he does about the life he observed in these churches. He describes these churches as:[11]

- Groups of vibrant and multiplying communities of believers.
- Places where every cell is seen as a church, set in its neighborhood to impact it. (This does not mean that these groups are separated from the authority and direction of a local church and large group celebration).
- Places where every cell leader is a pastor, who always has an assistant.
- Churches where growing groups launch new groups with trained leaders.

• Places where many different kinds of groups can be launched including family cells, children's cells, youth cells, business people cells, coffee-shop cells, and of course home cells.

Evidence does not reveal the existence of an ideal model. Different churches use different tactics to make cell groups work. But in every working cell group model are Green's five elements. With the diversity of models that have arisen over the last few years, it has become quite clear that the key is not found in one model but in the values and principles that support all of these models.

It is tempting for people looking at these spectacular models to fall prey to the "magic model" theory. They attend conferences and go home thinking that the answer is found in copying the model. Many churches have tried to force their members into a certain model and the people found cell groups artificial and controlling. Models help people visualize how cell groups work, but God did not design His church to be a clone of an ideal church, just as He did not design human beings to be clones of an ideal human.

Are We Properly Communicating the Vision?

TOUCH Outreach Ministries is known for helping churches develop a cell group structure, commonly called a cell church. In the past, many people have heard us saying that the structure is the main problem with the church; therefore if pastors will adopt the new cell group structure, their problems will disappear. While structure is important, we have seen that a new structure alone will not turn around a church. TOUCH had to reconsider the way to communicate the cell church vision to move beyond simply changing structures.

First we asked, "What makes a cell church work?" *Cell groups that work.* The structure is only a means for facilitating the transforming life in the cell groups. Many churches were calling themselves "cell churches" but their groups were not working. They were so focused on the cell church structure that they did not invest their energies into the relationships that make cell groups work. The focus of the vision should lie on the cell groups, not on the cell church structure. Cell groups, when done well, produce great results. Cell groups, when done poorly, prove anemic. If the cell groups are working, it is easy to expand them and transform the church structure. If the basic unit of the cell group is not working, it will prove impossible to change the church structure.

Second, TOUCH realized that the more life a church had before adopting the cell group structure, the more likely it was to make cell groups work. Of course, this makes sense, but it forced us to ask again, "What makes cell groups work?" A big part of the answer is the flow of the Holy Spirit through the people of those groups. The cell group structure alone is not enough. Churches need a fresh touch of God, not just a new structure.

How Does a Church Go from No Cell Groups to Expanding Cell Groups?

This question summarizes the purpose of this book. When pastors and church leaders travel to model cell-based churches and observe what they are doing, they leave with a sense of excitement and vision. They often leave with something else: a sense of being overwhelmed because the vision is so different and the methods are so radical. They often feel like they have been looking at a watermelon and must eat it whole.

Yet model churches did not develop overnight. They didn't try to eat the watermelon in one bite. They took a journey from no cell groups to expanding cell groups. It is not enough to understand what the final watermelon looks like. Pastors and church leaders need to understand the journeys of these model churches just as much as they need to grasp the end result. They need to hear how these churches began, the lessons they learned, the mistakes they made along the way, and the surprising successes they found. These model churches have pioneered the journey to making cell groups work. By hearing these journey stories, others can avoid many mistakes and quickly develop a working cell group base. When they only see the watermelon, they feel pressured to leapfrog over the journey and immediately force cell groups to work.

Making Cell Groups Work cuts the watermelon into eight stages so that other churches will be able to eat it one bite at a time. It provides an 8-stage process for leading a church from no cell groups to effective, expanding cell groups. This process aims to do four things:

Provide a chronological process to help a church get started with cell groups. These eight stages identify where to begin and provide steps for moving forward. They reveal the order in which watermelon should be eaten so that church leaders do not try to change everything at once.

Help a church that already has cell groups improve them. I recently talked with an experienced cell pastor who confessed, "I have to go back and address some key factors that I skipped in Stages 2 and 3." When pastors describe what is going on in their groups, they often express that cell groups are not yet expanding; they are more like "holding" cells. Many have implemented cell groups and inadvertently skipped key steps in the 8-stage process. When reading through each stage, pastors and leaders will be able to assess steps that they skipped and then make plans for addressing them.

Provide practical levers. Levers are "small, well-focused actions that can sometimes produce significant, enduring improvements, if they're in the right place."[12] It is not enough to do things right; leaders must do the right things right. At the end of each stage is a list of levers that will help propel a church through that stage and on toward the destination of making cell groups work. They point to other books, training resources, tools, and activities that will help a church on its journey.

Answer eight questions that pastors commonly ask when they are trying to understand cell groups.

Question	Answer
1. What is my first step?	Discover the Cell Group Vision (Stage 1)
2. How do I get people on board with the vision?	Develop Vision and Strategy as a Team (Stage 2)
3. Will cell groups work in my church?	Assess Your Church's Current Reality (Stage 3)
4. How do we prepare the church for cell group success?	Prepare the Church Through Transformation (Stage 4)
5. How do we start the first groups?	Launch the First Group(s) with Kingdom-Seekers (Stage 5)
6. How do we experience dynamic cell group community?	Generate Cell Group Momentum (Stage 6)
7. How do we establish cell groups as the base of the church?	Establish the Hidden Systems that Support the Cells (Stage 7)
8. How do we mobilize groups to reach people?	Expand the Cell Groups to Reach the Unreached (Stage 8)

This process will serve as a navigational guide for the journey toward making cell groups work in a church. This journey is similar to that of a ship sailing to a new destination. Much goes into a sea-going voyage, including pre-sailing preparation, gathering information, charting a course, recruiting crew members, navigating around islands and continents that impede the path to the port of call. The eight stages will serve as a travel guide for leading people into life-transforming, God-filled, adventure-loving, risk-taking, people-caring, lost-seeking, leader-developing cell groups.

What is the Basis for the 8-stage Process?

After Jim and I walked and talked that day, I realized that the next stage of training provided by TOUCH Outreach Ministries must be based on a much broader experience than those of us connected to TOUCH. While we were learning from our experience as cell leaders and pastors, we had to discover the lessons that other pastors were learning and create a larger pool of knowledge. Over the last three years, I have listened to the stories told by pastors of churches large and small, traditional and creative, across North America. I have asked questions to determine why groups work in some churches and fail in others. Pastors have shared their successes and their failures. They told me what they did right and what they wished they had done differently. These stories have revealed much about cell groups that has worked and much that has not. This book synthesizes the information from the stories.

These interviews led me to inquire about the ways leaders guide organizations through change. The eight stages presented in this book loosely correspond with the eight stages that John Kotter, a Harvard Business School professor, presents in his book, _Leading Change_. Principles from other key thinkers on leadership and change have been inserted throughout the eight stages. While this book draws from the best learning of the business world, the process is firmly based on experience in cell group leadership and interviews with pastors across North America, and is rooted in the theology of the Word of God.

TOUCH Outreach Ministries: The Cell Group People™, proclaims its mission in this way: "To empower pastors, group leaders, and members to transform their lives, churches, and the world through basic Christian community." I pray that this resource will help you propel your church toward this mission as you make cell groups work.

NAVIGATIONAL HAZARDS

With the explosion of the first modern cell church during the 1970s—the Yoido Full Gospel Church in Korea—a wave of church leaders traveled to Korea and returned with a vision to emulate Dr. Cho's pattern. Some, like Dale Galloway and the New Hope Community Church in Portland, Oregon, succeeded. Many others started home groups but never saw the same growth. Instead, they watched their groups become in-grown cliques. In other churches, the groups stalled out and church leaders shut them down.

In 1990, a new wave of cell group experiments burst forth. Much of this experimentation rose from the unexpected stir caused by Dr. Ralph W. Neighbour's book *Where Do We Go From Here?*. In it, Dr. Neighbour recorded personal insights that rose from his frustration with the American church. After twenty-one of the pastors he had helped develop cell groups were forced to resign, Dr. Neighbour stated that there was little hope for the traditional church to live out the values of cell groups.[1]

Instead of listening to Dr. Neighbour's caution about the traditional church, many church leaders were incited and challenged by his negative assessment. One pastor wrote: "I was frankly outraged at how easily Dr. Neighbour disposed of the traditional American church and described a new paradigm of church structure called the 'cell church.'"[2] During the 1990s, churches from every denomination—Baptist to Episcopal, Pentecostal to Presbyterian, Methodist to Church of God, Mennonite to Vineyard—experimented with cell groups. These churches were like ships taking a voyage into uncharted territory. They ventured into places where most had not dared to go 20 years before. On these voyages, these ships encountered almost every imaginable navigational hazard. As I listened to their stories, I kept hearing the same hazards being described. With the knowledge gained from the experiences of these churches, those churches that follow can avoid these hazards and sail more freely toward the destination of fruitful, dynamic, and growing cell groups.[3]

Hazard #1:
Misunderstanding the Destination

When a ship captain prepares for a sea-going journey, he takes the time to plan well. He studies ocean charts, determines destinations, plots courses, consults weather reports, purchases and stores provisions. No sailor dares a sea venture without a proper knowledge of his destination and what it will take to get there.

Many times pastors fail to thoroughly consider the destination toward which they travel. They call TOUCH or visit our offices and ask for help in starting ten groups within three months. While they come with a desire for biblical community, they do not know what it really looks like. They often have only read one book or heard about a big church that is doing cell groups. They have not done enough research to understand where they are going or how they can really get there.

Too many pastors have experienced the hazardous nature of this approach to starting cell groups. Reading one book or attending one conference is not enough to attain a clear vision for cell groups. Most pastors spend years in seminary learning how to follow patterns of traditional church ministry. It might not take three years to learn how to run a cell group ministry, but it will take considerably more than reading one book.

I can state this fact with a great deal of confidence because the churches that have done the best job of "making cell groups work" have this in common: they do their homework, and they do it before they make plans to start groups or announce those plans to the church congregation. They also hear God's call to cell ministry very clearly. They do not make the transition because it has made the church down the road grow large or because it seems like a good idea. They do it because they sense God calling their church to do it. *Stage 1: Discover the Cell Group Vision*, will deepen your understanding of cell groups and how churches organize themselves to facilitate cell groups.

Hazard #2:
Failing to Practice Team Leadership

Pastoral leaders cannot force cell groups to work through strength of will, knowledge, or diligent effort. Leading a cell group initiative will fail if it is a solo project. Cell groups work because people work together in relationships. This requires the commitment of more than one person.

Shouldering the transitional burden alone seems to be a common hazard in many churches. The senior pastor goes to his study, reads all of the available literature on cell groups, attends conferences, and develops a plan, often using fancy charts and illustrations. Then he announces the plan to the leadership.

When one person announces his cell group strategy to a group of people as if it is a done deal, he is asking for trouble. People do not adopt new ideas blindly. They need understanding, time, and much discussion. This means the senior pastor will need help in disseminating the idea to other members of the church. Seminars and sermons will not work in the early stages.

To overcome this hazard, the senior pastor must gather a team of key people who will help him discover how God is calling the church to navigate the waters of change. *Stage 2: Develop Vision and Strategy as a Team*, will guide you through this process.

Hazard #3:
Not Identifying the Starting Point

It is not enough for a ship captain to know his destination point when determining the proper course to steer at sea. Two vessels may have the same destination, but vastly different starting points. The issues and challenges each ship will face will be unique because of its unique starting point.

The same is true for the church. Two churches embarking from two starting points will take different courses to arrive at the same location. The journey toward making cell groups work will be very different for a 100-year-old Baptist church in rural east Texas than it will be for a 5-year-old non-denominational church in metropolitan Cleveland. Or imagine the difference between the journey of a church who has had three pastors in the last 8 years and that of a church who has had the same pastor for the last 20 years.

When churches fail to understand their starting points, they steer blindly into waters replete with hidden dangers and unseen hazards. *Stage 3: Assess Your Church's Current Reality*, will guide you in your quest to understanding your church's starting point so that you will be able to prepare your members and lead them in the God-directed steps toward the vision of cell ministry.

Hazard #4:
Putting Old Wine into New Wineskins

Many churches have embraced the new wineskin of cell groups, but the people of the church have not allowed their personal lives to be challenged, changed, and remade by the work of the Holy Spirit. Some have carried with them old patterns of ministry that stand in the way of what God is doing. Others have transported unbiblical ideas of what the church is. Most people entering the cell group wineskin struggle with simple things like becoming transparent, relating to nonbelievers, and mentoring future leaders.

One west coast denominational pastor caught the vision for cell groups. He received training on cell group ministry, brought in experts for consultation, and hosted seminars for his church members. The church started groups and the level of excitement rose. The church began reaching nonbelievers, and new Christians not only came to the groups but also started attending the worship services. The church discipled these new believers and even began reaching their friends. Everything was working well until the old guard started looking across the isle of the church and realized that they were losing control. The deacons started questioning the cell group strategy (one which they had endorsed and approved two years before) and then they began to pull in the reigns on the pastor, telling him that he needed to get back to pastoring and caring for the people. This pastor did most things right, but there was no change of heart on the part of his church's leadership.

I have yet to find a church that made cell groups work but did not develop a deep hunger for God. Each successful church sought to change not only the wineskin of cells, but also to change the wine that flows into the hearts of the people. In order to enter into what God is doing in our world today, you must go beyond a transition of structures; you must embrace God Himself and allow Him to transform you through repentance. *Stage 4: Prepare the Church Through Transformation*, provides practical ways to prepare people for successful cell group experiences.

Hazard #5:
Starting Too Abruptly

The average tenure of senior pastors in the United States is four years. Therefore, when pastors feel they have a God-given idea, they do not have much time to enact it and often encounter great resistance when doing so.

While pastors feel like they do not have a lot of time to do what God is calling them to do, cell groups begun too abruptly rarely work. Church after church over the last twenty years has tried to jump from Stage 1 to Stage 5, skipping Stages 2, 3, and 4. They dive into the deep end without considering whether or not they can swim.

Instead of launching groups recklessly, churches that succeed launch them intentionally. Pastors do not intend to be reckless; their motives are usually pure. But when leaders try to begin groups too quickly, they often find themselves picking up the pieces. Intentional start-ups are based on the realization that leaders must be prepared and the cell group members must be committed to the values that make cell groups work. Without such a commitment, cell members will be distracted from the vision and purpose of the groups.

I imagine that some readers will struggle as they read this section. They might believe that their church is unique, that they can start more quickly than others, that they will not encounter the hazards and the struggles of a quick start-up. Before your church decides to begin cell groups quickly, please consider the ramifications if you are wrong. Read through the information on the first five stages. These chapters will help you chart a course of action and determine how quickly you can begin.

As I have talked with pastors, I have discovered that the churches who loaded the front end of their start-up efforts with as much thought, preparation, and training as possible were more likely to launch effective start up groups. *Stage 5: Launch the First Group(s) with Kingdom Seekers*, will give you the confidence to know that when your church does start its cell groups, it will start them with great potential for success.

Hazard #6:
Viewing Cell Groups as a Program

Cell groups are not a panacea that will solve the ills of a church. The cell ministry strategy is not a program that a church can purchase and put on autopilot. Cell groups work because pastors and coaches are ministering to, mentoring, and releasing others into ministry.

Sadly, many churches have treated cell groups as a program that will run itself. Pastors promote cell groups from the pulpit, put charts on the walls, and hire a "cell pastor," assuming that everything will work itself out. An effective cell group ministry is not like an effective Sunday School program or a Bible Study group where the church can purchase curriculum and pass it out to teachers who have been teaching for 15 years. When you put cell groups on autopilot, they crash.

In the early 1990s, one early adopter of the cell group strategy had a goal posted on the walls of his worship facility. It read: "2,000 groups by 2000." I looked around his church and thought, "How?" The church was doing cells according to the proper structure, but the groups had not developed any momentum. The pastor had heard a cell pioneer state that a vision should be an impossible vision. This vision was so impossible that they didn't even come within shouting distance of it.

Cell groups do not grow and multiply just because they are meeting together. Cell group growth is a result of momentum generated by Christ-centered and Christ-empowered relationships. Momentum must be developed through cell group wins in three areas: personal victories, new Christians, and new cell groups. When Christ moves through the cell group relationships in these three ways, the cell system is propelled forward, creating more and more momentum. *Stage 6: Generate Cell Group Momentum,* will explain how to develop new leaders relationally and thereby create new groups.

Hazard #7: No Support Systems

An associate pastor took me out to lunch after a conference to pick my brain for ways he could turn around his 20 stagnating groups. I asked him how his cell group members were discipled. They were not. I asked him how he was coaching the cell group leaders. There were no coaches. I asked him how much energy he, as the cell group pastor, spent ministering to the groups and leaders. He told me about the other administrative responsibilities he had in the church and how he had no time to invest in the leaders. Then I asked him how the senior pastor fit into the vision of the cell groups. He confessed that the senior pastor gave little to no attention to the cell group vision.

Cell groups are not designed to work autonomously. When left alone, cell group leaders must do all of the work of setting direction, discipling members, training interns, and evangelizing the world. This leads to burnout and failed groups. Group members and group leaders need oversight, support, accountability, and direction. This is the biblical role of apostles, prophets, evangelists, pastors, and teachers. *Stage 7: Establish the Hidden Systems that Support Cells,* will help your church provide the needed support that comes in the form of training, pastoral staff oversight, organization, teaching, evangelistic harvest events, children's cell ministry, youth cell ministry, and much more.

Hazard #8: Failing To Maintain Focus and Expand the Ministry

A church leadership team recently asked me, "What percentage of our members should be participating in our cell groups? 70%? 80%? 100%?" I thought afterward, "That is not the right question." The mission of the church is not about getting current Christians into cell groups. The mission of the church is to transform the world by the power of the Holy Spirit flowing through us. Cell group ministry is one of the best ways to accomplish this mission.

But some churches have fallen to the temptation of shifting the focus of the church after 75% or more of the membership has joined a cell group. They assume that the job is done. There is nothing further from the truth. Groups are like roses in a garden. Weeds will invade and insects will destroy, leaving the rose bushes distorted or dying unless the gardener tends to the garden. Without the focus of church leadership, groups lose energy, people focus on other things, and Satan invades what is left unprotected.

In order to avoid this hazard, it is important for a pastor to understand that initiating change and then leaving the congregation for another ministry position is a recipe for cell group demise. Without the guidance of the leader who initiated the groups, the church members are pulled back toward the old ways of ministry. This is what they know, and without the leader, they will feel safer with the old style.

Cell groups do not work as a maintenance strategy. They only work when they exist to change the world. Cell groups are either growing or dying, just like a rose garden. Therefore the focus should lie on expanding the groups, starting new churches, training new pastors, and impacting the world. Churches that have a vision to impact their Jerusalem, Judea, Samaria, and the ends of the earth (Acts 1:8) have exciting cell groups full of people who are called to minister and see the hand of God transforming society. *Stage 8: Expand the Cell Groups to Reach the Unreached*, will provide practical ways to increase the impact of the cell groups to transform more than just your church and neighborhood.

Navigation is foundational to a successful sea-going voyage. Without a good navigator, a ship is likely to end up in trouble or even destroyed. Churches face a similar situation when trying to move God's people from no cell groups to expanding cell groups. Haphazard navigation will almost always lead a church into a head-on collision with a debilitating hazard. The eight stages found on the following pages provide the necessary tools for navigating around these eight hazards. The journey to making cell groups work will look differently in every church. These eight stages will provide broad parameters for navigating that stage, while at the same time allowing room for God to guide the church forward. So prepare yourself for the adventure of a lifetime. Your ministry will never be the same as God leads you and your church into the new territory of making cell groups work.

STAGE 1
Discover the
Cell Group Vision

Before a ship sets sail, its captain must prepare for the journey ahead. The first thing he does is discover as much as possible about his destination. He will roll out his chart and place a big X to identify where he wants to go. He will talk with other seamen who have taken the journey, study charts from other voyages, and read and reread captains' logs. The preparations for a successful sea voyage begin long before the ship embarks on the voyage itself.

The first thing pastors ask when they are looking at cell groups is, "Where do I begin?" My response is always the same: "Find out as much as you can about the final destination." Churches that have done the best job of making cell groups work began by focusing their energy and time on discovering everything they could about what lay ahead. The process of discovery is much easier today than it was 10 years ago, when there were only two or three books on cell groups. In fact, the amount of information available today can be overwhelming and even confusing. The sections in Stage 1 will help organize some of this information:

"Discover Cell Group Models" (Section 1.1). There are many different cell group models that have proven successful. This section provides an overview of each and highlights the major differences between them.

"Discover the Cell Group System" (Section 1.2). Effective cell group models are structured differently, but beneath these structures are common components that make the structures work. This section presents a system that identifies these components and introduces how they work.

"Discover How Cell Groups Fit in Tomorrow's Church" (Section 1.3). The church universally is going through a massive transformation as society at large is changing. This section demonstrates the ways in which cell groups must be a foundational component to this changing church.

"Discover How to Lead Change" (Section 1.4). Every leader needs to understand how to lead people through change, especially when dealing with the change to cell groups. This section demonstrates how people react to change and how to lead them through the change process.

SECTION 1.1 Discover
Cell Group Models

Every sea going voyage begins in the mind of the leader of the ship. Christopher Columbus had a vision to travel around the globe to China. Vasco de Gama dreamt of sailing around the Cape of Good Hope. Magellan wanted to sail around the world. For a ship to arrive at a new port of destination, the captain and his officers must first catch a vision for heading that direction. The same is true of the journey to making cell groups work. Key church leaders must embrace and understand the new vision if there is to be any hope of a successful journey. The senior pastor must have a clear vision of what God is calling the church to be. The pastoral staff and key lay leaders must begin to have a clear understanding of how the vision works.

As pastors shared their stories about starting cell groups, I found two basic patterns. First, there are the churches that launch groups without much thought or understanding. They know that cell groups are crucial and the senior pastor wants them, so they get started as soon as possible.

Although their urgency is admirable, such quick starts usually stall out or run into a series of obstacles.

The second pattern is one of deliberation. Pastors of many successful cell churches have told stories like this: "I read every book on cell groups I could get my hands on. I passed out a key book for our leaders to discuss. We went to conferences and visited churches that are doing cell groups. We learned as much as we could." This slower start-up lacks some of the urgency, but the preparations allow for much smoother sailing.

In Stage 1, the senior pastor and key leaders must invest time into learning as much as they can about the destination of cell groups. They must discover what happens in a cell group, how to best support cell groups, and how a church based on cell groups works. Bethany World Prayer Center understood this principle. Key pastors traveled to Korea, Singapore, and El Salvador to learn from the best cell-based churches in the world before announcing anything about cell groups to church members. On these research trips, they visited cell groups, talked with pastors, visited pastoral offices, and worshipped with the people. Bethany's leaders understood that cell group ministry is so different from the old way of doing ministry that they had to relearn everything from scratch.

In Fairbanks, Alaska, Door of Hope Church invested nearly $30,000 in advanced cell training to equip its staff. Bishop Robert Davis of Long Reach Church of God in Columbia Maryland traveled to ICM in Bogota, Faith Community Baptist Church in Singapore, and the Works and Mission Baptist Church in the Ivory Coast to discover what the final destination of cell groups looks like. Churches that have developed the best cell group systems have taken at least six months and some even up to one year to discover as much as they can about cell groups before they start a group.

While most churches do not have the resources to send pastors out to travel the globe or take lots of classroom courses, churches that make groups work will at the very least attend conferences held by model cell group churches, read books about these model churches, work through tested training materials, and read key survey resources that provide an overview of how the cell group system works.

Popular Cell/Small Group Models

The popularity of cell groups and small groups has grown exponentially over the last decade. This is due in part to the model churches and their pastors who are writing books and holding conferences. People flock to large churches to learn about each of these models and return home hoping to implement what they have learned through conferences and resources. There are four major cell group models that are being promoted as models for others to follow.[1]

1. David Yonggi Cho formed the first model at Yoido Full Gospel Church (YFGC) in Seoul, Korea. This model, often called the 5x5, stimulated interest in cell groups and attracted people, like Ralph W. Neighbour, Jr. who has propagated the model around the world. The elements of this model have been adopted by many churches, including the 100,000-member Elim Church in El Salvador, Clearpoint Church in Houston, Texas, and Faith Promise Church in Knoxville, Tennessee.

2. The International Charismatic Mission in Bogota, Colombia started cell groups using the Cho model but then developed a model of its own called the Groups of 12. With this model, the church has grown to over 20,000 cell groups, and now large churches in the United States have embraced the G-12 model, including Bethany World Prayer Center in Baton Rouge, Louisiana and Cornerstone Church in San Antonio, Texas.

3. Victory Christian Center in Tulsa, Oklahoma has established a third model that several churches are learning from. Karen Hurston calls it the Mixed Cell model because it uses elements from the Cho/Neighbour model, the G-12 model, and has borrowed some concepts from the Meta-church model discussed on page 51.

4. The fourth model is called the Congregationally-focused model. Pantego Bible Church in Ft. Worth, Texas has both developed a model that places a greater emphasis on the mid-sized grouping of 50 to 75 people, alongside cell groups and weekly celebration services.

In addition to these four, there are two small group models that share common traits with the four cell group models. The first is the Meta-church model, which was first introduced by Carl George in his landmark book *Preparing Your Church for the Future.* Influential churches like Willow Creek in South Barrington, Illinois, Saddleback Church in southern California, and Southeast Christian Fellowship in Louisville, Kentucky have adopted the principles of the Meta model, even though they may not necessarily call themselves Meta-churches.

Another small group model has arisen recently at New Life Church in Colorado Springs, Colorado. It is called the Free Market Model, and many churches are beginning to embrace its methods.

Understanding the Major Models

I, along with other TOUCH staff members, receive calls each week from pastors asking, "Which model is the best?" I wish this question were easy to answer. Each model has inherent strengths and weaknesses; none is perfect. They all seek to accomplish the same things, but they use different methods to do so. Each uses small groups as a basic foundation for its ministry, but each does small groups differently. It can prove confusing when trying to understand how the different models work. In order to understand the differences between the various models, a pastor should prepare a list of questions, questions that will probe to the heart of the differences. There are four broad questions that pastors should ask of the various models.

Question 1: What is the purpose of the cell group?

The term "cell group" is used for many different kinds of groups in the church, including home groups, evangelism target groups, task groups, and even Sunday school classes. Because different churches define their "cell groups" differently, deciding what is and what is not a cell group often proves confusing. Some models have developed a very specific purpose for their groups, while other models allow for greater flexibility.

This question marks the major difference between the first four models and the last two. The four "cell group" models define their groups as having a holistic purpose, in that they aim to see both edification and expansion happen through their groups. The two "small group" models create groups with more specific purposes based on a task, special interest, or Bible study.

Consider asking:

- Are the groups holistic in nature?
- Are there groups that meet for a task without an emphasis on mutual ministry to one another?
- Do the groups have a stated purpose of reaching nonbelievers?
- Do the groups have a plan for raising up new leaders and multiplying groups?

Question 2: How are cell group leaders supported?

All of the successful cell group models have developed extensive strategies for supporting their cell leaders. They dedicate resources, time, personal relationships, and money to the support and care of group leaders. But the methods for providing this support vary between the models. Here are a few questions to probe this issue further:

- How is the senior pastor involved in the oversight of the cell groups?
- What kind of personal support do cell leaders receive from the pastoral staff?

• Does every cell leader have a coach who invests personal time in mentoring him or her?
• How are networks of cell groups organized?
• How often do the cell leaders meet for continuing training?
• How often do cell leaders meet with their cell coaches?

Question 3: What priority is given to cell group life as compared to activities in the church?

This third question is one of priority. Few churches will state that cell groups are unimportant, but many will argue about the priority they should have in the ministry of the church. Model churches place a very high priority on cell groups. The cell groups are weekly groups and churches clearly articulate the importance of participating in a cell group as part of walking with the Lord. Here are a few additional questions:

• What degree of priority is given to the cell groups?
• Do other ministries compete with cell group participation?
• Are non-cell members allowed to take on ministry roles in the church?

Question 4: How does the church equip cell members and raise up new cell group leaders?

Almost every church that starts cell groups complains about a shortage of leadership. Model churches have developed patterns for equipping every member for ministry. This means providing more than leadership training for new cell group leaders; it means creating a discipleship track that will take cell members from "new Christian " to "minister" to "leader." In other words, model cell-based churches do not expect leaders to develop out of thin air. Instead, they have an intentional development process that disciples each person according to his or her level of maturity: new believer training for new believers, ministry training for growing Christians, and leadership training for future leaders. Additional questions include:

- How does the church equip new believers who join the cell groups?
- How does the church prepare cell members to minister to other people in the cell and to nonbelieving friends?
- How does the church train new cell group leaders?

Applying These Questions to the Major Models

Before proceeding, allow me to offer a disclaimer: I hesitate to include this section because my goal is not to offend or to promote one model over another. God is doing wonderful things in churches that follow any of the six major models I have listed. In the next several years, He will likely inspire others to create or adapt new ones, as He has done in the past. Yet I am compelled to include this section because so many pastors confess their confusion about the ways these models are different. The differences are often hard to identify because they use very similar language. What follows are my answers to the four questions for each of the models. Proponents of each model might answer differently. My purpose is to orient the reader to the differences between the models, not to provide a detailed analysis of each model; to that end, I have included a list of additional resources for those interested in learning more.

The Cho/Neighbour Model.

Cell Group Purpose—Pastor Cho teaches that there are two main purposes of cell groups. The first is evangelism; the second is spiritual growth. In a recent publication from YFGC, he writes, "There must be a balanced focus on outward evangelism and on inward spiritual growth."[2] Another way to state this is that groups have a two-fold purpose:

edification and expansion. Such groups are holistic in nature. Rather than focusing on one aspect of the Christian walk, they seek to build community so that group members experience both ministry to one another and to the unchurched. Groups usually meet in homes, but they are free to meet in a variety of non-church settings.

Cell Group Support—Support of cell group leaders and members is crucial. The senior pastor leads the vision and all of the staff pastors oversee networks of cell groups. The staff pastors are organized to spend most of their time visiting the homes of cell group leaders and members. Dr. Ralph Neighbour adapted Cho's support system and called it 5x5 (although the strict adherence to these numbers is not required.) The support structure might look something like this:

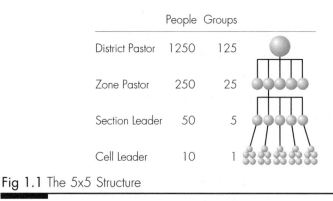

	People	Groups
District Pastor	1250	125
Zone Pastor	250	25
Section Leader	50	5
Cell Leader	10	1

Fig 1.1 The 5x5 Structure

Most churches have used this structure to organize their groups into geographic sections, i.e. an east zone, west zone, etc., but it can also be used to organize homogeneous networks, i.e. women's cells, men's cells, youth cells, etc.

Cell Group Priority—The cell groups are central to the vision and the life of the church. The cell group is the place where people connect with one another and where they are discipled. There is no competition with participation in the cell groups. In fact, many churches link church membership with cell group membership.

Equipping—This system emphasizes not only the training of new cell group leaders, but also the equipping of every cell group member for ministry. Churches develop a cell member equipping track that will help disciple new believers into maturity and ministry. Dr. Ralph W. Neighbour has developed such a track, called *Your Equipping Journey*, which includes one-on-one mentoring, discipleship books, and weekend retreats.

For more information on the Cho model, read:

Successful Home Cell Groups by David Yonggi Cho
Growing the World's Largest Church by Karen Hurston
Where Do We Go From Here? by Ralph W. Neighbour, Jr.

The Groups of 12 Model.

Cell Group Purpose—In the G-12 model, the cell groups have the same purpose as in the Cho model: edification and expansion. They are holistic, open groups that aim to minister to one another, reach the lost, and start new groups.

Cell group support—Each cell group leader receives support from a G-12 leader through a weekly meeting. Up to 12 cell group leaders gather to form a G-12. This G-12 meeting is separate from a cell group meeting, as it is reserved for those who are leading the cell group. A Group of 12 could be called a Group of Leaders. The G-12 oversight system looks something like this:

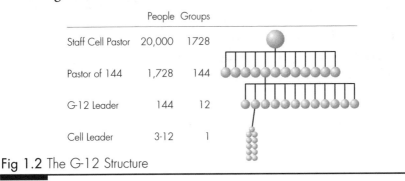

	People	Groups
Staff Cell Pastor	20,000	1728
Pastor of 144	1,728	144
G-12 Leader	144	12
Cell Leader	3-12	1

Fig 1.2 The G-12 Structure

A cell leader becomes a G-12 leader when one of her cell group members starts a new group. This means that the cell leader will attend two meetings per week: the first is the open cell group; the second is the G-12 support meeting.

The pure G-12 model emphasizes the importance of raising up 12 new cell group leaders to complete a G-12. For many, this is an overwhelming proposition. For volunteer leaders, a smaller number is a more attainable goal. Joel Comiskey has sought to understand the principles of the G-12 and has developed a G-12.3. In this model, a staff pastor raises up and oversees a G-12, and each of these 12 not on staff sets a goal to raise up three new leaders and form a G-3.

Cell Group Priority—The open cell group is the focus of this system. Many observers of the G-12 model have falsely equated the G-12 with a cell group and have taken the emphasis off the weekly cell meeting. Then they highlight a regular G-12 leadership training meeting. The G-12 is a weekly meeting to support the cell group leaders and the life of the cell groups. It is not a separate structure that runs beside the cell groups.

Equipping—The G-12 system places a heavy emphasis upon preparing every cell group member to one day lead a cell group. At International Charismatic Mission and in other churches who use the pure G-12 model, the equipping occurs through a series of retreats and classes which culminates in leading a group.

For more information on the G-12 model, read:

Groups of 12 by Joel Comiskey
From 12 to 3 by Joel Comiskey
The Jesus System by Rocky Malloy
Successful Leadership through the Government of 12 by César Castellanos
The Ladder of Success by César Castellanos

The Mixed Cell Model.

Cell Group Purpose—The mixed model combines many of the elements of the previous models. The emphasis lies on the holistic cell groups that have a stated purpose of edification and expansion. At the same time, churches that use this model have redesigned other areas of ministry around cell group principles. They have on-campus Sunday morning cell groups, with Sunday School teachers trained to lead their groups like cells. They have worship team cell groups that meet before worship practice. They have bus groups where leaders minister to kids while they are being bussed to church. They have hundreds of children's outreach groups that meet in apartment complexes, government projects, and subdivisions.

Cell Group Support—At certain levels, mixed model churches support their groups with the Cho model of oversight. Some are also developing G-12 oversight on the staff level. The strength of this model lies in the staff, as the cell pastors focus their energies on hands-on ministry by meeting with cell leaders and cell members outside the office.

Cell Group Priority—At Victory Christian Center, the originator of the Mixed cell model, cell groups are central to the life of the church and to the vision of the pastor. Victory Christian Center has been able to prioritize its cell groups while at the same time maintaining three large group services per week; most model cell group churches only have one large group service per week.

Equipping—There is a clear track for discipling cell members and training cell leaders. This model uses a combination of retreats, classes, and resources.

Read *Breakthrough Cell Groups* by Karen Hurston for more information.

The Congregationally-focused Model.

Cell Group Purpose—The small groups are geographically organized to create a place where people can be involved in a spiritual family. This model emphasizes the geographic groups because of the disparate lives that suburban Americans embrace. These groups are holistic small groups with two goals: "to function in interdependent relationships, assisting each other in growth toward Christlikeness" and "to practice their growing faith by reaching out to others outside the group."[3] All of the small groups are heterogenous and intergenerational. They seek to involve the entire family and to reach out to other families within walking distance.

Cell Group Support—For every five home groups, there is a Community Group Leader. For every five Community Group Leaders there is a staff Zone Pastor. This support structure is the same as the 5x5. The model is distinctive in what it does at the Community Group level, which consists of approximately 50 adults. Every Sunday for 1 hour and 15 minutes, Community Groups gather for instruction "in the core beliefs, practices, and virtues of the Christian life."[4] This mid-sized group experience connects groups with other groups, provides an avenue for gifted teachers to teach the Word, and alleviates the stress of home group multiplication because people are still connected in their Community Groups.

Cell Group Priority—The entire structure is designed to facilitate connecting people in community. The vision is to develop homes groups as a way of life for the church.

Equipping—This model uses an assessment tool where individuals can identify strengths and weaknesses in 30 core competencies in the areas of beliefs, practices, and virtues. The church organizes individual equipping, Community Group Instruction, and Worship Service sermons around these 30 core competencies to ensure that the people are being equipped in the basics of the Christian life.

For more information on the Congregationally-focused cell model, read *The Connecting Church* by Randy Frazee

The Meta-church Model.

Cell Group Purpose—The stated purpose of meta-groups is for members to minister to one another and reach out to the unconnected. While some groups in this system might be holistic small groups, also included are task groups like ushers and the choir, short-term Bible study groups, Sunday school groups, and activity groups like those that play volleyball or football together. Some groups meet weekly, while others meet biweekly or even once per month. This model therefore defines the small group a little differently than the models above.

Cell Group Support—Structurally the support is the same as that of the Cho/Neighbour model: 5x5. For every four to five groups, there is a volunteer coach. Pastoral staff members oversee the coaches.

Cell Group Priority—The small groups are given high priority in this system because the goal is to get everyone connected in a small group. Bill Donahue and Russ Robinson of Willow Creek state that their small groups have made their church "a place where nobody stands alone." Some Meta-churches connect people in small groups of every kind, whether they are task groups or holistic cell groups, placing all groups on the same level of priority. This means that a holistic small group that meets weekly to discuss the Word, pray for group members, and reach the lost is considered equal to a group that parks cars on Sunday morning. Other Meta-churches recognize the differences and prioritize holistic small groups (community groups, cell groups, care groups, and home groups), stating that these groups are where real life-change happens. Secondary groups, such as task groups, seeker groups, and recovery groups are used as bridges for people to cross into holistic small groups.

Equipping—Churches using this model focus energy on equipping new small group leaders through training and an internship process. They also develop equipping for members, i.e. new believer equipping, ministry training, spiritual gifts training, etc.

For more information on the Meta-church model, read:

Building a Church of Small Groups by Bill Donahue and Russ Robinson
Prepare Your Church for the Future by Carl George

Free-market Groups.

Cell Group Purpose—The groups in this system are short-term semester groups that meet around a shared interest. Some of the interests include fly-fishing, dog training, snow skiing, home-school classes for home-schooled children, and investment planning. Some groups are created for nonbelievers, while others are tailored to the interests of believers, like prayer groups. This system uses the Engel scale, which provides 12 points on a continuum from –8 to +3, to identify a person's relationship to Christ. A person at –8 has no knowledge of the Gospel, a person at 0 has just made a decision for Christ, and a person at +3 is a mature, reproducing Christian. "Every small-group leader knows that his job is to bring the people in his group up one point on the Engel scale every semester."[5] The goal is to build relationships around these shared interests so that people will take one step closer to Christ. Therefore the groups vary from evangelism groups where the leader is the only Christian to Bible study groups who gather to study Paul's Epistle to the Romans.

Cell Group Support—The support structure is the same as that in the Cho model. For every 5-8 groups, there is a Section Leader. A Zone Leader oversees 5-8 sections. A District Pastor oversees 3-5 zones.[6] The small group topics must be approved by a Section Leader.

Cell Group Priority—Haggard argues "everyone is already in a small group…The church's job isn't to rearrange those people; it's to give their groups God's purpose."[7] Because this model sees everyone as already belonging to a group, it recognizes many different kinds of groups, allowing people to be creative without placing limitations upon them.

Equipping—As a person's interests change, she will join a new small group. Likewise, as a person takes steps on the Engel scale, he will most likely join a group that will equip him at his point of need. The training for cell group leaders is very basic, with the emphasis on getting people started and then training them on the job.

For more information on the Free-market cell model, read *Dog Training, Flying Fishing and Sharing Christ in the 21st Century* by Ted Haggard.

Once your church has researched the models and understood what is involved, I recommend a visit to a church that uses the model that interests you. You can learn many interesting and important things seeing cell groups in action.

SECTION 1.2 Discover the
Cell Group System

Cell group models are like shining stars. They beckon other churches to become like them. Pastors anticipate copying what other churches are doing. A church seeks to become a mini Willow Creek if church leaders like the Meta model. Or a little version of Yoido Full Gospel Church if the leaders favor the Cho/Neighbour model. Or a replica of Bethany World Prayer Center or the International Charismatic Mission if they embrace the Groups of 12.

Most pastors begin their journey toward cell groups by observing what God is doing through cell group models. These models provide "snap-shots" of methods for doing cell groups, but these "snap-shots" often prove deceiving. They reveal only the visible practices, not the unseen system and various sub-systems that work together to make cell groups work. The cell groups in model churches work because all of the systems are functioning properly, not because the model is an "ideal" way to do cell groups. As one cell pastor who has developed over 90 groups told me, "There is no magic bullet." There is no perfect structure or magical formula for making cell groups work. It is not enough to understand the models; a pastor must understand the systems that uphold the models.

What Are Systems?

Systems fill our lives. On an average day, we will breathe air that is brought to us by a weather system, drink water from a water system, drive on a highway system, send mail through the postal system, surf the system of the worldwide web, and work with others in a business system. "A system is a perceived whole whose elements 'hang together' because they continually affect each other over time and operate toward a common purpose."[8]

All of the parts of a model church "hang together" to form a system. The Apostle Paul talked about systems when he described the church as a body, with each person as a different part, each affecting the other parts (1 Corinthians 12:12-26). Peter Senge, one of the foremost communicators in systems thinking, describes the ability to think in terms of systems as "a discipline for seeing wholes. It is a framework for seeing inter-relationships rather than things, for seeing patterns of change rather than static snapshots."[9] The diagram on the next page will help you see the "whole" and provide a framework for seeing the ways cell groups relate to other sub-systems.

The diagram highlights five major systems: the cell group, the corporate celebration or worship service, the pastor-mentored leadership team, pastoral mentoring and oversight, and facilitative functions. Every church that has made cell groups work has developed these five systems, each of which has various subsystems. This chapter will define these systems, while Stages 5, 6, and 7 will demonstrate how to develop them.

Fig 1.3 The Cell-Based System: A Macro View

The Cell Group

For decades, the church around the globe has used small groups: Bible study groups, care groups, fellowship groups, task groups, discipleship groups, mission groups. Small groups are not new, but the small groups of the past tended to focus on just one aspect of life in the church. True cell groups, on the other hand, are holistic. This chart illustrates the shift:

From	To
Groups are a function of the church	Groups experience church life
Groups have a singular focus	Groups have a holistic focus
Groups are a ministry option	Ministry flows through the groups
Groups are a church-growth mechanism	Groups are a Kingdom-growth organism

Christian Schwarz and Christoph Schalk preformed research on over 1000 churches in 32 countries to determine the factors that contribute to church health. One of their eight factors is Holistic Small Groups. They state,

Holistic small groups are the natural place for Christians to learn to serve others—both in and outside the group—with their spiritual gifts. The planned multiplication of small groups is made possible through the continual development of leaders as a by-product of the normal group life. The meaning of the term "discipleship" becomes practical in the context of holistic small groups; the transfer of life, not rote learning of abstract concepts.[10]

The church is experiencing a shift from small group programs to holistic small groups. The groups are no longer limited to one aspect of Christian life, such as discipleship, Bible study, or service. Instead, they seek to create the experience of basic Christian community, which goes beyond simply attending a weekly small group meeting. Basic Christian community is an experience of Christ in the midst of a group of people who know one another, love one another, and support one another. It is the knowledge that Jesus has come to life by His Spirit moving through every member of the body.

The ministry of edification is stated in the Great Commandment: "Love the Lord your God with all your heart and with all your soul and with all your mind. This is the first and greatest commandment. And the second is like it: Love your neighbor as yourself" (Matthew 22:37-39). The ministry of expansion is stated in the Great Commission: "Therefore go and make disciples of all nations, baptizing them in the name of the Father and of the Son and of the Holy Spirit, and teaching them to obey everything I have commanded you. And surely I am with you always, to the very end of the age" (Matthew 28:19-20). The ministry of edification and expansion is the call of every church. It is also the call of every believer. The same call should form the foundation for every cell group.

In the diagram, the cell groups are the smallest gray circles. Notice that cell groups are not an appendage to the system. Rather they lie at the heart of the church, alongside the weekly corporate celebration. In other words, cell groups are not tacked on to a plethora of other already existing programs. Connecting to a group of people in a small group is crucial to life in this system. In addition, each cell group is connected to other cell groups in "coaching networks" or clusters. Every cell group leader needs a coach in order to be successful.

Corporate Celebration

Some cell group advocates have taken the vision for cell groups to the extreme and elevated cell groups over the corporate celebration of the church. Yet this seems to go too far. Large group celebration is just as crucial as small group community. The book of Acts refers to this experience as Temple worship (Acts 5:42) or public worship (Acts 20:20). Cell groups work best when they work in tandem with a large group experience, not independent of it.

The world's best cell group churches also have some of the world's best corporate gatherings. Joel Comiskey writes: "Some people presume that the cell is more important than the celebration service. Yet successful cell churches tell a different story. Celebration and cell attendance are two sides of the same coin: One is not sufficient without the other."[11] Many claim that Pastor Yonggi Cho is one of the best preachers they have heard. The worship at Faith Community Baptist Church is phenomenal, and Laurence Khong is an incredible teacher. Ben Wong of Shepherd Community Church in Hong Kong leads corporate worship services with vision, strong biblical teaching, and the people experience the presence of God. The worship services at Victory Christian Center include first-rate worship, top-notch teaching, and a sense of meeting God face to face.

This large group worship experience is necessary because it is the place where people experience the God who is bigger than themselves. It is where people join in a movement that is much larger than personal goals or even a group's goals. It is where they hear a vision from one of the leaders of the church who is set apart to equip them for works of service (see Ephesians 4:11-12). In the large group, church leaders inspire the people to a life that is beyond what is known in the every day, to experience life that transcends the ordinary.

When churches elevate the cell group experience too high and fail to develop the experience of the inspiring transcendence of God, they are out of balance. They only have the experience of the immanent God, where God comes near to His people. In the cell group, people discover the touch of His personal love, His intimate forgiveness, and His loving vulnerability. They learn that they can reveal themselves to God and trust Him with their feelings, their thoughts, and the hidden stuff of life. People discover this personal God as they reveal themselves to other people. Then these people become the nearness of God, revealing His mercy. Cell groups allow people to become "Jesus with skin on" for each other. It is remarkable how the private experience of God's presence directly increases with the increase of God's presence while with other people.

This experience of the transcendence and the immanence of God through the large group and the small group is a balanced approach to church life. The small group is not emphasized over the large group, nor is the large group emphasized over the small group.

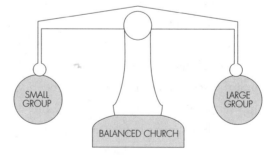

Fig 1.4 The Balanced Church

As churches work on developing the cell groups, they must also keep celebration strong. If the weekly celebration is weak, churches will find it necessary to strengthen it as they move through the 8-stage process.

Pastor-mentored Leadership Team

The vision and the anointing of God flow down from leadership, not up to it. Moses did not wait for the enslaved Israelites to come to him with leadership ideas. Jesus did not allow the disciples to set the vision for the Kingdom of God. Paul did not cower to those who opposed his vision of carrying the Gospel to the Gentiles. All three illustrate how leaders must catch vision and anointing from God for those they lead so that they can pass them down to others.

Not one of the churches I researched has implemented an effective cell group system without a visionary leader at the helm. This leader is a person set apart by God to lead the church, a person called to hear God's vision for the church, to communicate that vision, and to embody that vision.

The key to vision implementation is found in a pastor's ability to gather a team and then mentor team members in the vision. This team should be composed of those called to provide pastoral oversight to the corporate body. In a larger church, the team will be formed by staff members. In a smaller church, key volunteer leaders will work with the pastor to oversee the implementation of the vision.

Pastoral Mentoring and Oversight

The pastor carries the vision mantle given by God, and the leadership team works out what this vision will look like. But visions die if they are not transferred to the people who will carry them out.

The job of the leadership team is to mentor people and oversee front-line ministry. They must pass down the vision and the anointing they receive from God. Cell groups work as a part of a system of leadership interconnectivity. Cell leaders need mentoring from coaches. These coaches need mentoring from a pastor. These pastors must constantly focus on ways to mentor and develop the coaches and cell leaders under their care.

Such a sub-system is often called an oversight structure. There are two basic oversight structures currently in existence: the 5x5 and the G-12. The key to oversight success is not found in the structure. It is found in the relational mentoring that pastors and coaches provide to their leaders. This principle is so crucial and so often neglected by pastors as they develop groups that it will be highlighted over and over again in this book.

Facilitative Functions

The cell group structure and the weekly celebration are the visible systems that everyone sees when they attend a model cell group church. But there are many other systems that are necessary for these two visible structures to operate properly. Such sub-systems include nursery, worship leadership, assimilation, discipleship, leadership training, and many more. These I classify under the heading "Facilitative Functions."

Some churches have made the mistake of focusing solely upon the visible structures and sacrificing the crucial elements that facilitate the life in the large and small groups. Without greeters, nursery workers, an assimilation process, and a discipleship system, people do not know how to enter or grow in the life of the church. Stage 7 provides more information on facilitative functions and ways to develop them.

Articulate a Cell Group Vision

In Stage 1, a pastor should focus on learning as much as he can about how cell groups work. He must read books, attend conferences, and compare models. From these models, a pastor will recognize the systems that make the groups work. As God calls the church to develop cell groups, the vision for cell group ministry will grow in the senior pastor's heart and mind. He must then envision the ways to apply the cell group system to his church's context. Most likely, the vision will fall into one of these four categories:

A **vision to become cell-based**. This is the vision of the largest churches in the world. It is characterized by a senior pastor guiding the vision, holistic cell groups seeking to edify and expand, cell groups given priority alongside celebration, no other ministries competing with cell group participation, and the development of a clear track for discipling every cell member for ministry.

A **vision to try out holistic cell groups**. Many leaders are not ready to bite off the entire vision of becoming cell-based, but they do want to explore how cell groups might work. Such a vision is very wise for many churches because they are not ready for the radical shift of becoming completely cell-based.

A **focus on holistic cell groups**. The TOUCH staff developed a close relationship with a Vineyard pastor in southern California. He honestly told us, "I do not want to become a cell church. We are a Vineyard church. But I want to develop small groups that embrace the values you teach." We told him, "Great, just begin doing cell groups according to these patterns, and they will flourish. You don't have to have a vision to become a full-blown cell-based church." He has taken those steps and now is sold on cell groups. He wants more and more of them. At the same time, he does not want to change other parts of the church that are working well. Some churches already have many different kinds of groups and the pastor would like to see them shift to a holistic focus. This is happening in many innovative churches that have a variety of small groups, including task groups, Bible studies, evangelistic small groups, and even creative twists to Sunday school. In their attempts to improve their small group systems, they want to develop holistic cell groups, but they do not necessarily desire to become 100% cell-based. Stages 5-6 outline the key elements that churches like this need to focus on. If they want more of the vision, they can choose to go further later.

Including holistic cell groups as an optional type of small group. Some pastors will want to create holistic cell groups alongside other types of small groups. While the 8-Stage process does not provide a strategy for organizing other types of small groups, it will help in the development of the holistic groups that are a part of the vision.

A Relationship-based Church

Relationships lie at the heart of cell group life. All successful cell group models depend on relationships. One of the cell group leaders I oversee called me to share that the relationships in her group were going very well. She said that she does not want to confuse her leadership with her relationships, because she enjoys the relationships so much. She was making cell leadership much harder than it really is. I told her, "You are leading through your friendships, not apart from them. God uses friendships to bring people into maturity."

Dr. Phillip Sell, professor at Trinity Evangelical Divinity School and former pastor of a cell group church, calls this a relationship-based church. This model of church life contrasts with the program-based church, where a church creates programs to meet needs, the entertainment-based church where people come to catch a spiritual high every week, and the content-based church, where the church is a "teaching center" for people to attend every Sunday.

The goal of the cell group system is to develop a model for people to be connected to God, to be connected to one another, and to raise up disciples. This is the heart of the Great Commandment and the Great Commission. Some pastors have placed all their focus on the structure and made the change in structure the final goal. Some churches call themselves "cell churches" or G-12 churches, believing that they have found the ideal model and that other models don't measure up. Such churches take great pride in the fact that they are returning to a truly biblical model of church organization.

But in the end, labels matter very little. Being what God has called the church to be is everything. Floyd Schwanz, a former small groups pastor with Dale Galloway at one of the pioneering cell group churches in North America, puts it this way, "Don't talk about being cell-based because it sounds like another program (and we have too many of those already). Focus instead on being more relational through small groups." I consulted with one group of church elders a few years ago and illustrated the different models of cell groups. I shared with them how they could become a "pure" cell church. One elder piped up, "I have no interest in being a 'pure' cell church." The elders stated that they wanted to develop a structure that promoted the values of biblical relationships. They were not interested in labels, categories, or comparisons.

Pastors and church leaders must seek to understand the different structures and determine what will work best for them. But the vision ultimately is about relationships, not about fitting into the proper category or developing an ideal structure. The ways in which churches organize their cell group efforts will be different for almost every church. One way does not fit all.

SECTION 1.3 Discover
How Cell Groups Fit in Tomorrow's Church

I grew up attending the church that my father and mother attended. It was a church typical of the rural South. Membership averaged around 100 people; weekly attendance was about half that. The church was called Foote Baptist Church because the Foote family had donated the land in 1908. Because the church was the only public building, the neighborhood was called the Foote community.

Across the country are similar stories. A church's steeple was once the tallest man-made point for miles. A church served as the community center, not only for worship, but also for things like town meetings, social gatherings, and school. In the summer of 2001, my wife and I drove across western Kansas for vacation. As little towns surfaced on the horizon, I saw large grain silos and farmhouses surrounded by wheat fields. The most prominent features, however, were the steeples on church buildings. That architecture spoke loudly to me. The buildings were the tallest and most beautiful around, yet none of them were new. They stood as witnesses to the time of yesterday's church.

Such stories are also true in large cities. Look behind the new construction of steel and concrete and you will find cherished places of worship like First Baptist Church in Dallas, People's United Methodist in Chicago, and Park Street Church in Boston. In fact, when People's United Methodist Church was erected in 1924, its spire reached 568 feet into the air and was the tallest building in all of Chicago.[12]

People's United Methodist sat across from Chicago's city hall, symbolizing that the church watched over the life of the city. Outside my office window, a relatively successful Episcopal church in Houston has recently finished a new building. It stands in the shadow of two 12-story office buildings that sit at the edge of the "energy corridor," which includes companies like Exxon-Mobil, Shell, British Petroleum, and others. While the church of our fathers' youth stood above all aspects of life, it does so no longer. The church as we once knew it has disappeared.

The Church of Yesterday

The changes in church architecture only point to the surface of a deeper shift the church has undergone in the last 50 years. In fact, to understand the transformation of our culture and Christianity, we must capture a view of the role the church once played in society. To illustrate this role, we need to broaden our understanding of the church situation of the past. This diagram illustrates yesterday's church.

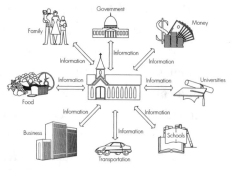

Fig 1.5 The Church of Yesterday

This was Christendom, which began with Emperor Constantine's Edict of Milan in 313 declaring Christianity a legal religion in the state of Rome. For the next 1,650 years, the church lived within the friendly confines of Christendom, where it held influence, authority, and the respect of the people.

Christendom was a period when Christianity was a cultural establishment, a marriage between the church and the majority culture. This marriage came in two basic forms. First, the establishment of state churches created governmental Christianity. This was the predominant model embraced by European Catholicism, German Lutheranism, British Anglicanism, and Swiss Calvinism. Second was social Christianity, which developed into the American form of Christianity. The state did not officially endorse any particular church; instead, denominations arose that were independent of the official government. The collective form of these denominations comprises Protestantism, which has been historically equated with Americanism. This is why so many Americans claim to be Christians even though they have not attended a church service in years.

Many times, it was very difficult to see where the majority culture stopped and the church started.[13] This is illustrated throughout the pages of history. Pope Leo III crowned Charlemagne as emperor in 800. Frederick of Saxony protected Martin Luther from Catholic persecution for political reasons more than religious ones. Because Henry VIII of England could not obtain permission for divorce from the Pope, he established Anglicanism. The Pilgrims founded Massachusetts Bay Colony to escape persecution in Europe, as well as to create a truly Christian society. The First Great Awakenings were not limited to the church; the movement also gave rise to the American Revolution. All but one U.S. President (who declared himself a Catholic) has claimed membership to a Protestant church. Throughout the history of Europe and North America, countless events illustrate the marriage of the church and society.

This church of yesterday sat in the middle of all of life, as the diagram illustrates. The points below delineate the meaning of the church in the middle of society.

View of Information: The church was the most respected institution in society. Therefore, the church's role was to inform, advise, and teach people about how to live. The people then would take this information with them as they went about their daily lives.

Influence: The Kingdom of God was viewed geographically, so when the impact of a Christian nation expanded, the impact of the church expanded. The church sought to expand its influence by erecting new buildings which people would come to for worship. This practice carried over into the missionary movements of the 19th and 20th centuries.

Role of the clergy: Clergymen were often the most educated, articulate, and respected men in society. They had traveled, they read, and they could teach. At the same time, they often played the role of a chaplain, in that they pastored those who came to them. For instance, a Baptist pastor often saw his role as pastoring the Baptists within a certain geographical setting.

Authority of the church: A church grew in its authority as it grew in size, thereby increasing its ability to influence the agendas of society.

View of Faith: Faith was a private affair, characterized by "personal conversion" and personal baptism. When a church did get involved in social issues, it did so at the expense of faith by trying to promote the well-being of the social structure.

Ministry Method: Church was viewed as a place where certain things happened. Church became a building on "1st and Main" where official services were held, led by official leaders.

Some might argue that this analysis of Christendom is too harsh. In some ways, they are right. Many people were saved and became vital parts of the Kingdom of God through this model of ministry. I am among those people. The United States was founded upon the principles of Christendom. Many great institutions were created under this ideology. Thank God for what He has done through His church!

But the fact remains that the age of Christendom exists no longer. The aim of Christendom was to make "faith credible to the powers-that-be so that Christians might now have a share in those powers."[14] But that was yesterday. The "powers-that-be" care little about what the church today has to offer.

The Church of Today

If Christendom is dead, how do we know when it died? The authors of the book *Resident Aliens*, Stanley Hauerwas and William Willimon, pinpoint the death of Christendom to 1963 when the Fox Theater ran a picture show on Sunday night. They write, "Before the Fox Theater opened on Sunday, we could convince ourselves that, with an adapted and domesticated gospel, we could fit American values into a loosely Christian framework, and we could thereby be culturally significant."[15] This diagram illustrates the situation of the church of today.

Fig 1.6 The Church of Today

Whether or not the exact date of the death of Christendom occurred in 1963 matters little. The fact remains that the church is no longer at the center of society. It has been marginalized and included alongside every other element of society, forced to compete for the attention of individuals who have to choose between the myriad options that bombard them every day. The church finds itself competing for time, influence, and power. And often it finds itself competing with the rules that society has established. Here are some characteristics of the church today:

View of Information: There is no dominant or single respected source of information. All sources of information are viewed as equally credible, depending upon how different people view life. The newspapers, internet, paparazzi, television talk shows, fashion magazines, and cable all compete with the Gospel of the church.

Influence: The church competes for influence with cultural icons like rock stars or basketball players. These cult-like icons often have more direct influence on what is seen as right or wrong than do church leaders.

Role of the minister: Ministers are no longer the most educated or articulate leaders, even in small towns. They are relegated to the role of "spiritual" experts and are not viewed as having any knowledge about real life.

Authority: Often churches have sought authority by adopting the practices of business marketing and promotion. Other churches have tried to compete by embracing the practices of the entertainment world. But it is impossible to compete with Madison Avenue or Hollywood.

View of Faith: Faith is no longer a private affair, instead being discussed in such forums as afternoon talk-shows, Internet chat-rooms, coffee shops, even lecture halls. People can even find Jesus outside established churches.

Ministry Method: Ministry includes high-class productions, super-star preaching, entertaining music, expensive promotions, anything that will attract people to attend weekly services. In other words, the church has become a vendor of religious goods and services.

Many churches are seeing results as they minister in this highly competitive environment. We live in the age of the super-church. These churches are led by especially gifted leaders and communicators who have discovered ways to compete with the options of life. Praise God for these pioneering leaders and churches! These very large and successful churches are needed in our society. We need significant churches that can have influence upon the culture, upon politics, and upon larger cultural issues. They serve as towers of light in very dark places.

Yet these churches are the exception rather than the rule. Most churches are failing as they try to compete with the forces that pull people ten different directions in turn-of-the-century society. Churches do not have the leadership skills, the resources, or the vision to become super-churches. While some churches can compete, most cannot keep up.

The Church of Tomorrow

Not everyone believes that the church must be in competition with the rest of the world. There is a model of ministry arising that sees the church on mission, penetrating and taking church to the ordinary stuff of life. This view of the church on mission requires a mental shift in our understanding of the church. Church is not something that people do one day a week. Church is something people belong to and take with them wherever they go. Church must become a way of life, not just a meeting. Church can be held wherever two or three are gathered, not just in a building specifically set aside for religious purposes. This church on mission might be illustrated like this:

Fig 1.7 The Church of Tomorrow

If the church is going to be the church of God, it must become a church on mission. With this shift, people are not limited to attending fixed church activities; the church goes to the people. The church invades schools, businesses, families, colleges, even the government. It infects all of life, not just the official "services" that happen at official buildings. The church on mission recognizes that Christians aren't cars to be topped off with spiritual gas once a week. Here are some further characteristics of the church of the future:

View of Information: This kind of church realizes that the church cannot compete nor can it convince; therefore it seeks to demonstrate the Gospel in life by allowing God to move through its members. When others see the reality of life-change, the door is open for the Gospel message.

Influence: Because positions of ministry are not respected in society, personal relationships are the primary means of having influence on others. People will discuss their beliefs with friends.

Role of the minister: The minister's role is no longer that of "doing the ministry" of the church but that of leading, equipping, and mentoring. The new goal is to mobilize others so that they can minister in their respective worlds.

Authority: The church does not seek to attain authority in the world. Instead, it understands that its only authority is found in weakness. This weakness leads the church on mission to depend upon the Spirit of God, because without Him, the people only look like fools.

Faith: Faith is understood to penetrate all of life, all the time. People are mobilized as faith missionaries or faith ministers to their respective 'worlds.' These 'worlds' include neighborhoods, places of employment, clubs, and any other activities where people have relationships with nonbelievers.

Ministry Method: The church on mission chooses, mentors, and releases people for ministry. It does this by building community in relational small groups and then helps people practice their gifts. In this way, the church becomes a body of people sent on mission.

The church on mission is a church of opportunity. Its purpose is to equip and send people to act as missionary platoons, not to limit itself to inviting people to come to a building or to just provide excellent professional ministry. The church on mission is not limited to any specific type or size of church. A 25-member rural church can enter into God's mission on this earth just as well as a 2,500-member suburban church can. Its focus is not upon building a huge church but on following God to touch the world. It seeks to follow Christ into the unknown and take the life of the Gospel where it has yet to go.

Missions vs. Mission

The church at the center of society (Christendom) practiced the principle of missions, which involved missions giving, missions trips, missions reporting, and missionary commissioning. Missions was an activity that special people did in places outside of Christendom.

Local churches supported these missions activities, but they were seen as something separate and ancillary from the central activities of the local church.

Missionaries have accomplished great deeds in the name of Jesus. Servants like St. Patrick, William Carey, Hudson Taylor, John R. Mott, Jim Elliot, and many others have taken the Gospel to places of darkness and established churches that are now impacting entire nations. Being involved in missions and sending missionaries is not the point where the church fell short; it fell short because it divorced the work of mission from what it meant to be the church of God. Because it viewed the church as sitting within the walls of Christendom, missions work was something that happened outside the church. The church limited its purpose to ministering to those within Christendom. This practice tended to keep the missionary call of the church at arms length and kept the focus on maintaining the ministry at home.

While the church still sends money, missions teams, and missionaries to do missions work, the church has realized that mission is something that is integrally tied to the meaning of being the church in this world. "The church is not the sending agency; it is the sent agency."[16] The church is sent by God to represent life in the Kingdom of God and thereby show the principalities and the powers of this world what it means to truly live.

Churches that are impacting people through cell groups understand that the call of the church is to send itself. They know that cell groups are designed to do much more than close the back door or get people already in the church connected by relationships. These churches have a vision that is much bigger than themselves. They have a vision to impact the world.

Often people think that only large churches have the luxury of participating in mission. Grass-roots movements like The Sycamore Network in Savannah, Georgia are taking up the challenge to enter this mission. This network is formed by a group of four congregations located in different parts of the city. While each congregation worships separately, they share leadership, resources, and training. They do this because their aim is not to build a big church. That vision is too small. They want to launch cell congregations all over the city. They have developed a training school for future leaders and are even praying about planting new churches overseas that will be part of the network.

Three Options for the Church

The church is standing at a crossroads. One pastor states it this way:

We are living at an important and fruitful moment right now, for it is clear to church leaders that the images of Christian leadership given by the religious subculture are worn out; a minister can no longer depend on them. By the time a person in professional ministry reaches thirty-five, he or she knows that the images of the knowledgeable, doctrinally sound, politically correct, and above all successful pastor that were learned in seminary (and at the Christian bookstore or leadership conference) simply do not work in life. Such a Christian leader is open to new vision of what a Christian and a church leader is or could be.[17]

No leader is exempt from the choice set before the church. As Leonard Sweet writes, "Whether we like it or not, God has chosen you and me to live in interesting times."[18] We as church leaders do not have a choice about the times that we live in, but we do have options about how we respond to this situation. Our options are three.

We can fight to reestablish the church as a physical place where certain things happen. Many churches across North America have adopted this strategy on the assumption that society remains basically Christian. They quote statistics that support the fact that people claim to be Christians. They even look to the shift in the return to morals in political leadership. They assume that the government, big business, and education are looking to the opinions of the church to make their decisions. Douglas John Hall, a theologian who has sought to understand the church in turn-of-the-century society wrote, "I believe that commitment to the established institutional model of the church is the single most important cause of inertia and the retardation of intentional and creative responses to this great transition."[19]

These institutional churches even try to use cell groups to hold on to or get back what they once had. These groups become holding cells for those who are already in the church. Their group meetings focus on "deep" Bible knowledge without any reference to practical ways the groups can live out what they discuss. Such attempts at cell groups leave people with the feeling that cell groups will not work in the church. The problem is not the cell group strategy, but the approach to the strategy. When a church tries to put new clothes on a lifeless skeleton from yesterday's closet, it remains lifeless, no matter how it is dressed up.

We can work harder to compete with society, to out-entertain and lure people in with as much pomp and circumstance as a church can afford. Some will be won to the Lord this way. Many will find this option very exciting. Some very large churches have the resources to make this strategy work. Many will even include cell groups in this option, but cells often only serve as holding pens for people who attend the church. They prove effective at "closing the back door," but they lack the ability to mobilize people for mission. At best, this strategy will only maintain the status quo.

We can lead our churches to become churches on mission. In reality, this is the only choice. God is not interested in returning to yesterday and He does not have a maintenance strategy. He is a God on mission. He is going places and doing things that we would never imagine. And He longs for His church to go with Him.

Joining the God of Mission

David Bosch, author of *Transforming Mission* stated, "Mission [is] understood as being derived from the very nature of God…The classical doctrine of the missio Dei as God the Father sending the Son, and God the Father and the Son sending the Spirit [is] expanded to include yet another "movement": Father, Son, and Holy Spirit sending the church into the world."[20] Simply put, God is a God of mission. His very nature as Father, Son, and Holy Spirit is to send Himself into the world in order to save the world. God did not sit in heaven, waiting for us to reach up to Him. He first sent His Son and then the Spirit with a mission to reveal Him to us.

Paul said the same thing when he wrote, "Who, being in very nature God, did not consider equality with God something to be grasped, but made himself nothing, taking the very nature of a servant, being made in human likeness. And being found in appearance as a man, he humbled himself and became obedient to death—even death on a cross" (Philippians 2:6-8).

Paul tells the church to have this "same mind," which was also in Christ Jesus. The mission of the church and of every cell group is the same as the mission of Christ: we must give up our rights and privileges and become servants for the sake of showing others what it means to live in Christ. We have a mission to give away the life that we have received. Jesus clearly articulated this when he inaugurated his ministry with these words:

'The Spirit of the Lord is on me,
because he has anointed me
to preach good news to the poor.
He has sent me to proclaim freedom for the prisoners

and recovery of sight for the blind,
to release the oppressed,
to proclaim the year of the Lord's favor' (Luke 4:18-19).

It is time again to embrace the Spirit of the Lord, to bring good news to the poor. We must go out and bring freedom to the prisoners and sight to the blind. We must bring release to the oppressed in every city, state, and nation. We must go and proclaim the Lord's favor in our neighborhoods and our communities. Together, we can impact the world for Christ.

A pastor of a small Baptist church in Georgia gathered a team of core leaders. Through the reading of *The Purpose-Driven Church* by Rick Warren, they were prompted to develop a new vision for the church. After working for 18 months on this vision, they concluded that their current structures would not accomplish the vision that God had given them. This led the pastor on a search for a new structure, which led him to cell groups.

Cell Groups on Mission

Bosch states, "There is a church because there is a mission, not vice versa. To participate in mission is to participate in the movement of God's love toward people, since God is a fountain of sending love."[21] There are cell groups because there is a mission. Having cell groups simply for the sake of having cell groups results in disappointing lifelessness.

Cell groups on mission take their mission personally, because they know the God who took His mission personally. They act as conduits of God's sending love, touching the unloved. They enter His mission by reaching out to friends and neighbors. They see people in need and seek to minister to them. They work together to reach out to a homeless person. They minister to a sick cell member and take her children into their homes. They start a group at work and invite unsaved colleagues.

They reach out to single mothers who need a family. In other words, they take the life of God to people, instead of waiting for people to come to them. Such a mission is costly. Howard Snyder reveals part of the cost:

> In the church business, people are concerned with church activities, religious behavior, and spiritual things. In the Kingdom business, people are concerned with Kingdom activities, all human behavior and everything God has made, visible and invisible. Kingdom people see human affairs as saturated with spiritual meaning and Kingdom significance.[22]

On the day that Jesus announced the "Year of the Lord's Favor," He did not receive warm applause. No one invited Him to speak at a religious leaders' conference. He did not receive a book contract. Instead, He was escorted to the brow of a hill to be thrown down a cliff, a foreshadowing of His coming death. The cost to participate in Jesus' mission ("Kingdom business" as Snyder calls it) is nothing less than death, death to "church activities," death to "religious behavior," death to "spiritual things." It means death to self-preservation. It is impossible to join in God's mission when the church clings to its own agenda. The church and cell groups were made for mission. Anything else leads to a lifeless existence.

Revelation 12:11 reads, "They overcame him by the blood of the Lamb and by the word of their testimony; they did not love their lives so much as to shrink from death." People do not die for structures. People will not die for cell group organization. People die because they are in love with the One who calls them on mission. This mission calls them to give their lives up for others in cell group community. When people experience this kind of Christ-life through their cell groups, they press on to discover how to share this life with more and more people, giving them a reason to live and to die.

SECTION 1.4 Discover
How to Lead Change

Leading change in the church is one of the biggest danger points of any pastor's career. Dr. Ralph Neighbour wrote a book in 1973 entitled *The Seven Last Words of the Church: "We Never Tried It That Way Before."*[23] If you want to develop a Top 10 List of Least Innovative Organizations in your city, look first at the local churches. This struggle remains true even with the advent of creative ministries like cell groups, seeker services, worship bands, and Friday night worship. Since most churches look at change with suspicion, they must undergo a shift regarding change itself. One author puts it this way: "Change your church's attitude toward change and everything else will change as it should."[24]

Life in cell groups is about change: changing people, changing the church culture, and changing the structure. It is not enough for a church leader to know that cell groups will work, nor is it enough for him to understand how cell groups work all over the world. Church leaders must understand how to lead people on the journey from no cell groups to expanding cell groups. They must discover how to guide people through change if the vision for cell groups will work in a particular church setting.

Constraints of Change

Cell group proponents have used the J-curve to illustrate the expansion potential that cell groups possess. Supposing that a church starts with one group and that group along with subsequent groups will multiply annually, the math would be as follows:

Year 1—	1 group
Year 2—	2 groups
Year 3—	4 groups
Year 4—	8 groups
Year 5—	16 groups
Year 6—	32 groups
Year 7—	64 groups
Year 8—	128 groups
Year 9—	256 groups
Year 10—	512 groups
Year 11—	1,024 groups
Year 12—	2,048 groups

In the beginning, the expansion of groups is slow, but then it takes off in years seven and eight. Some churches have seen this kind of explosive expansion of their cell groups and have growth curves in the form of a J.

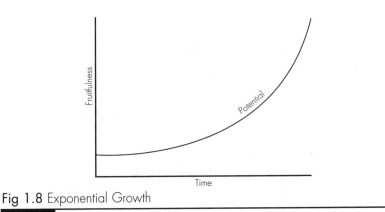

Fig 1.8 Exponential Growth

Some people might state that adopting the new structure of cell groups means seeing incredible growth. But if growth were as simple as doing the math, there would be hundreds of churches across the United States with more than 500 cell groups. There is more to cell group fruitfulness than mathematical equations.

Fighting against change are constraints. Constraints might include an associate pastor who has no experience with cell group ministry and no desire to work with groups, elders who are legalistic and critical of the pastor's leadership, or cell group members who have no desire to care for one another or reach out to those who don't know Jesus. These constraints prevent churches from seeing exponential growth.

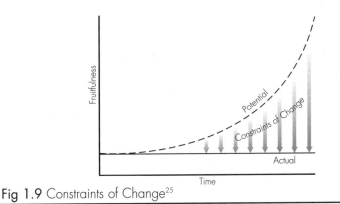

Fig 1.9 Constraints of Change[25]

Making cell groups work is not about mathematical equations. Cell group growth comes because people put effort into making cell groups work. Cell group members and leaders must go through a change process before they can put their energy behind the new cell groups. If a pastor fails to understand the ways people process change, he will add one more constraint to the list of forces fighting against cell groups.

Levels of Change

When people enter a change process, they must wrestle with many different levels of change all at once. Imagine the suburban church of 200 people that has been doing Sunday school since its inception twenty years ago. The pastor learns about cell groups and sees the structural differences between the two strategies. But the changed structure is only the visible level of change. Beneath the surface lie two elements that must also change because they support the structural change. Without a change of culture and of individual values, a change of structures will fail.

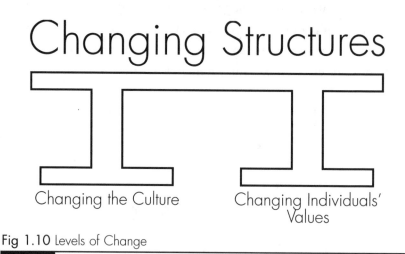

Changing Structures

Changing the Culture   Changing Individuals' Values

Fig 1.10 Levels of Change

Changing Structures. Changing the structure stands out the most when a church begins cell groups, because the structure is what people can see. For many churches, cell group ministry is radically different from the ministry of the traditional church. The change to a cell group strategy involves reorganization of leadership, development of new training, meeting away from the church building, and refocusing the vision. These are the visible trappings.

Every week, people call TOUCH or come to a conference asking questions like, "How do I start cell groups?" or "How do I do Groups of 12?" These are vital questions, but when the issues that underlie the structure are not addressed, the structure will crumble.

While changing the structure of an organization can happen as quickly as a leader chooses to make the announcement, changing the underlying factors can take years. Think about it. Moses led the Israelites out of slavery, but he did not lead the slavery out of the culture. It took 40 years of wandering through the wilderness before the people were prepared to enter the Promised Land.

Changing the Culture. Culture can be described as the set of beliefs, feelings, and values that a group of people shares. The culture of a group of people is so much a part of who they are that it is impossible for them to define it. It is like asking a fish to explain water to a mammal. It cannot understand water because water is its culture.[26]

Likewise, Christians are a part of a church culture. Some share a culture that understands church as programs, committee meetings, and congregational voting. Others share a culture that views the church as a building where people come for weekly spiritual feeding and entertainment. Still others share a culture of a church where people get saved and walk the aisle, but the relationships end when the pastor says, "Amen."

When Don Tillman planted his first cell group church, he had the help of many people who had been a part of a Sunday school system for decades. They could not imagine meeting anywhere else than in a church building. One group refused to meet in a home. They met for months on the sidewalk outside the school building the church rented for worship celebration, until the weather turned so cold they could do so no more. Reluctantly, they moved their meetings into a home. Once they had experienced the new environment, they became some of the strongest proponents for doing things in new ways.

Many cell group initiatives have stalled because pastors failed to address the beliefs, feelings, and values that hide beneath the surface. Some hope that the culture will shift as the structure changes, but this is rarely the case.

Changing Individuals' Values. Without the third level of change, that of changing individuals' values, neither the strategy nor the culture will ever change to be what God is calling it to be. Imagine the cell group leader who has been an elder for 20 years but has blocked every leadership initiative that every pastor has suggested. Imagine the former seminarian who is leading a new group but talks for two hours because he is the only one who knows Greek. Imagine the Sunday school superintendent who does not know where he fits into the new system, the music minister who does not want to pastor people, or the youth minister who does not want to change what he is doing. Picture the deacon who is judgmental of "sinners" and has no desire to build relationships with the lost and invite them to a cell group.

Individual change occurs as the Lord moves to transform individual hearts and lives. As people change, the culture changes. As the culture changes, the structure can change all the more. This individual change must happen at three levels. First, individuals need to change their knowledge. For this they need new information. They need to understand the basic vision of cell groups and how they work. Second, they need to change their attitudes and values. For this they need to see how present attitudes and values fail to line up with the Word of God.

The final change must occur at the level of behavior. People need to practice church life in a different way to see different results.[27]

Why People Change

Why do church members view change with an air of suspicion? Some might argue that they lack faith or don't love the lost. Others are living in nostalgia or stuck in old forms of ministry. These are outward expressions of the underlying response that people have to a new idea. When you get into the mind of a person who is evaluating a new idea, you will notice that there are many thoughts that contribute to the final decision to accept or reject change. People evaluate opportunities according to this change formula:

$$(A + B + C) > D = Change^{28}$$

A = a significant dissatisfaction with current reality

B = an awareness of a better condition

C = a knowledge of the first step(s) to take

D = the anticipated loss as a result of the change

People prefer the status quo because it is safe. In order for a person to adopt a new idea, he must experience dissatisfaction with the status quo. He must know of a better way. And he must see the first steps to take. These three things must add up to be greater than the anticipated loss or pain that will result from the change.

Consider Bob, the head deacon and leader of the largest Sunday school class. His level of dissatisfaction with current reality is low because his ministry is going well. He has read about cell groups because the pastor gave him a book, but he is using those principles to grow his class. The pastor knows that few lost people are being reached, but Bob is unwilling to change. He cares little about the first steps. He would lose the opportunity to lead his class if the church shifted to cell groups. Therefore, he will not embrace this new vision.

Next consider Sue, the leader of the women's Bible studies for the last 10 years. Lately, she has realized that these groups are going nowhere and that the women are starting to get bored. She has tried a new curriculum, videos, and special speakers, but nothing makes any difference. She read the same book as Bob about cell groups and began to see a different way of doing ministry. She talked with the pastor about the future, and he explained what the next steps were. Then she realized that if they did this right, they could start women's cell groups. Sue called her pastor and asked if he had any more books on cell groups.

This combination of factors clarifies why some people explore cell groups while others resist them. In order to get key leaders to embrace this change, pastors must take the time to help them work through their issues concerning the change instead of trying to force-feed the change. This requires the hard work of communication—listening and sharing while allowing time to process the idea—which is the only way to get people on board with a new idea.

Rules for Communicating Change

Joel Barker, a researcher in implementing change, has developed a video called *Tactics of Innovation*.[29] In the video, he presents five sets of communication tactics that increase the adoption rate of a new idea. He applies these to the business world. I have applied them to the adoption of cell groups.

Upside, Yes—Downside, No. People will be much more likely to adopt cell groups when they see the incredible upside of the strategy. This is very easy to communicate. Cell groups allow everyone to get involved in ministry. They are much more cost effective than building more classrooms. They connect people in relationships. And they provide a natural place for nonbelievers to explore Christ. Initial communication should also address the consequences if cell groups do not work or fail to live up to expectations. People must see that there is little downside to the new vision.

Seemingly Simple—Small Steps. Cell groups are based on a very simple principle—"Love one another." If people in the groups learn to love one another, the groups will work. Vision communication should focus on this and not the complex details concerning the theology, structures, and strategy. Most people in the pews do not care. They just want to experience the life of the groups and taste their fruit. They want to know the basic steps to get started loving one another. They do not want to get bogged down with cell group theory or theology.

Clear Message—Compatible Fit. The message of cell groups must be clear. What will they look like? What is their purpose? How will people be involved? These are questions a potential adopter wants answered. After she understands what cell groups are, she will determine if the groups fit with the vision and the values that the church has expressed to this point.

Credible Messenger—Reliable Performance. If the cell group visionary does not have credibility, church members will not follow. This is why it is so crucial that the senior pastor cast the vision for cell groups. As the credible messenger sharing the vision of groups, he must communicate the reliable performance of cell groups in other settings to help prove that they will work in his church. This can occur by visiting another church or inviting an experienced cell group practitioner to share the vision.

Easy In—Easy Out. People are more likely to change when there is an easy way to begin. If the change requires huge up-front investments before people can try it out, they will not likely change. Likewise, if people feel that they will not have the opportunity to get out of cell groups if they do not like them, they will often fight them.

These five sets of communication tactics serve as guidelines for getting people to consider a new idea. In fact, these tactics can be found in Jesus' ministry. For instance, Jesus introduced his ministry as "preaching the good news of the kingdom of God" (Luke 4:43), *Upside, Yes*. If the message failed for them, they could return home just as the disciples did after Jesus' crucifixion, *Downside, No*. Then he invited the first disciples to be "fishers of men" (Luke 5:10); He did not tell them about the cross from day one, *Seemingly Simple* and *Small Steps*. His message was very *Clear* when he said, "It is not the healthy who need a doctor, but the sick." And his ministry was a *Compatible Fit* when he said, "I have not come to call the righteous, but sinners to repentance" (Luke 5: 31-2). If there was ever a *Credible Messenger*, Jesus proved himself to be just that—"He spoke with authority"—and he practiced *Reliable Performance*, working seemingly countless miracles. He never forced anyone to change; rather He invited people to participate and even told those who were not ready to go back home, *Easy In—Easy Out.*

People make cell groups work. It takes people to make the church work. Jesus realized this. He came to help people reinvent their lives through His grace. Jesus communicated in such a way that the people who needed His grace could hear it.

Leading the Charge

Just as ships have captains who guide the crew, churches moving into cell groups have leaders at their helms. Churches do not enter into mission without a mission leader. In fact, if a church body is left without a mission leader, it will always choose the path of least resistance, and the course of cell groups on mission is definitely not that.

If there is one thing that all the research shows regarding making cell groups work, it is this: the senior pastor leads the charge. Whether the church is large or small, rural or urban, traditional or creative, each one that has had a fruitful experience with cell groups has had the senior pastor guiding the church and the cell groups on a mission. The pastors possess a few common traits of leaders.

Leaders are Compelled. The greater the conviction the pastor has about the importance of cell group ministry, the greater the chance of making cell groups work. Model cell church leaders felt a biblical mandate to guide their churches into a missional cell group system. For them, it was not just a good idea or a creative shift in ministry. It was a response to God's call to be the church. Tony Plummer, pastor of Venice Bible Church in Florida states, "I had to do cell groups without question. I wanted to stop building structures and start building people." Bill Henning, associate pastor at Abundant Life Church in Maryland, puts it this way, "You need to know that this is a strategy of the Holy Spirit for you." Pastors that feel this kind of conviction are motivated. They are hungry to see God move in the church no matter the personal cost.

Leaders Envision. Leaders see what others cannot see. They know something in their hearts that has not been made real yet. They possess a picture of what the church can be and it grabs their hearts so deeply that they are not satisfied until that picture becomes reality. The cell group pioneers saw a vision for cell groups in their hearts and minds. Now that models of effective cell group ministry have arisen, leaders can see the vision in action in other places. The vision does not have to originate entirely new from within the heart of a leader; he only needs see the missional cell group vision so that he can lead his people there.

Leaders Learn. To learn how to pastor in the traditional church, pastors attend seminary for three years, learning theology, biblical exegesis, preaching skills, and evangelism. If such an emphasis is placed upon learning how to lead the traditional church model, why should leaders not place just as much or more emphasis on learning about leading the church into missional cell groups? One of the gravest mistakes that leaders make is to stop learning. The pastors that have made cell groups work are voracious learners, seeking every avenue available to discover new insight about the journey.

Leaders Lead. Many pastors find themselves doing what Peter Wagner calls "one-on-one" ministry while a few church members actually set the course for the church. This is not leadership. Pastors are called to be mission leaders, not church caretakers. To lead means to go before, to set the course, establish the vision, and to have others follow on that vision path. Kennon Callahan, a church consultant, states this well:

> Leaders lead. Leaders lead toward discovery and fulfillment. Leaders do not manage or administrate, manipulate or dictate, process or enable, mandate or command, threaten or scare. They do not push, prod, or poke—they lead. Leaders lead. And the grouping—whether a local church, a subcultural grouping, a movement, or a nation—senses that this person is helping them toward discovery and fulfillment.[30]

To lead the cell group vision, the pastor must do just that—lead it. He must take the time to initiate and guide the vision. Even more, he must participate in the vision by embracing the values of cell group life. People do what the pastor does. They don't do what he says. If the pastor is relational, the people will follow. If the pastor hides from people, church members will hide from one another.

Leaders Equip. Churches that make cell groups work are led by pastors who have shifted their understanding of ministry from that of "doing" ministry to that of equipping others to do ministry. Ephesians 4:11-12 makes it very clear that the leadership of the church is not to be paid to perform ministry, but to equip or prepare the church for ministry. One pastor describes his role as a coach and the leaders and members of the church are the players. His job is to prepare the people to win in ministry.

This requires a big shift for most pastors. Traditionally, the full-time pastor is paid to study, preach, visit the sick and elderly, counsel, manage the church property, and take care of crises. Rarely do pastoral job descriptions include things like developing a leadership team, recruiting, training, and mentoring future leaders, or releasing people to operate in spiritual gifts. An equipping pastor understands that all ministry does not need to go through him.

Leaders Stay. Kent Hunter, a church consultant, argues that it takes seven years before a pastor enters into his most effective time of ministry. Unfortunately, the average tenure of a senior pastor is less than four years. Hunter states that most pastors move on to brighter pastures in years four and five because the "alligators" of the church start to bite and tear him down. These "alligators" are usually a small contingency, while the majority who have no complaints sit silently by.

What is a pastor to do? Hunter encourages pastors to "hang in there" and show the "alligators" that they cannot be pushed around. Most of the time, these "alligators" will find other ponds where they can cause trouble or else become harmless bullfrogs.[31]

Senior pastors that are leading their churches on the journey toward making cell groups work must understand this crucial point: without the initiating leader, a church will revert back to the old vision because the people do not understand the new vision. Over and over churches have moved into effective cell group ministry, and then the pastor moved on to another church. Within a year, the churches set cell groups aside and returned to what they knew best. The only exceptions to this: churches where the new senior pastor had a strong cell group vision and had been a staff member under the former senior pastor.

Leaders Know their Limitations. The most effective pastors do not fall to the temptation that they can lead the change by themselves. They seek counsel, learn from other pastors, and seek help where it is needed. Some churches have invested in consultants. Many pastors receive on-going coaching from an experienced cell group expert or pastor. Others secure outside speakers to promote the vision and train their people. Such outside help has proven especially important for those pastors who have had little success in leading change in the past.

Cell Group Change Strategies

The journeys of various churches in transition typically fall into one of four categories.

Instant Cell Church Strategy.

In this strategy, innovative leaders get the vision and run with it. One of the characteristics of this strategy is that cell groups are legislated by the pastor. I heard the story of one pastor who stood before his church on a Sunday morning and held up Ralph Neighbour's book *Where Do We Go From Here?*. He told church members that the book represented the new direction of the church. Then he said, "Either you are going with me or I am leaving to go somewhere else." The good news is that this pastor had served this church for over 20 years and had enough credibility with the people to make such a statement. The bad news is that most people did not understand what the vision entailed, and consequently the church has struggled to get cell groups on the right track. Another pastor used a similar tactic and was fired by his deacon board before the day was out. He works at a secular job today.

Legislating change in a church rarely works, even if a pastor has the power of the Pope. There are two reasons this is true. The first reason is because persuasive arguments cannot convince someone that one way of life is better than another. No matter how much data you give people that cell groups are a better form of ministry, those who have ties to other styles of ministry will still resist the change. Human persuasion alone will not get people to give up the stability of what they have today to change to something that is unknown.

Secondly, even if people are persuaded that cell groups are better, enforcement of cell groups will not lead to changed values. When groups are legislated and people are assigned to join groups, people become a part of a programmic cell group system. It might have all the trappings of a working cell group system, but it has little life because the people see cell groups as a different way of doing the same kind of church. This will lead to stagnant groups, the very thing that churches need to leave behind them.

The Blueprint Strategy.

This strategy happens when one church tries to replicate the strategy of another church. Sadly, this is a very popular strategy. People read a book on cells or go to a conference. They return to their churches and try to mimic the strategy of the church they have learned about. This happened when people went to Singapore to learn from Faith Community Baptist Church, to Korea to learn from Yoido Full Gospel Church, and to Baton Rouge, LA to learn from Bethany World Prayer Center. Now people are doing this with International Charismatic Mission in Bogota, Colombia.

To illustrate the weakness of this strategy, imagine an owner of a small manufacturing company visiting General Electric to learn how they run their operation. He purchases all of its manuals, interviews key leaders, and reads every book available on this great "model" business. He returns home to implement everything that GE does. But he soon discovers that it is impossible. First, GE does business on such a grand scale that no small business owner could copy all of its methods. Second, GE has refined its methods over a period of decades. The small business owner needs time to learn how the methods work. He cannot force them to work overnight.

Most churches are small. Most model churches are large and they have been refining their ministry methods so long that they have internalized them. It is crucial for small churches to learn from these large model churches. Even seeing what they do with cell groups and adapting that strategy to one's own setting will prove vital. But to mimic or impersonate another's cell group strategy is often a recipe for disaster. Leonard Sweet offers this advice: "Every successful church is successful in its own way. However we may try to pass ministries off as our own 'intuitive' insights, settling for mimicry and impersonation only offers up a recipe for extinction."[32]

I encourage pastors to go to the conferences of model cell group churches like Bethany World Prayer Center, Long Reach Church of God, Victory Christian Center, and others. But to try to reproduce exactly what these pastors are doing is impossible. It is important to read about the Groups of 12 strategy and other cell group models, but to force a church into a predetermined structural blueprint will limit the creativity that God desires to express in a church.

The Roadmap Strategy.

This strategy assumes that leading people into cell groups is a linear process of going from step A to step B, etc. With this assumption, people look to books and churches for a logical place to start. Many experts have said that the best place to begin with cell groups is with one group (often called a prototype or pilot group) led by the pastor. After the first group, there are predetermined steps.

But the journeys of most model churches did not progress in straight lines. Almost every one started a little differently. Some began with one group, others with a few, and others with many. Each of the churches progressed on the journey differently. Some moved very quickly, while others moved slowly. And still others took more than a year to prepare themselves for the initial cell group start-up.

Pastors often adopt the Roadmap Strategy because they see it as a way to control the change process. They do not want people to get out of hand or get too creative. Therefore they take charge of everything and make sure that the entire cell group system lines up with preconceived ideas about what it should look like. This is a quick way to get stuck in the land of mediocrity.

Another reason for adopting this strategy is that pastors see the process of changing to cell group ministry as a simple shift from what they have been doing in previous ministry. In other words, if a church plans to transform its Sunday school classes and committees by using cell group principles, the leadership can see this kind of change as progressive and linear. It is a simple shift in what they have been doing. But if a church is trying to reorient itself to transform the church from an inward-focused program ministry to life-transforming, missional cell group ministry, the change process is not linear and map-like. This kind of change is too fluid to fit on a map.

The Charting Strategy.

This strategy draws from life on a ship. When a captain determines that he needs to change course in order to arrive at a new set of coordinates, he uses a very different kind of map. A nautical chart shows water depths, surface obstacles, common sea lanes, and navigational aids. The captain charts a course that is unique to his position, his destination, and the particular capabilities of his vessel. On the sea there are an infinite number of courses to take and each is unique to each trip, not just to each ship. In other words, no two trips will be the same, even if they begin at the same starting point and end at the same destination. Weather, water currents, prevailing winds, and other factors will constantly impact the course a ship steers. As the voyage progresses, the crew will regularly re-evaluate the course and make adjustments as necessary to ensure that they arrive at the proper destination.

Leonard Sweet states, "Maps and blueprints are useless on water, never the same. The sea knows no boundaries. The only way one gets anywhere on the water is not through marked-off routes one follows but through navigational skills and nautical trajectories."[33]

One of the navigational skills serving ship captains and crew over the centuries has been the ability to read the charts of the captains who have gone before them. They listened to the explorers who charted unknown islands. They were skilled at reading the stars. They were navigators, not map readers.

8 Stages to Charting Cell Group Change

The only way to journey to the land of making cell groups work is to lead change with a chart. The Charting Strategy gives leaders the freedom to creatively lead while at the same time learning from the journey of other churches. Visually, it looks like this:

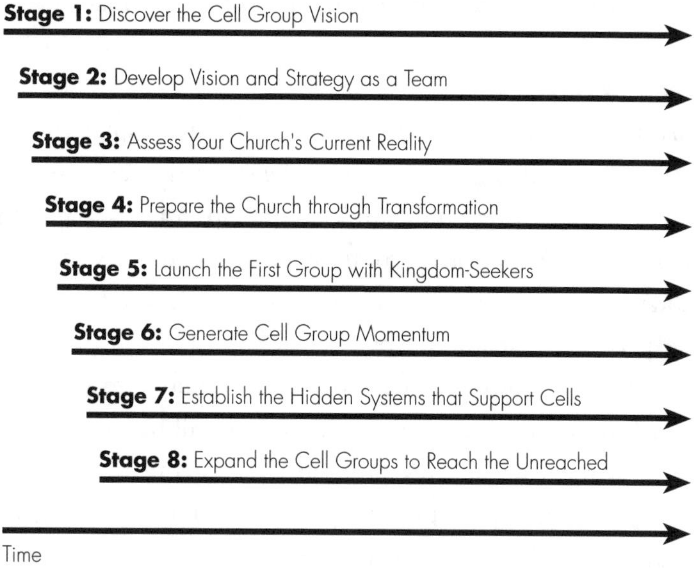

Stage 1: Discover the Cell Group Vision

Stage 2: Develop Vision and Strategy as a Team

Stage 3: Assess Your Church's Current Reality

Stage 4: Prepare the Church through Transformation

Stage 5: Launch the First Group with Kingdom-Seekers

Stage 6: Generate Cell Group Momentum

Stage 7: Establish the Hidden Systems that Support Cells

Stage 8: Expand the Cell Groups to Reach the Unreached

Time

Fig 1.11 The 8-stage Process for Charting Cell Groups

Notice that the stages start in a logical order: Stage 1 before Stage 2, Stage 2 before Stage 3, etc. Each stage has specific goals that should be accomplished before moving to the next stage. Charting a sea voyage has a logical process and so does charting change in a church. Also notice that these stages are ongoing. A church does not complete one and then move to the next one. Rather, the stages are like eight different practices that the captain, the crew, and the passengers must initiate in order for the ship to move toward its destination. All eight stages work together to propel the church and the cell groups toward God's calling.

Levers

Just as a sea captain will chart the destination first and then sit down with his key crew members to process it, so will most church pastors. Usually, God begins to lead the pastor through the discovery process in Stage 1 by himself and then he will begin to share what he is discovering with a few key leaders.

Articulate the mission of your church and how cell groups fit into that vision.

Key Resource:

– *The Missional Church* by Darrel Guder, et. al. This book provides a theological foundation for the church on mission in the North American culture.

Read as much as you can about cell groups and churches that have made cell groups work.

Key Resources:

—*Reap the Harvest* by Joel Comiskey. Based on findings from the world's best cell-based churches, this book identifies the common components found in these churches.

—*Home Cell Group Explosion* by Joel Comiskey. Based on interviews and surveys with cell group leaders around the world, this book identifies the key components for effective cell group leadership.

—*The Cell Church* by Larry Stockstill. The pastor of Bethany World Prayer Center describes the vision and strategy behind one of the best cell group models.

—*The Second Reformation* by William Beckham. Provides a strong theological and philosophical foundation for cell group ministry.

—*Where Do We Go from Here?* by Ralph W. Neighbour, Jr. contrasts the church based on relationships in cell groups with that of the church based upon programs. Provides practical insight on how to organize and structure the cell groups for success.

—*Life in His Body* by David Finnel. Articulates the vision for cell groups in a very simple fashion, introducing the basic structure and the values that support it. Chapters include discussion questions.

Attend conferences sponsored by model cell group churches. These conferences are great sources of learning about what churches have found successful. Do not be afraid to ask them hard questions about what they are doing and how they got to that point. Use some of the questions in Section 1.2 to help guide your questions.

Attend conferences sponsored by TOUCH Outreach Ministries or another non-church resourcing agency. This information is not limited to the experience of one church, but will reveal synthesized insight from a multitude of churches.

Befriend pastors in your area who have experience with cell groups. Take them out to lunch and pick their brains. Ask them questions like:
- What is your vision for your church?
- What was your church like before cell groups?
- How did you begin your first cell groups?
- How did you recruit your first leaders?
- What do you wish you had done differently?

Discover principles about leading change.
>   Key Resources:
>   —*Leading Change* by John Kotter
>   —*How to Change Your Church without Killing It* by Alan Nelson and Gene Appel

Vision Team Discussion

These questions can be used to stimulate discussion with key leaders in the church. After a cell group vision team has been chosen (Stage 2), these questions will prove helpful in getting the vision team on the same page.

1. Identify the state of your church. Is it a church
   —aimed at yesterday?
   —trying to compete with modern life?
   —seeking to invade all of life?
2. How do cell groups fit with a missional focus of the church?
3. What is the mission of your church? Does this mission serve as a plumb line against which every activity and program is measured?
4. What is most attractive to you about the cell groups system?
5. What concerns do you have about cell groups?
6. What do you think it means to change the church culture and individual values?

STAGE 2
Develop
Vision and Strategy
as a Team

A captain does not try to sail a ship by himself. It is not enough for him to know how the ship works; he needs a crew to perform the necessary tasks. It is not enough for a captain to understand the ship's destination and the course to get there; he needs an officer core to help him plot the course and steer the ship. Everything requires teamwork.

Pastors often ask, "How do I get people on board with the vision?" The best way is to recruit and build a team of people who work together to lead the church toward the cell group vision. If a senior pastor cannot gather three or four people to help him move toward the cell group vision, it will prove even more difficult, maybe even impossible, for him to get a larger group heading in that direction. Stage 2 in this process addresses key areas of Vision Team development.

• "Develop a Cell Vision Team" (Section 2.1). Pastors begin by gathering a team of three to seven people who have the commitment and the propensity to work on the cell group vision. The first section provides a clear rationale for working with a team and specific instructions on who should be a part of this team.

• "Develop Vision and Strategy" (Section 2.2). The vision team must have a clear picture of its goals. This chapter outlines the major goals of the vision team.

• "Develop a Cell Group Definition" (Sections 2.3). One of the most crucial goals of the vision team is to attain a clear understanding of a cell group and articulate the way God is calling that specific church to live out the values of basic Christian community.

SECTION 2.1 Develop A Cell Vision Team

Martin Luther nailed the 95 theses on the Wittenberg Church door. John Wesley started a movement of churches across England. Jonathan Edwards began the Great Awakenings in America. Martin Luther King Jr. led African Americans into the experience of freedom. Billy Graham set the standard of what a preacher should be. These men have modeled what it means to be a Christian leader. They were bold communicators, premier organizers, and excellent motivators. In many ways, these men were uniquely gifted for specific times. Problems arise, however, when pastors today elevate them to superstar status and try to emulate them. Howard Snyder paints an excellent picture of the superstar pastor:

Meet Pastor Jones, Superstar.
He can preach, counsel, evangelize, administrate, conciliate, communicate, and sometimes even integrate. He can also raise the budget.

He handles Sunday morning better than any talk-show host on weekday TV. He is better with words than most political candidates. As a scholar he surpasses many seminary professors. No church social function would be complete without him.

His church, of course, Counts Itself Fortunate. Alas, not many churches can boast such talent.[1]

Few pastors live up to the superstar image. Trying to is no longer necessary. The day of the isolated superstar leader has disappeared, and the day of collaboration has come. No longer do military heroes lead as isolated dictators. Gone are the days of business tycoons who control the economy in solitary confinement. Yesterday's science had mythical figures like Sir Isaac Newton and Albert Einstein, while today's science has creative teams with coordinating leaders forging the path.

Team leadership is how business gets done today, even in the church. The pastor need not be a superstar for a church to enter the mission of God. George Hunter, author of the book *Church for the Unchurched*, analyzed churches that are effective at reaching nonbelievers. He states, "Leadership in these churches is team leadership and most pastors are unskilled in this approach, and yet it is much more fun."[2] Similarly, the churches that have made cell groups work practice team leadership.

Cell Groups and Teamwork

Cell groups do not work just because ten people gather once each week for a meeting. Life together in cell groups is a result of the flow of the Spirit into and through the people in the groups. Such life is characterized by words like community, shared leadership, collaboration, family, brotherhood and sisterhood: in other words, teamwork. This life is a mutual experience where individuals tear down the walls that divide them and work together to accomplish a purpose that is beyond themselves.

Cell groups will copy the style of ministry they see modeled by the leadership of the church. If the pastor works in isolation and does not collaborate with others in his leadership, the cell group leaders will do the same, producing groups of individuals rather than groups in community. If the pastor works with a team to lead the church, practicing shared leadership, transparency, and delegation, then cell leaders will be more likely to lead their groups in community.

The difficulty is that most pastors have been trained to lead from isolation. A pastor learns of cell groups through a conference or book. He feels God leading him to move in that direction. He enters his study to develop a strategy, which he subsequently presents to his leaders. Much to his surprise, they respond less than favorably.

Even when church leaders consent to the cell group vision presented by an individualistic pastor, the vision rarely works. The issues related to leading people into cell group life are too complex for one person to recognize and evaluate. Different kinds of leaders with different kinds of giftings are required to make sure the right factors are recognized, spiritually discerned, and acted upon. In addition, most pastors do not have the time to give to cell groups because they are called to lead the entire church, prepare sermons, and provide direction for people not yet in cell groups. Also, when multiple people contribute to a vision and strategy, the rest of the church will be more likely to trust its validity.

The churches that have developed the most effective cell group systems have developed teams to work on cells. In some churches, the team effort was deliberate, while in many it was an informal accident. A vision team is quite different from a committee. Committees are empowered to make decisions but are not responsible for carrying out those decisions. Vision teams, on the other hand, guide the entire process from research to decision making to implementation and evaluation. The vision team is set apart to guide the entire cell ministry integration process. It is an action team, not an idea team.

Recruiting the Cell Vision Team

Inviting the right people to participate on the team will prove to be one of the most crucial decisions in the process. Putting the wrong people on the team will set back cell development for months or even years. This team should be handpicked by the senior pastor, not open to anyone who is interested.

Furthermore, the team should be no smaller than three people because any fewer would not make a team, and it should be no larger than seven because any more and it would be difficult to manage. Those selected should be people who enjoy working "on" a project, not "in" a project. The difference is significant. "On" people like to discover possibilities and search out boundaries of what could be. They see the whole perspective of the project and are good at manipulating the systems involved in order to reach the intended conclusion. "In" people like to work within the project. They are hands-on and enjoy the step-by-step process. "In" people get frustrated when the "on" people begin to discuss ideas, concepts, and vision. They only want to know what the finished project will look like and what they are supposed to do. If "in" people are recruited for the vision team, the integration process will prove very frustrating.

Leadership aptitudes are another important consideration when forming a vision team. I once participated on a cell vision team with my pastor at that time. We were both visionary strategists. We liked to sit in a room and come up with a vision, but we were not especially strong at carrying out strategies or getting other people involved. We did not realize that our team needed more balance to successfully disseminate the vision and include others in its implementation.

George Barna provides helpful insight on the different leadership aptitudes in his book, *The Power of Team Leadership.* He identifies four different aptitudes that should be understood when putting together a team.[3]

Directing Leaders have the ability to develop vision, inspire people to enter that vision, and see how people fit into that vision. This leader is not good with details and does not have the ability to implement the vision.

Strategic Leaders focus on developing the plans for implementing the vision. They are concerned with details, analyzing progress toward the vision and doing whatever it takes to make the vision a reality. These leaders are often accused of being more concerned about the vision than they are about people, and they tend not to make decisions quickly. My former pastor and I had unusual strengths as strategists.

Team-building Leaders complement Strategic Leaders because they focus on people. They are great at communicating the vision to individuals and at mobilizing people for the vision. These leaders tend to ignore details and strategic planning because they place so much value on relationships.

Operational Leaders help develop the systems that make the cell groups run over the long haul. This type of leader sees what is falling through the cracks and seeks to find ways to change the system to close the crack.

While the cell vision team may not have four different people, variety is important. One of the best vision teams I have seen was composed of a senior pastor who was a directing and strategic leader, an associate pastor who was a team-building leader, and volunteer retiree who was an operational leader. There are some additional questions that must be addressed when recruiting a vision team, which are listed on the following page.

Vision Team Recruitment Questions[4]

Position Power: Are enough key players on board, especially key leaders, so that those left out cannot easily block progress?

Expertise: Are the various points of view—in terms of discipline, work experience, nationality, etc.—represented so that informed, intelligent decisions will be made?

Credibility: Does the group have enough people with good reputations in the church so that its strategies will be taken seriously by church members?

Leadership: Does the group include enough proven leaders to be able to drive the change process?

Submission: Do the group members demonstrate submission to the leadership of the church?

Availability: Do the members have the available time to commit to this process?

Aptitude: Do the members have a propensity to work on the cell ministry and think critically about the big picture strategy and future development? In other words, are these people leaders or practitioners?

Prayer Life: Do the members have a passionate prayer life and love for God?

The Role of the Senior Pastor

As has been previously stated, the vision for cell groups cannot be delegated to someone other than the vision carrier, the senior pastor. From Pastor Yonggi Cho in Korea to Pastor César Castellanos in Colombia to Pastor Larry Stockstill in Louisiana to dozens of other effective pastors across America, pastors serve as the primary carriers of the cell group vision. When the vision for cell groups is delegated, church members quickly realize that cell groups are not a priority.

Carrying the vision for cell groups means much more than being the person to tell people to get into groups. Senior pastors must set the model for cell group life. The people will do as he does, not as he says. There are five areas of commitment that the senior pastor must be willing to enter if he truly wants to see his church move into a fruitful cell group ministry:

✓ **Participation**. At the very least the senior pastor must be committed to full participation in a cell group. He cannot say that he does not have time to be a part of a group. If he does, other people will make the same argument.

✓**Modeling**. More than participation, it is best that the senior pastor lead a cell group, at least until the groups get off the ground. He will show people how to lead groups by leading one himself. He must be committed to modeling community life, relationship evangelism, and leadership development.

Oversight. The senior pastor must serve as the ultimate overseer of the groups in his church.

Focusing on the Vision. It is the responsibility of the senior pastor to ensure that all eyes are kept on the vision for cell groups. Many senior pastors fail to realize this and quickly get distracted by the next interesting program that comes along. When this happens, the vision gets confused in the eyes of the members and new visions start competing with cell groups.

Setting the Strategy. The senior pastor must be involved in setting the strategy with his vision team. He cannot delegate this vital role to the team and then remain disconnected from the strategy team members develop. To do so is a recipe for a multiple-vision church.

A Cell Group Champion

Carrying the cell group vision might be hard for some pastors to swallow. Thoughts of constantly working, strategizing, and laying the relationship foundation needed to develop strong cell groups might seem overwhelming. A senior pastor cannot drop every other aspect of ministry in the church and focus solely upon group development. He still must preach, administer the affairs of the church, and counsel if he wants to keep his job.

Over the past 40 years, researchers have discovered patterns for the successful implementation of new ideas. One of the keys is called an innovation champion. "The champion is a charismatic individual who throws his/her weight behind the innovation, thus overcoming the indifference or resistance that a new idea often provokes in an organization."[5] The new idea of cell groups needs a champion, someone who wakes up every morning praying and thinking about how cell groups will work in the church.

A cell group champion is a person with a special passion for cell group ministry, who has a submissive heart and can work in unity with the senior pastor. This frees the senior pastor to oversee the vision of the entire church, including cell groups, and it frees the person with a special passion for cell groups to focus on what God has laid upon his or her heart.

One day I answered my phone and the man on the other end said, "Hello, my name is Dawson McAllister." After overcoming my shock (I grew up listening to this man who kept 20,000 students held in rapt attention), I listened as he shared his calling to start a cell group-based church. Over the next few months of working with him, it became obvious that Dawson has gifts of vision, teaching, and preaching, but he is not strong in the areas of administration, mobilizing leaders, or developing systems. He knew he needed help. After a long process, he recruited Ross McGary to serve as his co-pastor. Dawson is 51% in charge of the large group worship, and Ross is 51% in charge of the cell groups. Even though Dawson's strengths do not lie in overseeing the cell groups, he has a vested interest in them and carries the vision for them. If he did not, his personal vision would distract the church from making the cell groups work. The responsibilities of the senior pastor and the cell champion might look like this:

	Senior Pastor	**Cell Champion**
Participation	At least a member	At least a member
Modeling	Models cell leadership	Always models cell leadership
Oversight	Oversees entire church	Oversees cell group development
Vision	Focus on cells	Helps pastor focus on cells
Strategy	Involved	Central strategy developer

My former colleague, Jim Egli, is the cell group champion at the Champaign, IL Vineyard. Senior pastor Happy Lehman is vitally involved in the vision of the cells, but he is not concerned with their day to day operations, the training of new leaders, or how new groups will be started. Jim is the cell group expert, and Happy is the leadership expert. They allow each other the room to operate according to their giftings.

Some senior pastors have chosen to play the role of the cell group champion. For instance, Van Ducote of Northwood Christian Center in Gulfport, Mississippi feels the special calling to champion the groups, but he has also recruited 12 other key leaders to be champions over other areas of the church's vision.

What if Key Influencers Are Against the Cell Group Vision?

A vision team should consist of people with a passion to see their church enter into cell group community. No one should be included simply because he or she has a position of authority or control in the church. A vision team needs spiritual calling, not fleshly dominance. At the same time, the team should contain people of influence in the church, or church members will never enter into cell groups. Therefore, an ideal group would include the senior pastor, at least one official lay leader (deacon, elder, etc.), key staff pastors, and key influencers in the church.

This team must consist of godly, praying, and spiritually growing people. Unfortunately, in many churches the key influencers are not always godly people. They are not open to the vision of cell groups and they don't want to change the ways they have always done church. In one church, the pastor began cell groups. One of the primary elders was a cell group member but never attended. He guarded himself and did not practice transparency; instead he acted like a know-it-all because he had a traveling evangelistic ministry. The pastor and this elder were not in unity. Eventually, the elder and his family chose to attend another church that fit his style of ministry.

I have also seen this in staff members who feel threatened by the possibility of their jobs becoming irrelevant because of the new way of ministering. Such feelings are valid and must be processed if their support of the vision is desired. Even with such processing, some staff members have found it so difficult to make the change that they seek other places where God will allow them to do the ministry they know.

If the key influencers of the church are against the cell group vision, the pastor *must not* force cell groups upon them. This is the time for either one of two options:

- Pray that God will change the hearts of the key leaders, and that they will embrace the values that make cell groups work.
- Determine if God is calling the pastor to be a part of that church or if He wants him to follow Him to a place where people are ready to develop basic Christian community.

Don Tillman came to such a point in his ministry. He asked God, "Am I called to stay and lead my congregation at the pace they are able and willing to go? Or am I called to a mission that would require a change in ministry position?" He intensely sought God's heart for many months before seeing His will. Instead of trying to transition a church whose key influencers were not willing to change, he was sent out by that church with a team of 20 people to plant a new, cell-based church.

How to Recruit the Cell Vision Team

Most likely the people who would work well on such a team will be very obvious. Yet before plunging head-first into recruitment, a pastor should invest significant time in listening to the Lord. He might take a couple of days away from the office to listen and pray, following the model of Jesus in choosing His key leaders (Luke 6:12ff). After receiving God's direction, the pastor should set up individual meetings with each of the potential vision team members. He should begin to share the cell group vision and determine the level of interest. He might share one of the resources listed at the end of Stage 1 or watch the video *Cell Church Revolution*. After a person shows a significant level of interest in the cell vision, then the pastor should begin to share the idea of a vision team.

Strong teams make pastors look brilliant. When God puts the right team together, His vision becomes clear. When the vision team assembles, the pastor must communicate its goals, which are outlined in the next section.

SECTION 2.2 Develop
Vision and Strategy

The cell vision team is a group of leaders who are called to develop the vision and strategy for cell groups, to oversee implementation, and to evaluate the progress of development. In the larger churches that have made cell groups work, the vision team process was very natural because many, if not all, of the team members were on staff. They worked together on the cell group vision on a daily basis. In smaller churches, the vision team process must be more intentional. If team members do not purposely work together, one person will end up developing the entire vision and strategy. This means that every member of the vision team must understand the goals of the team and commit to accomplishing these goals.

Goal #1: Discover the Vision As a Team

First the team must attain a shared understanding of the cell group vision. This means that the team should process through the material in

Stage 1 as a group. While individually each team member might already understand the basics of the cell group vision, together they will be able to wrestle with these concepts and internalize them further.

An essential tool for accomplishing this goal is dialogue. Dialogue is the process by which a team accesses a pool of common learning that cannot be accessed individually. A team practices dialogue when the members contribute to a free flow of thought, resulting in team learning. This concept has been developed for team leadership by MIT business professor Peter Senge.

Senge contrasts dialogue with discussion. "In a discussion, different views are presented and defended, and…may provide useful analysis of the whole situation. In dialogue different views are presented as a means toward discovering a new view. In discussion, decisions are made. In a dialogue, complex issues are explored."[6] Most leaders, including pastors, are comfortable with discussion because they want to argue and defend their points of view. Dialogue can prove threatening because "the purpose of dialogue is to go beyond one individual's understanding."[7] Its goal is not to win, but to discover.

Senge outlines the three basic conditions necessary for dialogue:

1. All participants must "suspend" their assumptions while at the same time communicating their assumptions about the topic. In other words, team members disclose the logic behind their opinions and hold them up for examination.
2. All participants must regard one another as colleagues and friends on an equal plane. Dialogue does not occur when some team members feel that their opinions are less important than the opinions of others. Every team member must be granted permission to share honestly, even if it means sharing concerns about an idea from the pastor or a senior elder.

3. There must be a facilitator who guides the context of dialogue. Most people do not know how to dialogue. They know how to discuss, arguing their point. For the team members to practice dialogue, there must be someone who opens the door to dialogue and keeps that door open.

Discussion is not evil, but the vision team will quickly stagnate if it gets caught trying to argue one point against another. Dialogue will allow each team member to verbalize assumptions, deal with nagging questions, express concerns, and articulate points of view. This will establish a foundation for the vision and set the stage for each person to share how he or she sees the vision.

Goal #2: Articulate the Purpose of Cell Groups

To begin groups without a clear picture of the biblical purpose and mission of cell groups breeds confusion. Hundreds of churches have done just this, resulting in cancerous groups that lead to death instead of life. The vision team should articulate a clear purpose for cell groups that will become the measuring stick by which they evaluate the groups as they develop (See Section 2.3).

Beyond the development of a biblical purpose for the groups, the vision team must translate this purpose into a vision that has meaning to everyday Christians in a specific local church. One cell pastor in Georgia said, "Our biggest mistake was that we adopted more than we adapted." Many churches have copied a cell group structure that they saw in another church without understanding how to make it their own. The result was stagnating groups, groups without a purpose that was important to members. The vision team is responsible for articulating the cell group vision in terms that have meaning to their church.

Goal #3: Write a Vision Statement that Includes Cell Groups

The vision for cell groups flows out of the mission of the church discussed in Stage 1. The vision puts feet on the mission. It is not enough to create a vision for cell group development if the church does not feel the call of God to be on mission to impact the world.

The vision team should contribute to the development of a vision statement for the church that includes cell groups. The senior pastor should initiate this process by writing the first draft, and then the vision team should provide feedback about how cell groups fit into that vision statement. The following process, developed by John Kotter, will help the team create an effective vision statement:[8]

- **Write a First Draft**: The process often starts with an initial statement from the visionary leader, reflecting what he sees God calling the church to be.
- **Massage the First Draft**: The first draft is reshaped over time by the vision team or an even larger group of people.
- **Analyze with Honesty**: The group process never works well without honest feedback. This requires that the team members take risks by presenting their thoughts, even though the pastor is the one who developed the original vision statement.
- **Dream**: This requires that the team members listen with their hearts and minds to the Holy Spirit throughout the process.
- **Ignore the Mess**: Vision creation is not a clean, logical process. It is often a dance of "two steps forward and one step back, movement to the left and then the right."
- **Stick with It**: A compelling vision cannot be developed in one meeting.

The vision team will not be the only group who speaks into the development of the vision. The vision team's goal is to make sure that cell groups and the values espoused by them fit into that vision.

Some churches have developed very specific vision statements. For instance, Pantego Bible Church has developed a vision that reads: "to reach the 74% unchurched by establishing at least one fully functioning Biblical Community in the 20 high school zones within a 10 mile radius of our church campus by the year 2010." Vision statements like this are like rifles; they focus all energy on very specific and measurable elements. They are also based upon a much broader mission statement. The Pantego mission is to "transform people through the work of the Holy Spirit into fully developing followers of Christ."

The leadership of Belmont Church has articulated the purpose or mission of the church as "to prepare and equip God's people to edify one another and to do the work of ministry." The more specific vision statement of Belmont Church is "to equip every member to passionately live with Jesus, walk in community, and advance God's Kingdom."

The vision development process will involve the creation of a broad mission directive, followed by a more specific vision focus. The team will not complete this process in one meeting. In fact, most will make adjustments to the vision as they hear God while walking through Stages 3-8.

Goal #4: Chart a Strategy for Stages 3-8

It is impossible to develop a strategic plan that maps out every step of the process. Instead of a comprehensive strategic plan, this group should seek to chart a course with checkpoints along the way. These checkpoints will be established as the team works through the information in Stages 3-8. Here are a few of the key questions the team will be working through on an ongoing basis:

- How will you communicate the vision of cell groups to the church?
- How will you create urgency to prepare people for a new vision?
- How will you prepare people to be successful in group life?
- How will you begin groups?
- How will you train leaders?
- How will you equip cell members for ministry?
- How will you provide ongoing coaching for the leaders?
- How will you multiply groups?
- How will evangelism be incorporated into group life?

These questions need not be answered up front. The levers and the questions at the end of each stage will help facilitate this process.

Goal #5: Monitor Progress and Deal with Hazards

Once the course is set on a voyage at sea, a navigator's work is not over. Constantly changing conditions require diligent attention. Sea conditions, currents, and wind have a dramatic impact on the ship's progress. Adjustments to course and speed are necessary to ensure that the ship reaches the proper destination. Unexpected hazards impede the journey.

The same is true with cell ministry. There is the ideal vision set on paper, and then there is reality. This process involves people, and people change. Leaders move to new cities. Cell groups grow much faster than expected. New Christians need special ministry. The team will need to evaluate the situation and adjust the course accordingly. Some of the adjustments might include:

- Seeking a greater understanding about how to lead people through this process.
- Providing more training for new leaders.
- Slowing down (because most go too fast).

Launching a Vision Team

Many teams have found it helpful to begin the journey together with a retreat. Others have gone to cell group conferences together. Still others have met weekly to work through one of the books listed in Stage 1.

A retreat has proven to be the quickest way to get a vision team launched. This will allow members to establish unity and determine how they will work with one another. The goals of this retreat are to:

- Work through Goal #1
- Dialogue about the purpose of the cell groups (Goal #3)
- Begin to develop a navigational chart for the journey ahead
- Determine guidelines for how the team will work together

From there, the team should meet at least once a month. At these meetings, specific work will be assigned to each member of the team, most of which the cell group champion will do. Every six months the team should meet for an extended time to re-evaluate the progress.

SECTION 2.3 Develop a Cell Group Definition

On Tuesday nights, college-aged students gather in a west Houston home to discuss the Scripture, pray for one another, and grow in friendship. In Fort Worth, Texas, entire families meet on Sunday nights for a meal, followed by Bible discussion and ministry. In urban Chicago, divorced men meet on Wednesday nights, rotating between their homes. Busy mothers gather on Thursday mornings in a coffee shop in a San Francisco suburb. All of these groups are cell groups, but all are quite different.

What constitutes a cell group and what does not? This is one of the most crucial questions a vision team can address. Without a clear definition, cell group leaders become confused, pastors lack a clear standard for measuring group success, and groups will be more likely to develop cancerous habits. One change consultant writes, "When the leadership [vision] team reaches alignment on vision, strategy, and values, it also needs to define the behaviors that will support the strategy and those that will be considered unacceptable."[9]

To arrive at a clear definition of a cell group, leaders need more than simple "how-to" answers to questions of what cell groups do. Learning about the external practices is not enough. Vision team members need tools so that they can think creatively about cell groups, not just do cell groups. Creative thinking is supported by answers to "what" questions, not just "how-to" questions. The answers to the "what" questions are intentionally theological. At first these answers might not seem entirely practical, but when all of the pieces are assembled, the vision team will have a clear picture of what cell groups should produce and of creative ways to produce it.

Digging Beneath the External Practices

On a visit to Faith Community Baptist Church in Singapore, I attended a cell group. I took an elevator up to the tenth floor of a high-rise apartment and entered a room full of people in their 20s and 30s. When the meeting started, we shared our answers to a simple ice-breaker, sang together, prayed, discussed a Bible passage, and then the group members practiced sharing the salvation message with one another.

When trying to define a cell group, pastors and leaders are tempted to look no further than the visible practices that different churches embrace. But the practices of Faith Community Baptist Church are different from those of Elim Church in El Salvador, which has grown to over 120,000 people. Both are different from Baptist Works and Mission Church in the Ivory Coast, again with over 120,000 members.

For instance, at Yoido Full Gospel Church, a typical cell group meeting consists of a time of praise which usually consists of reciting the Apostle's Creed and singing, Bible discussion and prayer, receiving an offering, intercessory prayer, and singing of the Lord's prayer to close the meeting.[10] While these cell group practices work in Korea, they may or may not work elsewhere.

The magic does not lie in the specific practices. The vision team must dig beneath the practices to understand the elements that make the practices work. Underneath the practices of model cell group churches are the priorities that focus the cell groups in the right direction, the values that give life to cell groups, the principles that differentiate Christian cell groups from other small groups, and finally the theological foundation which is the very nature of who God is.

By pressing down beneath the surface of the practices, the vision team will be able to articulate not only the methods of cell group ministry, but also the foundation upon which these methods are built. They will be able to define a holistic cell group. They will be able to express how a holistic cell group is much more than a weekly meeting, but a group that experiences basic Christian community.

A Theology
of Basic Christian Community

Theology is founded on the nature of God. Everything the church does should be rooted in God's nature and purpose. One image used in Scripture to help us understand God's nature is the body. The church as a group of believers is His body in the world; He is the head. Paul called Christ the Head, "from whom the whole body, supported and held together by its ligaments and sinews, grows as God causes it to grow" (Colossians 2:19). Our human bodies exist to carry out the desires and demands of our brains. We have feet to take our brains where they want to go, hands to manipulate the things our brains want to investigate or control, and eyes to behold the things our brains desire or need to look at. Even our internal organs exist to keep the whole body working properly so the brain can do the things it wants to do. The church as a spiritual body exists for the same reason: to carry out the purposes of the

Head. Aside from that, it really has no purpose. It is Christ who gives us our nature, our purpose, and our mission. We exist solely to carry out His desires and commands.

John 16:13-15 says,

> But when he, the Spirit of truth, comes, he will guide you into all truth. He will not speak on his own; he will speak only what he hears, and he will tell you what is yet to come. He will bring glory to me by taking from what is mine and making it known to you. All that belongs to the Father is mine. That is why I said the Spirit will take from what is mine and make it known to you.

In these three verses, Jesus expounds on the doctrine of the Trinity. He makes it very clear that the three Persons of the Father, Son, and Spirit work in perfect unity with one another. They are interdependent, in that one member of the Trinity cannot perform His duty without the other two. This interdependency is often called perichorisis or a holy dance.

The foundation of basic Christian community goes all the way to the point of who God is. God is not an individual, nor is He a plurality. God is a unity of life: Father, Son, and Holy Spirit. For the people of God to line up under the Head in His body, the people of God must also experience the life of interdependency, just as God does. Paul wrote at the end of 2 Corinthians, "May the grace of the Lord Jesus Christ, and the love of God, and the fellowship of the Holy Spirit be with you all," expressing his desire that the complete experience of God be realized by the church.

Jesus prayed in John 17:21, "...that all of them [believers] may be one, Father, just as you are in me and I am in you. May they also be in us...May they be brought together to complete unity..." It is not enough that the church know doctrinally that God is a triune God. Jesus knew that the only way we would know the fullness of God would be through the experience of being unified with one another.

In addition, it is not enough to have several good cell groups that do whatever is right in their own eyes. The ultimate purpose of the church is to know Christ, the Head of the church, becoming like Him. The cell group must be a place where group members participate with God and one another in His holy dance. Basic Christian community then is not simply a method or an option for the church. It is a way to experience and know who God is.

The Principles of Basic Christian Community

A principle is "an important underlying law or assumption required in a system of thought." One of the guiding principles found in the Word of God is the principle of covenant. Without an understanding of covenant, it is impossible to understand God's relationship with Abraham, Samuel's anointing of David, or the Cross. God set in motion a covenant with His people, which lays down a basic principle for life with God and with one another.

Basic Christian community is based upon God's covenant with His people. One of the cornerstones of the Old Testament Covenant was the 10 Commandments. These 10 Words, as they were often called, delineated 10 ways that the people of God were to relate to the LORD and to one another. All ten are relational commands, not instructions for a private individual on how to relate to himself. But the Old Testament provides continuous evidence for man's inability to keep the covenant. The Law lacked the ability to change the heart of man (Romans 8:3). Through Jeremiah, God promised a new covenant that would be written upon hearts because covenant keeping could not be enforced.

Likewise, basic Christian community cannot be legislated. It can only be entered into as a gift. Man cannot make it happen. Cell group members can only enter into the community that God has established for them because He creates community; the group does not. This is what happens when a cell group recognizes Jesus' words in Matthew 18:20: "For where two or three come together in my name, there am I with them."

The presence of Christ is already in the midst of a group, because He has completed the covenant with man. His presence is a gift to all who will receive it. The principle of His presence is what allows cell group members to keep covenant with God and with one another. Without His empowering presence, cell groups only have laws, rules for doing cell groups the "right" way. Such rules never produce life.

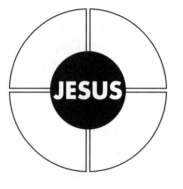

Fig 2.1 Jesus Is the Center

The presence of Christ is the only unique contribution that cell groups have to offer to the world. But what does it mean to experience Christ in the midst of a cell group? The verse above provides two keys. The first key is found in "come together in my name." So many cell groups meet in the name of everything but the name of Jesus. They meet in the name of "Bible study," in the name of "fixing people's problems," in the name of "having no conflicts," or in the name of "multiplication." To meet in the name of Jesus means that people die to their own agendas. To meet in the name of Jesus means that a group listens to what He is saying and heeds His voice. To meet in the name of Jesus means that Jesus is living through the people and moving through them to minister to one another. When a group meets in this name, Jesus becomes the agenda.[11]

The second key to meeting in the name of Jesus is found in the words "two or three." Many cell groups gather every week with one person, the cell leader, meeting in the name of Jesus. He or she is trying to lead the other 5-15 people into His presence. The other cell members have their hearts set on the problems of the day, guilt over recent sins, gossip someone just heard, marital problems, or emotional pain. Most cell group members are not meeting in the name of Jesus; they are meeting in the name of whatever is on their minds at the time. One person meeting in the name of Jesus does not set the pattern of community for others to enter; instead, the group becomes a battle of wills. It takes two or three people in a cell group who can commit to meeting in the name of Jesus to establish the model of His covenant with them.

When two or three gather in the name of Jesus, Jesus comes to life in the group. Worship takes on a different, almost supernatural feel; personal problems, sin, and guilt come under the powerful force of conviction and the freeing essence of forgiveness; relationships bridge over petty interpersonal issues to join with others in forming a healing community. In other words, the requirements of the covenant are realized in His presence.

The Values
of Basic Christian Community

Values are those underlying assumptions assigning worth to the elements of life. The value that a person assigns to different aspects of life determines the pursuit, the promotion, and the preference of certain aspects over others.[12]

Many pastors receive negative feedback when they address their church members' values. When a pastor tells a workaholic that his work stands in the way of serving God, the workaholic may argue that he serves God through work. If he tells a mother that she is so focused on her children that she cannot see God or anyone else, she may assume the church is trying to pull her away from her family. Our values are precious to us, and we cling to them.

But the values of the Kingdom of God are established by the King, not the servants. A cell group does not dictate the values that it will base its life upon. Jim Egli has performed extensive research on what makes cell groups work. He has discovered four values that must flow through the group in order for it to fully work. These values are summarized in the words Upward, Inward, Outward, Forward (UIOF).[13]

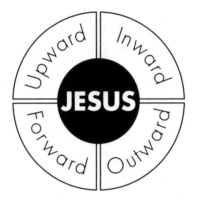

Fig 2.2 The Values of UIOF

These values flow out of the presence of Jesus as he empowers people to live out the values of His Kingdom. These are not values that people can force upon themselves. Remember that values flow out of principles, and if the principle is the presence of Christ, then without the presence of Christ there is no Upward, Inward, Outward, or Forward.

Jesus himself summarized these four values:

Upward: *"Love the Lord your God* with all your heart and with all your soul and with all your mind" (Matthew 22:38).

Inward: *"Love your neighbor* as your self" (Matthew 22:39).

Outward: "Therefore go and *make disciples* of all nations…" (Matthew 28:19).

Forward: "Teaching them to *obey all that I have commanded you…*" (Matthew 28:20).

The *Upward* value is the regular experience of God. Cell groups work when people encounter Him; they fail when group members simply go through religious motions, praying religious prayers. This kind of encounter with God is based on an authentic passion for Him, a desire to be with Him, and a yearning to share what He is doing with other people.

The *Inward* value is expressed by love for one another in the group, as group members make covenants with one another. They become committed to living in community together. I love the movie *Forrest Gump*. In one of the most memorable scenes, Private Gump runs out of a Vietnam jungle while bombs crash around him. When he gets to safety, he realizes that his friend Bubba is still in the jungle. Forrest runs back to find Bubba and in doing so, he finds other wounded soldiers. He carries each one out to safety. On his last trip in, Forrest finds Bubba and carries him out, risking bombs, bullets, and berating from his lieutenant. The Inward value in cell groups is realized when cell members discover that they have a Forrest Gump or when they have an opportunity to be a Forrest Gump for someone else. This value begins in the cell meeting, but it extends outside the meeting because life happens outside official meetings. Without this commitment to community outside the meeting, relationships will be very weak and the meetings will be artificial and stale.

The *Outward* value is found in groups that understand that they are on mission in this world. "As you are going, make disciples." The command is to make disciples. It is the only imperative found in the entire commission (Matthew 18-20). Our mission in the world is to perform as disciple-making disciples. As followers of Christ, we are to lead others to Christ.

The *Forward* value is seen when Christ's followers are taught to obey all things Christ taught us. Unfortunately, the church has too long left the word obey out of this Scripture. Being taught information has been equated with obeying. Jesus just gave a command—make disciples—which, if ignored, becomes an immediate act of disobedience. A disciple who fails to produce disciples is not fully discipled! The entire Forward value centers on growing followers of Christ to be disciple-making disciples. Rather than focusing on training leaders to fill certain positions in the church, the focus should be on growing biblical disciples. This will naturally result in a multiplication of leaders.

The Priorities of Basic Christian Community

Priorities are those activities people actually arrange their lives around. Priorities are not priorities when people talk about them or even when they feel deeply about them. Priorities become real when people actually do them. In the cell group, they flow from the values of Upward, Inward, Outward, Forward.

Cell groups that value Upward life prioritize prayer. They do this by making room for prayer in the meetings and outside of the meetings. The group meetings focus on Christ, and members allow the Holy Spirit to move through them to minister to one another. The meetings do not limit themselves to focusing on an activity like Bible study or even a common interest. These groups discover "Christ in the midst" of two or three gathered in His name. Some will use worship songs to make prayer a priority. Others will praise God spontaneously.

The type of prayer that is not prioritized is the kind of prayer where cell members spend 20 minutes sharing prayer requests, most of which are about sick relatives or hurting people outside the group. Cell group prayer focuses on praying for the needs of the people in the group and seeing God minister to them.

Cell groups express the Inward value by prioritizing relationships. Cell group meetings must make room for relationships. People should have the freedom to express their personalities, their desires, and their unique qualities. This can be done with things like icebreakers, shared conversations over snacks, and laughing together during the meetings. Recently, my cell group needed to bond, so we took some time to play a board game before we entered into the cell group lesson. But relationships only begin in the weekly cell group meetings. Real relationships are developed outside the meetings: at lunch, in phone conversations, shopping together, playing golf, going for a walk. When cell group members connect with one another outside the meeting, the Inward value comes to life. People learn to hold one another accountable. They share one another's burdens. They spontaneously care for each other.

Cell groups practice the Outward value by prioritizing love for nonbelievers. This love is expressed by such things as praying as a group for lost friends, making sure the group is open and welcoming to newcomers, and providing an opportunity during the cell group meetings for cell members to share how they are ministering to lost friends. Prioritizing love for nonbelievers means that cell group members will make time for their unsaved friends, family members, co-workers, and neighbors. It is not enough to say that we love the lost. We must actually befriend them and love them.

Cell groups enter into the Forward value by prioritizing mentoring. A cell leader must mentor his intern or apprentice. This is the most basic element. But there are other ways to prioritize mentoring. Different parts of the meeting can be delegated to various cell group members who are ready for small responsibilities. A cell leader should seek to understand where each cell group member is in his or her walk with the Lord and help him or her take the next step on the journey. When mentoring is prioritized, cell members see themselves as more than cell group attendees. They see themselves as ministers.

Combining the values and the practices creates a simple definition for a cell group:

> *A holistic cell group is a group of 5-15 people who form the basic unit of Christian community. It functions to provide a place where members gather weekly around the presence of Christ, support one another as a family, reach out to the hurting world, and mentor and release new leaders, all of which results in the multiplication of groups as others are added.*

The Practices of Basic Christian Community

The Theology, Principles, Values, and Priorities define the boundaries for cell groups living in basic Christian community. The goal of the vision team is to understand these boundaries and define them for others. When these boundaries are clear, the vision team, the pastoral overseers, and cell group leaders can creatively develop unique practices to make cell groups work. All groups do not have to look alike within these boundaries, but they will be operating according to the same vision.

Homogeneous or heterogeneous: must cell groups be composed of both men and women or can they be gender-based? Some people make an issue out of gender and argue that cell groups only create basic Christian communities when they involved both men and women.[14] Others will argue that homogeneous men's and women's groups are the best way to organize cells.[15] Either kind of group can live out the values of UIOF. A church does not have to limit itself to one or the other.

Intergenerational or not: should the kids be included to create family groups? Some argue that basic Christian community only happens when the family unit is involved in the same group. Some groups will include children and they will do it well (See Section 7.3). Others will choose to minister to children in other ways.

Move from house to house: "house to house" describes the practice of the New Testament church because the church did not have elaborate buildings. Homes are a very natural place to hold cell groups because the members can get to know one another more easily in a home environment. Additionally, when the cell meets in every member's home, the members will more easily take ownership of the group and call it "my group." But there is no law about the practice. Some groups will meet from house to house. Other groups will practice rotating homes monthly rather than weekly. Others will meet in just one home. Still others will meet in coffee shops, country clubs, or conference rooms at work. The one practice that tends to limit the values of UIOF is meeting at the church building. When in the familiar Sunday school environment, people tend to revert to the practices they used in that environment. Associations of Bible learning and limited discussion will hamper true "one-another" ministry.

Sunday sermon discussion or not: this practice seems to be a sore spot with many. TOUCH encourages pastors to write "Cell Discussion Guides" based on their sermons because it simplifies the work for the cell leaders, keeps churches flowing in the vision that God has given each pastor, and increases quality control. At the same time, it is not mandatory for all groups to discuss the same topic every week forever. Living out the values of UIOF may require a group to work on a specific issue together for a few weeks. One practice here that does not work: allowing the cell leader to do whatever he or she wants in the cell group. This places a lot of pressure on the group leader, makes it far more difficult to reproduce qualified leaders, and leaves too many doors open for aberrant teaching.

Frequency of meetings: research in this area has clearly shown that cell groups meeting weekly experience the values of UIOF much more fully than groups meeting biweekly or monthly. In addition, the Bible prioritizes relationships and "one-another ministry." If this is the case, why should the cell groups be any less important to church life than the weekly celebration? Few pastors would dare move to a biweekly celebration, even if the people of the church wanted it. But many churches adopt cell groups that only meet biweekly because the people do not want weekly groups. They might even argue that the frequency of the meetings is not crucial as long as the group members are loving one another. A few churches might be able to pull this off, but in a less than ideal world, most cell groups will not be able to enter UIOF through biweekly meetings. At the same time, I have friends who pastor churches with biweekly meetings because the people do not want more than this. A biweekly meeting is better than no meeting, especially if the group can develop some life between the meetings.

The order of the meeting: Dr. Ralph Neighbour developed a meeting order around four Ws: Welcome, Word, Worship, and Witness (See *How to Lead a Great Cell Group Meeting* or *Cell Group Leader Training* for a full explanation of these meeting components). Many cell groups get stuck in this pattern, resulting in a boring, predictable format that cell members eventually resent. First, this pattern is not the only one that churches use. It just easily communicates the basic elements of a meeting. Second, all four elements do not have to be included every week. Third, the order is not fixed. Fourth, there are many creative ways to facilitate each of these elements. Cell leaders will receive training in how to creatively lead the meeting, but it is important that the pastoral team and the vision team not fixate on a magical formula for what must transpire in every cell group meeting.

Rate of multiplication: multiplication is a result of a group living out the values of UIOF. It cannot be forced. Launching a new group is not a result of working harder, strategic planning, or setting goals. Some have felt great pressure to multiply within "six months" or "nine months" because that is what the books say. Such pressure often works against cell life. Goals are important, but groups should focus on seeking Jesus and His UIOF life. When He is alive in the group, new groups will come forth. If Jesus is not moving in a group, it will not give birth to a new group. Usually if a group does not birth a group in a year, it never will. The signs of a stagnant group should be easily recognizable by the sixth month.

When basic Christian community comes to life, the creativity will flow at all levels. Cell group members will come to the leader and ask to lead an all night prayer session. New Christians will confess sins and get set free. Quiet Christians who thought they would never do anything for God will suddenly demonstrate leadership skills. Basic Christian community is nothing less than a miracle. It is revealed by the Spirit of God. It makes life rich beyond the wildest dreams. You feel so loved that it seems unreal. You feel like you can do anything for God, but you are humbled because you know you can do nothing. I pray that your church will taste this life.

Levers

Identify potential vision team members according to the guidelines in Section 2.1.
> Key Resource:
> > —*Leading the Team-Based Church* by George Cladis

Determine who will serve as the cell group champion, whether it be the senior pastor or another person.

Recruit the vision team.

Launch the vision team and begin to work through the goals outlined in Section 2.2. Use the Levers and the Discussion Questions at the end of Stages 1 and 2 to facilitate this process.

Define the kind of cell group that God is calling your church to develop.
> Key Resources:
> > —*Home Cell Group Explosion* by Joel Comiskey
> > —*The Shepherd's Guidebook* by Ralph W. Neighbour

Vision Team Questions

1. What does it mean for a team to practice dialogue?
2. Each vision team member should take about five minutes to describe his or her previous small group experience, both the positive and negative aspects of it.
3. Each member should share how he or she feels about the cell group vision as he or she understands it.
4. How is the cell group vision different than that of traditional small groups?
5. Articulate clearly the goals of the vision team so that all the team members understand them.
6. The senior pastor should communicate his role as a member of the vision team.
7. The cell group champion should articulate his role, if this person is not the senior pastor.
8. Determine how often the vision team will meet.

STAGE 3
Assess
Your Church's Current Reality

Imagine two ships, both with orders to land at the same destination. One is only 20 nautical miles from the destination and heading toward it. The second is 300 nautical miles and there is a very large island directly in its path. Both plan to sail to the same point, but each will take very different routes. A ship's captain must plot his current location before he can plot the correct steering course.

The same is true for a church. Once the destination of the cell group vision has been charted (Stage 1), a church must determine its current location. The location of every church is unique. Denominational background, leadership style, history, culture, and socio-economic make-up all contribute to the differences. As a result, every church will take a unique path to arrive at the final destination of making cell groups work.

Many pastors ask, "Will cell groups work in my church?" The answer to this question is found by assessing a church's current location with respect to the final destination. Some churches are relatively close to making cell groups work. Others are further away. This does not mean that some churches cannot do cell groups. It only means that the journey for some churches will take longer than in others. Stage 3 demonstrates how to:

• "Assess the Readiness for the Journey" (Section 3.1). Some churches are primed and ready to start groups. God has prepared a strong foundation upon which to build strong cell groups. Other churches must work on their foundations before launching into groups.

• "Assess the Current Small Group System" (Section 3.2). Every church has some kind of small group system. It is important to obtain a clear understanding of the historical experience of small groups so that the new vision of holistic cell groups is clearly differentiated.

• "Assess to Create Urgency" (Section 3.3). Most pastors do not have the freedom to stand before their congregations and proclaim the new vision of cell groups. They must develop buy-in that will motivate people to embrace the new vision. Leaders develop this by increasing the urgency through assessing the current state of church health.

SECTION 3.1 Assess
the Readiness
for the Journey

When Dennis Wadley accepted the leadership of Community Covenant Church in Santa Barbara, California, he faced a troubled situation. Once a prominent influence in the community, the church had become a group of about 50 elderly people who knew that the church would die when they passed on. They called Dennis to turn around the church and lead it in new directions.

In 1995, David Parish assumed leadership of Christian Fellowship Church in Benton, Kentucky, following in the footsteps of his father, the founding pastor. David had established himself as a leader after serving in the church 11 years. The church was a strong, worship-based church with effective programs and over 500 members.

The first church was on the verge of shutting the doors; the second was a success by any standard. The first had a new and young leader working with an elderly congregation. The second had a trusted leader who had proven himself over many years. The first knew little about worshipping in the presence of God. The second experienced God's presence on a weekly basis. The first had not seen a conversion in years. The second had been reaching the lost for years.

Dennis Wadley and David Parish shared a common vision for cell groups when they started. But their commonalities did not extend beyond the vision. Dennis had to lead Community Covenant Church in turning around almost everything. The church could not depend upon a new cell group structure to save the day. Christian Fellowship, on the other hand, already had many strong elements in place. These strengths stimulated the cell groups.

Cell Group Readiness

Dennis Wadley's strategy for sailing toward cell groups was different than David Parish's because both pastors started at different places. Some churches have failed to recognize this. They falsely assume that if they do the cell group strategy correctly (usually as seen in a model church), they will see cell group success. In order to determine the proper strategy, a church must determine where it sits today. The best way to do this is to assess the church's readiness for cell groups. Assessment is crucial because most people tend to assume that the situation is better than it is. Peter Senge concludes, "An accurate insightful view of current reality is as important as clear vision. Unfortunately, most of us are in the habit of imposing biases on our perception of current reality."[1] In other words, most church leaders falsely assume that the church is better off than it really is.

Pastors and other church leaders often fail to take the time to assess reality before they embark upon the journey of cell groups. They only see the value of the vision and move forward. I have found three reasons why this is the case.

Pastors are committed to action. Most pastors get to where they are today because they have acted, not because they waited. They hear a vision from God and they want to put it into practice. Recently, a couple came into TOUCH's office looking for materials to start 10 cell groups in three months. The pastor had sent them on this assignment. I explained that this strategy would produce mediocre cell groups. It was hard for them to hear this message because they knew that it would frustrate their pastor.

Pastors do not want to see the dirt. Some argue that leading a church is the hardest job in existence. Answering to elder or deacon boards for decisions, recruiting volunteers, enduring criticisms, and the lies of the enemy can all make a pastor afraid of seeing the dirt. They might think, "What if the elder board questions my leadership if I raise these issues?" or, "What if there is so much dirt under the carpet that it scares everyone?"

Pastors don't know what to do with reality. Often the dirt gets swept under the carpet because no one knows what to do with it. It is not enough to see the dirt; someone must know how to address it.

A group of business consultants have recognized that all kinds of leaders are prone to skip over the assessment. They write:

> Often, executives are ready to launch, or have already launched, changes designed to move toward a new organization. Diagnosis and self-assessment seem unnecessary, like backtracking and delay. However, plunging ahead without some common understanding of the current baseline creates substantial rework later on. Even worse, the rush to action creates an impression of impulsive leadership and, consequently, the change enlists few supporters.[2]

Some churches, like Christian Fellowship, are primed and ready to start cell groups. Others have more in common with Community Covenant Church and must address other issues in addition to the development of cell groups. Churches find themselves somewhere along a cell group readiness spectrum. On the far left lies the Life-Depleted Church. On the right lies the Life-Giving Church.

Life-Depleted
Churches

Life-Giving
Churches

Fig 3.1 The Readiness Spectrum

Life-Giving Churches

Over the past three years, I have heard stories of cell success, stories of cell mediocrity, and stories of cell failure. By and large, the churches who were most likely to succeed with cell groups were those churches who already had strength in their corner. They were ready for cell groups because they had four strong areas:

- Primary church leaders ready to embrace the interpersonal model of ministry that cell groups require.
- Permission given to the pastor to lead instead of being bogged down with administrative duties.
- Worship services where people are inspired by the presence of God.
- A passion for God expressed through prayer.

This does not mean that churches strong in these areas are the only churches that have made cell groups work. It means that such churches have the shortest distance to navigate. In addition to Christian Fellowship Church, churches like Bethany World Prayer Center in Baton

Rouge, Louisiana; Victory Christian Center in Tulsa, Oklahoma; Long Reach Church of God in Columbia, Maryland; and Belmont Church in Nashville, Tennessee built their groups on this kind of strong foundation.

Bethany World Prayer Center was in many ways a model Life-Giving Church before embarking upon the cell group journey. The church has a long heritage of great worship and preaching. The worship services led people to experience the presence of God and inspired them to serve Him. In 1982, they changed the name of the church from Bethany Baptist Church to Bethany World Prayer Center because of their conviction on the importance of prayer. Pastor Larry Stockstill wrote: "God spoke to us that our church was to be a center for intercessory prayer for the nations, and we established a twenty-four hour 'World Prayer Center' to pray for our missionaries, pastors, and government leaders. This center has been in operation round-the-clock ever since, except for a brief period of remodeling."[3]

Pastor Larry Stockstill is an inspiring leader. When leading his church into cell groups, Pastor Larry had the permission and the trust of church members. His father had founded the church. He was committed to being Bethany's pastor, as he focused on his home church, and his people loved him for it. He was also clearly the leader of the church. The vision of the church was not controlled by a committee or board. He was not bogged down with endless meetings to ensure that the "power brokers" of the church were kept happy. At the same time, he had developed a team of top-notch pastors and a board of elders to maintain accountability.

Finally, the key leaders of the church were open and ready to embrace the lifestyle required to make cell groups work. The staff members were willing to change how they ministered. Key leaders were willing to lead cell groups. They were ready to do relational ministry, love one another, and love the lost.

Churches that define themselves as Life-Giving are able to move relatively quickly into the development of cell groups. They need not focus as much on Stages 1-4 and can focus their energies on Stages 5-8.

Life-Depleted Churches

On the other end of the spectrum are Life-Depleted Churches. Almost every Christian in North America has experienced or known of this kind of church. Life-Depleted Churches often have difficulty starting cell groups because certain areas are weak. These churches are often characterized by:

- Church leaders who are unwilling to change their lives and embrace the values of interpersonal ministry.
- Committees or a board that control the church program; the pastor does not actually lead the church.
- Worship services that possess little energy or momentum.
- A non-existent or perfunctory prayer life.

When Dennis Wadley arrived at Community Covenant Church in Santa Barbara, he found the church weak on the last two points: fortunately, he had permission to lead the church, and the key leaders were hungry for change. Many pastors are not so lucky. One pastor started a cell group and began to see nonbelievers coming to the Lord through it. He then shared the vision with church leaders. They also realized how much cell groups had to offer, and they endorsed his vision. But as the pastor tried to lead the people into the vision, the committees continued to enact programs that sapped the energy from the cell groups. Key leaders, while willing to participate in cell groups, were unable to change the ways they related to other people. One of the most outspoken leaders of the church read all the books on cells, loved the vision, but could not let go of his dogmatic, judgmental, and critical ways. He wasn't able to get close enough to an immature believer or a non-Christian to minister to them.

Many pastors of Life-Depleted Churches have tried to use cell groups to revive their churches. Doing so is a recipe for failure. While cell groups are crucial to the health of a church, the cell group structure will not bring a church to life. If a church is dead, sick, or cancerous, the addition of cell groups will only create dead, ailing, or cancerous cell groups. Cell groups are not the answer: Jesus is. Many churches in North America need revival. They need a fresh touch from the Spirit of God. These churches need a fresh vision from God before they need a new structure.

Some have argued that God has moved beyond churches that have a lot in common with Life-Depleted Churches. But the people of these churches are children of God. No good father abandons His children. Just as God called Moses to lead His people out of Egypt, God is raising up courageous leaders to lead these children into His promises. But these leaders need more than cell group strategies. They need the information that is found in Stages 1-4, especially Stage 4. Only as the Spirit of God brings new life to the church will it be ready to produce healthy cell groups that are developed in Stages 5-8.

Somewhere In-Between

Most churches lie somewhere between these two extremes. They are not like Bethany World Prayer Center, but neither are they sick or dying. A church need not be classified as a completely Life-Giving Church in order to do cell groups well.

Venice Bible Church located just south of Tampa, Florida was a good church of 500 people when Pastor Tony Plummer assumed leadership. The church leadership felt the Lord calling them to guide the church in new directions, recognizing that old methods were not living up to expectations. The church began with two cell groups in 1997 and by 2002 has developed 50 cell groups. Along the way, Tony has worked with the pastoral team and elder board to build unity around the vision.

Highland Baptist Church in Waco, Texas was a successful church with established leadership and excellent teaching when the college pastor, Jimmy Siebert, caught a vision for cell groups. The church as a whole was not ready to embrace cell ministry, but the college department was primed and ready. For ten years, Jimmy and his team developed an extensive network of college cells. These cell groups were developed around six passions: a passion for prayer, a passion for worship, a passion for cell community, a passion for holiness, a passion for ministry, and a passion for evangelism and missions.[4] In June 1999, Highland birthed out the college department into a separate church, called Antioch Church, which now has over 1,000 people participating in cell group life.

Every church will encounter hazards on its journey. These hazards do not mean that cell groups will not work in a particular church. Churches that recognize these hazards for what they are and develop a plan for navigating around them are much more likely to develop working cell groups.

Church Plants

Church planters call TOUCH and want material that addresses the specific needs of planting a cell-based church. Bob Logan and Jeannette Buller developed the *Cell Church Planter's Guide* to meet such a need. This guide is based upon the best-selling *Church Planter's Toolkit* and has been adapted for the cell-based structure. While there are many differences between planting a new church and changing an old church, Logan and Buller outline a seven-phase process for cell church planting.

Phase 1: Envisioning
Phase 2: Initial leadership team
Phase 3: Prototype cell group begun
Phase 4: Two to four cell groups, monthly private worship
Phase 5: Four to seven cell groups, weekly private worship
Phase 6: Seven to ten cell groups, public celebration
Phase 7: Planting a new church

Their church planting phases roughly correlate with the eight stages of *Making Cell Groups Work*, except for Stage 3. While there is not an official phase for assessing, it is included in the process. The assessment of a church planting team is a little different than the assessment of an established church. The church planter must take a self-assessment. Logan and Buller have included such a tool in their resource. This assessment identifies the essential characteristics found in effective church planters.[5] Strong, visionary leadership is required to plant a vibrant, missional cell-based church. Church planters who do not possess the characteristics of effective church planters will most likely find the process very frustrating, as will the team.

Whether starting from scratch or introducing cell groups to a church, an important step in the process is assessment. Determining a church's current position will help the pastor and the vision team make important decisions about the steps ahead. Some churches can proceed full-steam; others must spend more time transforming the lives of church members. The only way to know what comes next is to find out where you currently are.

SECTION 3.2 Assess the Current Small Group System

It is hard to find anyone who has attended church for more than two years who has not had some kind of small group experience. From Bible studies to choir groups, task groups to discipleship groups, care groups, prayer groups, fellowship groups, recovery groups, mission groups, and Sunday school groups, the church made small groups a focus of its ministry.

Because of a church's prior experience with small groups, pastors, church leaders, and church members brings with them differing ideas of what constitutes a good small group. Some of these ideas will prove beneficial, others detrimental. For instance, people with a strong Bible study background will often see deep Bible study as crucial. Others have experience with groups that had great worship, and still others have seen the power of open sharing and transparency in groups. These good things can become predetermined agendas that create expectations that limit the leadership and what Christ wants to do in cell groups.

Because these hidden expectations are unavoidable, it is helpful to understand the small group experiences before starting cell groups. To help you assess the history of groups, I have summarized six basic types of groups that churches have used.

The No Group System

The first group system is the simplest because it has no formal small groups. The focus of this church is solely on the large group life. This system might look like this:

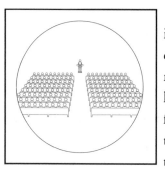

This kind of church places almost all of its focus on the large group meeting, where church members watch leaders perform ministry. This system occurs in churches large and small. Some Bible churches might fit this category when they behave like teaching centers where expert Bible teachers train the crowds. Some charismatic churches fall into this system because they place a heavy emphasis on spectacular praise and very energetic preaching. A few seeker churches embrace this model when the leadership puts almost all of its energy into the Sunday morning seeker service.

The positive side of this system is that it limits heresy and misdirected ministry, but this is the only positive point that I can find. This system tends to place all of the responsibility for ministry on the shoulders of a super-star pastor. The church is limited to what happens in a building at certain times and it tends to create sit-and-soak Christians who are looking for their next spiritual high.

In reality, this is a No Group System in an official sense only. When you look below the official structures, these churches have many groups, "cliques" which are limited to those who are already connected to the inner workings of the church. People looking into this system often find it difficult to penetrate these groups and feel left out.

Those who are accustomed to the No Group System often bring with them ideals, language, and lifestyles that exclude the less informed. They have little experience with immature believers or nonbelievers. Don Tillman was using the 8-stage process to train a No Group System church. He arrived in Dockers and an Oxford shirt. They arrived in dresses or suits. Their language was exclusive. They had lost touch with anything outside the walls of the church. He asked them, "How many of you have been to the Starbucks down the road in the last month? The last year? Ever?" No one raised a hand. He stated, "Do you realize you have lost touch with the culture around you? You live in a Starbucks generation and you have no concept of it. If you want to reach this world, you need to understand the people who frequent Starbucks." Churches with a No Group System have to undergo many shifts before they are prepared to launch cell groups.

The Programmed Group System

The Programmed Group System describes the Sunday school experience. It is still the most popular type of small group experienced in the church. Sunday school was a development that rose out of the 19th century program for training children how to read. This age-graded approach was applied to religious education in the early part of the twentieth century and took off in the church, especially in North America.

Sunday school systems work best when they are highly structured, even to the point of electing officers. Sunday school classes usually are larger than other kinds of small groups, sometimes averaging 25 in number, and are highly dependent upon curriculum and structure.[6]

Sunday school splits each category of people into a series of classes, who meet every Sunday morning before celebration.

The Programmed System achieves very good results on the surface, with participation of church members at 60-80%. Some people argue that the best resource for evangelism and discipleship is still the Sunday school system. They state that Sunday school is easy to manage, assimilates people into the church, and should be used as an evangelistic tool.

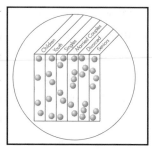

Evidence is mixed about the success of Sunday school. Many highly organized churches are able to make it work. Others are floundering in stagnation. Sunday school advocate Ken Hemphill writes:

> It is my conviction that the beginning of the so-called demise of Sunday School can be traced to a time when denominations and local churches failed to use Sunday School with evangelistic intentionality and purpose. When the design was forgotten, the Sunday School became a maintenance tool rather than a growth tool.[7]

Hemphill continues his argument by stating that Sunday school classes are just cell groups that meet on the church campus on Sunday mornings and that cell groups are just Sunday school classes that meet in the homes during the week. On the surface this might appear to be the case, but there are significant differences between the two structures.

	Sunday School	**Cell Groups**
Location	Church classroom	Where people live
Time	Fixed	Flexible
Focus	Bible study	One-another ministry
Limitations	Size of the building	Number of leaders
Attracts	Those willing to come to a building	Those who are sought

Sunday school is a "come" system. Cell groups are a "go" system. In most churches, Sunday school has become a nice place for Christian relationships to develop, but it is not a place for people to deal with the hard questions of life. Nor is it a place for nonbelievers, because they are no longer willing to come to religious buildings to find God. For those who have been raised in the Programmed Group System, a shift in mindset is necessary to experience life in cell group. There must be a shift in purpose, from "come" to "go." It demands a shift in participation, from "attendance" to "ministry." And it requires a shift in point of view, from "us" to "them."

The Associated Group System

On the surface, this system might look at first like a balanced church. But notice that the groups are not integrated at the center of the church; they are extra. They fall outside the view of church leaders.

This system is also quite common in North America. These groups are connected to the church but they are not given vision by church leaders. This system might look something like this:

Associated groups meet for fellowship and Bible study in the home. Usually a volunteer lay person helps to administrate these groups, but he or she does not regularly meet with the pastoral leadership to make sure the vision of the groups fits the vision of the church. Groups are limited to the highly committed who like to participate in deep Bible study. Usually only 10-20% of the church participates in the meetings, which meet anywhere from one to four times each month.

These groups are great at connecting people in deep fellowship, but they often fail to participate in the call of the Great Commission because they are not connected to the vision of the church. Groups tend to be ingrown.

People from this group system often struggle with the shift to life in cell groups. They tend to be independent in their thinking and they do not want to be guided by the church leadership. Because they have become ingrown, they feel threatened by the vision that the groups might open up to nonbelievers. Many times the best strategy for these groups is to let them continue as they are and to start new groups that will model holistic cell group life for them.

The Optional Participation Group System

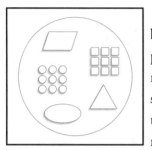 In this system, groups are given a higher priority because they are organized by the church. But participation in these groups is an option set beside many other options which do not break down into smaller groups, like the youth ministry, worship team, missions outreach, etc. The unbroken shapes represent these other ministry options.

A staff pastor or the senior pastor usually oversees these groups. Yet this pastor will also have many other responsibilities and cannot focus on the groups' direction; therefore, the groups tend to lack the support needed to be healthy and growing.

The groups within this system will have different purposes. Some might be fellowship groups, others Bible discussion groups, and others discipleship groups. These groups provide on-going pastoral care, but many times this system is limited because the small groups must compete with participation in other ministries. This hinders long-term growth and contributes to leadership discouragement.

The Church of Small Groups System

This system has become quite popular over the last decade. Carl George introduced it on wide scale when he argued that because a church is already comprised of small groups, the leadership need only recognize these small group units and organize and support them as such.[8] This system organizes people into small groups who are already connected.

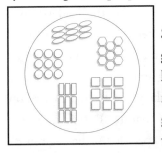

George argues that these groups can be Sunday school classes, choir groups, deacon groups, task groups, leadership groups, or home Bible studies. Each of the shapes represent a different kind of group. Any group that is small is considered of equal value.

In *Building a Church of Small Groups*, Bill Donahue and Russ Robinson reported the way they developed this system at Willow Creek Community Church. In their book, they argue that the purpose of these groups is to experience authentic life-transforming community with the end result of a "well-ordered heart."[9] Donahue and Robinson list five major types of groups: disciple-making groups, community groups, service groups, seeker groups, and support groups. Groups have a choice as to how often them meet, from weekly to monthly.[10]

Each type of group has a focus that is determined by its purpose. Service groups include task groups like "money counter groups," "parking lot groups," etc. Other groups might include sports groups, common interest groups like quilting, or even book-reading groups.

This system also includes home small groups which have much in common with cell groups. Some churches using this system prioritize these home groups over the other groups. In order to shift from this system to a cell group system, the focus should lie on developing basic Christian community in all groups.

The House Church System

The proponents of this system claim that people are looking for a deeper sense of community along with a lower commitment to institutions. House churches come in one of two forms: independent house churches and house church networks. The latter option is a growing phenomenon as leaders are developing oversight structures that connect house churches with one another. In these networks, the leaders work together and the house church members gather periodically for worship.

At first glance, the house church might seem to be the same thing as a cell group. Both meet in homes (although cell groups can meet in many different places). Both can meet at any time of the week. Both are based on interpersonal relationships and are informal in nature. But there is one major difference: house churches can grow to 50 people. At the beginning, house churches might be small in number, but they can become small churches that meet in homes. When this happens, the cell dynamic is lost and the sharing and interaction between church members deteriorates. The house church with more than 15 people needs to understand that multiple cell groups must be developed within the church.

As a house church grows over 15 people, the leaders must begin to wrestle with ways to continue to promote interpersonal ministry and accountability. One option is to create cell groups that parallel the house group meeting. House churches should find it quite easy to develop leaders for these groups because of the emphasis placed upon relationships.

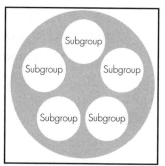

Previous Small Group Experiences

Former small group experiences can either enhance or impede the progress of cell groups. Church leaders must build upon the positive experiences and deal with the negative ones. Some people have had less than positive experiences in small groups. Boredom in meetings, members who talk uncontrollably, or leaders who make people feel stupid or unspiritual are common problems. When such issues are not addressed, the members will begin to resent small groups.

Some people have had small group experiences that border on the absurd. For instance, some leaders have sought to control cell members by dictating God's will and handing out punishment. A few people might even feel that small groups in homes might turn into cults. Such issues can be addressed through conversation, but if people have deep hurts, it will take time for them to trust the cell group vision.

Another common negative experience is past cell group failure. Such failures provide rich learning and can stimulate church leaders to discover the right ways to do it next time. The only way to deal with people's emotions about the failure is to talk honestly about the mistakes, and then address the ways things will be done differently.

Most people will bring positive experiences from their previous participation in small groups. These experiences should not be denigrated because they were not the full expression of basic Christian community. Instead, they should be capitalized upon because people will be able to connect these positive experiences with the vision of cell groups. College dorm Bible studies, street ministry with an outreach team, and fellowship groups all contain elements that can be built upon.

SECTION 3.3 Assess to Create Urgency

First Church Middle City, USA still meets in the building that the founders built in 1946. The remodeling project in 1975 and the expansion in 1983 to build a gymnasium both created new excitement and new growth. Jerry assumed the role of senior pastor three years ago, and he has become frustrated with the lack of real ministry within the church. He feels that people are merely going through the motions without a true experience of God's presence. But the people are content. They still have one of the largest church buildings in town. They still minister to the kids every summer in the government projects. And they have one of the highest baptism rates of any church in the county.

Just down the road sits Second Church. It is about the same size and age as First Church. The leadership has realized that its buildings are dated, but they cannot afford to renovate or build a new building. Giving has decreased over the last five years and attendance has started to drop. Sam, the pastor, has been leading the church for about 15 years and key leaders were starting to express concern over the church's direction. One elder has even suggested a pastor's conference at a nearby church. They know something has to change.

Urgency and Buy-In

The change formula I presented in Section 1.3 is instrumental for understanding the differences between these two churches:

(A + B + C) > D = Change
A = a significant dissatisfaction with current reality
B = an awareness of a better condition
C = a knowledge of the first step(s) to take
D = the anticipated loss as a result of the change

First Church does not have a significant level of dissatisfaction; the people are satisfied and have grown complacent. If Jerry tries to start cell groups without dealing with the lack of urgency, church members will not buy into the vision. On the other hand, Second Church has a significant level of dissatisfaction and therefore feels an urgency to look for new ways to minister. In such a church, it is much easier to get people to buy into the vision of cell groups.

On a ship, resistance to leadership is called mutiny. In the church, the mutiny sometimes comes in the form of active resistance. People ridicule the idea, spread rumors about cell groups, manipulate people and the system, and even accuse the pastor of being controlling. More often, mutiny comes in the form of passive resistance where people agree verbally but fail to follow through. Some might withhold their help and support because they do not like the idea, so they just look on to see the groups fail.

Pastors see this resistance. They attack it. They avoid it. They give up because of it. Mostly, they do not know how to deal with it. One pastor led his congregation through a three month process of developing purpose, vision, and mission statements. The process was well-designed, involved many key leaders, and resulted in a well-stated, challenging focus for the church. The entire package was presented at a major celebrative event that was to be used as a five-year ministry kick-off. The event was well attended and the vote was unanimous in favor of the vision. Within six months, the pastor left the congregation with a small group of people to begin a new church.

Except for one simple step, his process was nearly flawless. He assumed the congregation at large had a strong desire to move forward into new territory. He had preached, taught, prayed, shared, and thought they got it. A few did. A few key leaders were opposed. In fact, they were opposed to anything he did. But they went along with the vote. If the pastor and those who supported his vision had created a sense of urgency, the people's reaction would have been quite different.

Levels of Corporate Urgency

In some churches the urgency is felt. When one Mississippi church moved into its new building, it quickly filled up all of the new Sunday school space. Church leaders soon realized that they could not build enough buildings to hold the people they were called to reach. Church members didn't like crowding into classrooms. Cell groups were an obvious choice for them because cells are not building-dependent.

Other churches need help developing a sense of urgency. The methods for developing urgency depend upon the level of urgency already felt by the staff, the church leaders, and the people. I have identified four points along the spectrum of urgency:

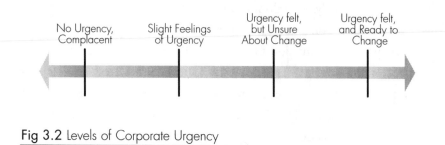

Fig 3.2 Levels of Corporate Urgency

No urgency, complacent. This church needs to take a hard look in the mirror. It is not ready to hear about the cell group vision. First, the pastor should focus the church on developing a biblical vision of the Kingdom of God and an understanding of the mission of the church. Second, the leadership should assess its strengths and weaknesses. Also, many times the church will require a spark from the outside, a confrontational speaker and/or a consultant who will speak honestly about the issues that are holding the church back.

Slight feelings of urgency. This kind of church feels the need to be different but is not ready to do anything radical. The people need an increased sense of urgency. This can be done through assessment, dialogue among key leaders about the direction of the church, and seeing what is happening in other churches who are using cell groups.

Urgency felt, but unsure about change. These churches know that something new is needed, but they lack the confidence about what to do differently. They do not understand the new idea and they do not understand the first steps. Pastors should capitalize upon this urgency before it turns into despair. They should mobilize key leaders to learn more about cell groups and gather as much information as possible to bring some security to the change process. Outside consultants and assessments both prove very helpful to these churches.

Urgency felt and ready for change. These churches are primed to move forward to implement cell groups. They need leaders who will build a team to clarify the cell group vision. They need to learn as much as possible about cell groups and get started with them.

Sources of Complacency

The enemy of urgency is complacency. The more complacent the congregation, the harder it will be to get members to see the potential of a new vision. Many times, it is more fruitful to address the cause of the complacency in order to prepare the hearts of people to hear the new vision. Here are some common sources of complacency:[11]

The absence of crisis. Moderation can be one of the greatest enemies of faith. Risk leads people into crisis situations and causes them to depend on the Lord. Churches that fail to take many risks do not experience crises and will not feel much urgency.

Too many visible resources. Buildings and money provide safety for churches. If a church has plenty of money and the buildings are relatively new, then people will feel like the church is doing well. On the other end of the spectrum, the same complacency can result from having too few resources. In such a case, the congregation becomes discouraged and no longer perceives the hand of God at work. Eventually, church members accept the place they are in and even tend to protect it.

Low expectations. A deacon once said to Don Tillman, "Pastors come and go around here. We have to live with all the changes each one tries to impose on us. You'll do good if you just preach good, visit our sick, bury our dead, and marry our kids. Please don't try to change us!"

Internal evaluation that focuses on the wrong factors. The mark of a successful church today is "respectable numbers." If a church has more than 250 people in regular attendance, it is above average, even considered by many as a success. But God is not interested in how one church performs in comparison to another. He is concerned about whether or not His church is working at His mission.

The lack of feedback from external sources. An unbelieving man confessed to a pastor that he did not attend church because he did not want people telling him what was wrong with his life. He already knew that he was messed up. The pastor took these words to heart and shared them with his leaders to illustrate how those outside the church view Christians. If the church plans to take the Gospel—"good news"—to those who need it, it had better learn to listen to nonbelievers, not just preach to them.

A kill-the-messenger-of-bad-news culture. Sometimes honest feedback is received as being critical, and the pastor's insecurity causes him to reject those who bring bad news. Doing so limits the level of confrontation and honesty.

Too much "happy talk" from senior leadership. Happy talk is the habit of only talking about the good stuff and making out like everything is grand. Pastors often fall prey to this because they want to be an encouragement to the church, but it can result in a false reality.

Emotional attachments to old ways of doing church. Because people attach great amounts of emotion to the ways of the past, choosing to change involves as much or more emotion as logic. Some will elevate Sunday school to biblical levels. Changing worship styles can create outright war. Remodeling a building can cause church splits. Why? Not because these people are necessarily ungodly, but because they experienced God in those ways and to change them causes doubt, pain, and discomfort.

Expecting the church to be safe. Change is happening so fast in today's culture that people are overwhelmed by it. The church is the one place where people expect or demand to feel safe. When people feel like the pastor is forcing them to change before they are ready, they revert into complacency, which serves as a protective mechanism from the pain that comes with change.

Lack of processing time. Pastors often feel the urgency to change and are motivated to explore cell groups. They present the idea expecting people to love it, not realizing that everyone needs time to process the idea and see its potential. People do not follow anyone blindly, especially church leaders, and they need time to wrestle with the idea and develop urgency.

Complacency, the place where most churches exist today, is ignoring reality in order to continue operating within the accepted or familiar boundaries. The emotion that established church leaders and members feel about established traditions is stronger than their belief in their pastor's vision. Pastors come and go, but the members have baptized their children and grandchildren in that same church, sweated over the construction of the building, taught Sunday school for 25 years, and pressed through the ups and downs of the past. Such long-term commitments come with deep feelings.

Communicating Urgency

Urgency cannot be developed in the entire church at once. Rather, it should be developed on the different levels, beginning with the pastoral staff, moving to volunteer leaders, and then the church body. Within each of these three groups there are key stakeholders. These are the leaders that carry the most influence. They are the leaders even though they might not have the title. These people will likely block the idea of cell groups if they are not involved in the development process. If a pastor does not get these stake-holders to buy-in and feel an urgency for change, doing so for others will prove difficult.

After identifying the stakeholders, the pastor must determine how to communicate the sense of urgency with them. Different people will process the new idea of cell ministry in different ways. Some respond well to new ideas and change, while others need more time and information before they embrace it. There are five basic responses to change.[12]

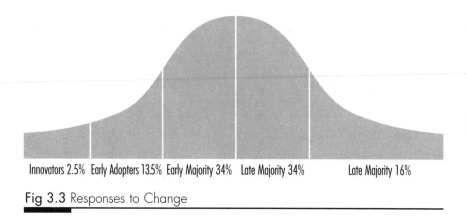

Innovators 2.5% Early Adopters 13.5% Early Majority 34% Late Majority 34%   Late Majority 16%

Fig 3.3 Responses to Change

Innovators. These people are obsessed with being venturesome. They challenge the status quo and expand the current boundaries by introducing new ideas. While not all of their ideas are practical or workable, their concern is to explore new territory. Innovators make many mistakes because they will adopt new ideas simply because they are new.

Innovators are able to visualize a new idea without ever seeing it. They do not need to increase their dissatisfaction with current reality, because they are always dissatisfied with the old. They continually feel a sense of urgency and embrace change just because it is change. To introduce a new idea to an innovator, a simple meeting is often sufficient, followed up with some reading material.

Early Adopters. These people are characterized by respectability. They are ahead of the pack, but not too far ahead: therefore, they have the greatest degree of influence upon others in the church. Most likely, the stakeholders are early adopters.

The vision cannot survive without the Early Adopters. These are the people who can understand what the Innovators are doing and then turn the new idea into action. Many times, it is best for Early Adopters to see the vision in another church, either through a conference or through a case study book. Honest discussion about current reality, with the help of assessment tools, will often develop a sense of urgency in an early adopter. They will need time, but it will pay off in the long run.

Early Majority. These people are deliberate individuals who make up one third of the population. They adhere to the motto, "Be not the first by which the new is tried, nor the last to lay the old aside." They will follow with deliberate willingness, but they will seldom lead.

It takes longer for members of the Early Majority to develop urgency. They need time to process current reality and a leader who will make them feel safe in this process. They have a limited ability to understand a new vision by reading about it or seeing it at another church. Primarily they need to experience it in order to adopt it. They will follow people they trust into a new vision and then they will take it on as their own.

Late Majority. Making up another third of the population, these people view new ideas with skepticism and caution. The pressure of peers and obvious circumstantial pointers must lead them to see the necessity of change before they will change.

Because those in the Late Majority category only adopt a new idea after other people are doing it and thereby proving it successful, pastors cannot expect this group to feel much urgency until they see it working in their church. To see cell groups working in another church is not enough.

Laggards. These are the last to adopt new ideas, as they are traditional and their reference point is in the past. They tend to be suspicious of the new and those who promote new ideas. This group rarely feels an urgency to change until they see that the cell group train has left the station and they realize that they are being left behind. They will change only because everyone else has.

Urgency Through Church Health Assessment

Urgency cannot be forced upon people, even if the pastor feels so much urgency for cell groups that he cannot sleep at night. The best way to develop a sense of urgency is when a pastor facilitates a process that allows people to discover the urgency on their own. Such urgency will create an internal motivation rather than one that is superimposed on them. "The one convinced against his will is of the same opinion still."

One of the best ways to facilitate this discovery is through the use of church health assessments. They provide expertise that has been gathered from the experience of many churches over the last 30 years. People tend to be much more receptive to bad news when it comes from an objective outsider who has nothing to gain than from an insider who might be perceived as having much to gain. Such tools not only present information, but they do so in a manner that allows the recipients to process and analyze the information. Elder and deacon boards, special teams, and staff members can work through the assessment tools and process the conclusions. They will point out weak areas and identify elements that must be changed. The conclusions that assessments discover are the conclusions of the participants, not those of the leader.

Natural Church Development Assessment developed by Christian Schwarz and Christof Schlalk is one of the best. These researchers assessed over 1000 churches in 32 different countries to determine the eight key factors that impact church health. These factors are:

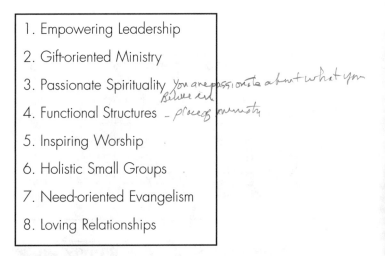

1. Empowering Leadership
2. Gift-oriented Ministry
3. Passionate Spirituality *You are passionate about what you Believe in*
4. Functional Structures *– process ministry*
5. Inspiring Worship
6. Holistic Small Groups
7. Need-oriented Evangelism
8. Loving Relationships

One pastor was given the book *Natural Church Development* and devoured it. He passed out a short booklet on the eight factors to his staff members and told them to rank the highest and the lowest factor. Every one of them ranked Inspiring Worship as the highest and Holistic Small Groups as the lowest. Almost immediately, the leadership of the church felt an urgency to change.

Assessment is an excellent way to stimulate urgency, but it is not the only way. Nor is it the primary way. One question that I have asked every pastor that I interviewed: "What would you do differently if you were to lead your church into cell groups again." Over 50% of them responded, "I would pray more." Ultimately, urgency is developed as the Holy Spirit convicts people. No pastor, church leader, assessment, or church consultant can develop the kind of urgency that the Holy Spirit can. Therefore, if you find your church stuck in complacency, stop reading this book and ask the Lord to breathe upon your church and stir it up to hunger and thirst after Him and His ways.

Additional Ways to Create Urgency

To Increase Urgency with the Staff:

• Lead a study on the church in Acts.
• Increase the expectations for actual results rather than busyness.
• Provide honest feedback on the state of the church.
• Paint a picture of what the church and their jobs could be like.
• Take them to a church that is changing the world through cell groups.

To Increase Urgency with Key Leaders:

• Evaluate the trends of the church over the past 10 years.
  —Membership
  —Worship attendance
  —Giving
  —Number of leaders developed
  —Number of people discipled and enfolded into the life of the church
  —Number of people won to Christ
  —Number of visitors who did not come back
  —Number of regular attenders who left the church
• Evaluate the impact of the church on the community.
  —Collect data on gang involvement, crime, etc.
  —Compare the population growth of the community with the growth of the church
  —Visit <www.barna.org> for statistics to share.
• Share the success other churches are having in reaching their worlds with cell groups.
• Share Jethro's advice to Moses in Exodus 18. Explain that one man or woman cannot minister to all the people alone.

To Increase Urgency with the Church Body:
- Preach a series of sermons on the purpose of the church in the world.
- Lead a special course that teaches different spiritual principles than church members are accustomed to hearing, (e.g. *Experiencing God* by Henry Blackaby).
- Share the data that reveals the impotence of the church today.
- Cast a vision for every person a minister.
- Call the people to prayer.
- Do not tell them about cell groups yet.

Levers

Evaluate the readiness of your church based on the spectrum of life-giving churches and life-depleted churches.

If you are a church planter, complete the church planter assessment.
Key Resource:
   —*Cell Church Planter's Guide* by Jeannette Buller and Bob Logan.

Identify the kind of group experiences that your church has had.

Identify the level of urgency felt by staff, by lay leaders, and by the people.

Assess the overall church health.
Key Resource:
   —*Natural Church Development* by Christian Schwarz
   —*NCD Church Health Assessment* available through
   <www.churchsmart.com>.

Develop a plan to create a sense of urgency at the appropriate level for your church.

Discussion Questions

1. How ready do you feel the church is for cell groups?
2. How ready do you feel the leaders are for cell groups?
3. What barriers do you feel are impeding the journey to cell groups?
4. Describe the historical experience of small groups in the church.
5. What positive emotions do people feel about small groups?
6. What negative emotions do they feel about small groups?
7. What is the level of urgency for change felt by:
   a. the staff?
   b. key leaders?
   c. the church overall?
8. What does the church health assessment reveal about the church?
9. Can this church health assessment be used to increase a sense of urgency?
10. What other methods can be used to increase a sense of urgency?

STAGE 4
Prepare
the Church Through
Transformation

A ship's captain occasionally must go to sea with a crew that is less than ideal. Imagine trying to sail a ship when the crew cannot hoist a sail or even lift the anchor. When a captain is stuck with a group of novices, he does not scream his commands and expect the people to automatically respond in the correct way. Instead, he shows them the ropes before setting sail and teaches them as the ship moves through the gentle waters close to the harbor. The captain must prepare the crew in the calm before the storm-filled voyage ahead. Likewise, a pastor must prepare church members for the new life in cell groups before the groups are actually started.

Many churches have leapt into the cell group structure only to realize that church members were not prepared for it. Church leaders copy a cell structure that they have found in a successful church, but the church members have not prepared their values to make the cell structure work. This is called pouring old wine into new wineskins.

Every pastor must ask, "How do we prepare the church for cell group success?" before he begins his first cell group. In Stage 3, the vision team should work together to determine the church's readiness for cell groups. In Stage 4, the vision team and other leaders will work to improve the areas of weakness that would undermine the cell group implementation. This stage contains three sections that will guide the preparation process:

• "Prepare People Through Transformation" (Section 4.1). This section lays the groundwork for leading people through the process of values-transformation, which is rooted in the biblical term "repentance." Without repentance, the cell group structure will not endure.

• "Prepare Individuals for Cell Group Life" (Section 4.2). One important, but often overlooked, person is the cell member. This section provides practical patterns for preparing not only the first cell group leaders, but also the first cell group members.

• "Prepare the Corporate Life for Cell Groups" (Section 4.3). There are hidden systems that often undermine the success of cell groups, and this section provides practical ways to address them.

SECTION 4.1 Prepare People Through Transformation

Over the last decade much has been written, taught, and discussed about the transition to effective cell group ministry and to the cell-based church. For instance, Ralph Neighbour developed a pastoral training series called *The Year of Transition*, which provided excellent resources explaining how to implement the cell group structure. Steve Fitch, the Superintendent of the Free Methodist Church in Southern California, has coached many churches into the development of cell groups through a process that he calls the Cell Transition Network. In each case, the word transition is used to describe the journey from no cell groups to a working cell group system.

While the word transition is not wrong, it does not completely illustrate the kind of change that most churches experience as they successfully implement cell groups. A transition focuses upon a change in external structures. Cell group church consultants who use the word "transition" do not limit their teaching to the changing of external structures. They recognize that most churches need more than a transition of the external structure to cell groups; church members need an internal lifestyle transformation in order to make cell groups work. The problem is that churches only see the structural change. Therefore, I choose to use the word transformation to highlight the need for more.

Three Depths of Change

Everyday we experience change. We observe, test, and purchase new car models. We use new computer programs. Try new restaurants. Visit new movie theaters. Everyday, we experience more change than entire countries experienced 500 years ago. But all change is not the same. Learning how to use the internet is a landmark change for this generation, but it is a different kind of change than switching from a PC platform to a Macintosh platform. An even more substantial change in this digital age is the virtual reality technology that is coming down the road.

To help understand these differences, change can be classified into three different categories or depths of change: Developmental, Transitional, and Transformational.[1] These depths of change can be illustrated with the ways a gardener addresses three different levels of change in a garden.

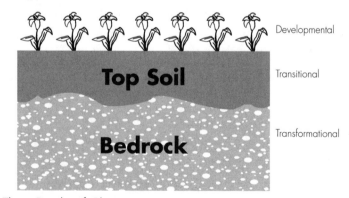

Fig 4.1 Three Depths of Change

Developmental Change.

The most basic of the three, it occurs when the gardener seeks to improve the growth of the flowers. She might do this by learning new pruning techniques, increasing the amounts of fertilizer and water, and pulling away the weeds.

A salesman develops his skills when he learns new techniques to sell his product. School teachers attend training courses every year to become better teachers. Business leaders read expensive books to improve their leadership skills. Developmental change looks like this:

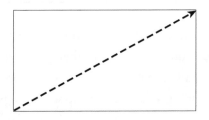

Fig 4.2 Developmental Change-A Linear Process

Churches experience developmental change when they seek to improve what they are already doing. Pastors read a book on preaching. Sunday school teachers attend a workshop. Children's workers travel to a conference. Prayer coordinators visit a church to learn about a new prayer ministry.

Transitional change.

Much more complex than developmental change, it occurs when the gardener realizes that she wants to replace the old flowers with new ones. This kind of change requires the old flowers to be pulled up and tossed away. The topsoil is in good condition; it only needs preparation for the new flowers. This might require the addition of mulch, fertilizer, and some tilling of the soil. After the old is gone, the new flowers can be planted and watered.

A salesman experiences transitional change when he accepts a job as a sales manager. A teacher must go through a transition when she teaches with new curriculum. Business executives experience transition when they purchase a new subsidiary. This type of change can be illustrated like this:

Fig 4.3 Transitional Change

In the church, transitional changes transpire when leaders discover that current methods do not work and that new methods are required. Examples might include the adoption of a new worship style, hiring a new staff member, adding a second worship service, replacing the Sunday evening service with a training center, or building a larger worship center. Transitional changes have set beginning and completion dates. They can be managed with the use of budgets and timelines.

Transformational change.

This is the most complex. Returning to the garden analogy, transformational change occurs when a garden needs a complete overhaul before it will be ready for flowers to be planted. Imagine a garden that is overrun with weeds, soil that is very poor, and rocks that must be removed. In addition, it does not have a source of water. No right-minded gardener would spend the money on flowers to have them choked by weeds, sickened by the soil, and starved from the lack of water. Instead, the gardener prepares the soil by removing the weeds, carrying off the rocks, plowing the ground (usually over and over), and tapping into a water source. Many times, this requires the gardener to work the soil deeply, going all the way down to the bedrock. If the soil is poor or rocky, she replaces it with new soil and only then adds mulch and fertilizer. After all of this work, the garden is ready for the flowers.

A salesman experiences transformational change by moving out of sales and into the corporate offices. A teacher goes through transformation by deciding to go back to school and get an advanced degree to teach on the college level. An executive feels the effects of transformation when the demand for his company's product disappears and the business has to close doors.

Churches encounter transformational change when they sell property and move to a different area of town, when a new pastor is hired and he changes the direction of the church, or when God reaches down His hand and touches His people through revival.

Transformational change in the church deals with two levels. First, it deals with external structures of programs, training, and systems. Second, it deals with the human values that drive the church. Unless God changes the human values that drive these external structures, the people will not be transformed and will continue simply to go through religious motions. The process of transformational change can be illustrated this way:

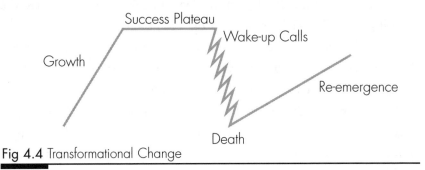

Fig 4.4 Transformational Change

First, a church experiences growth, which is followed by a success plateau. This is illustrated by the growth that accompanied Sunday school in the 1940s and 1950s, followed by the plateau in the 1960s through the 1980s. After a plateau, the church begins to experience wake-up calls. Not only is growth not occurring, but people are leaving, teachers are growing scarce, and nonbelievers avoid coming to church buildings at 10:00 A.M. on Sunday mornings. Finally, the church realizes that it must do things differently as members die to the old ways of ministry. From this emerges not only new structures, but also new energy and life.

Is it a Cell Group Transition or Cell Group Transformation?

For some churches, the journey toward making cell groups work looks much like a transition because they never missed a beat between the old ways of ministry and the new cell groups that they started. For instance, Bethany World Prayer Center began their cell groups in 1995 with 54 groups. These 54 groups were filled with 455 people who had been meeting weekly on Saturday mornings and during worship services to intercede for the church, the pastors, and the nonbelievers the church was trying to reach. This group was called Gideon's Army. After 18 months of praying together, Larry Stockstill trained this army in the vision of the church and cell ministry for 10 weeks. Then, he started the 54 cell groups. The cell groups took off from there.[2]

These people were prepared to do the work to make cell groups work. The soil was ready. On the outside, Bethany's process looks like a transition, but when you look into Bethany's history, it becomes clear that God had brought this group of 455 people and the staff through a process of transformation. They did not limit their focus to developing a new cell group structure. They focused on the Lord and allowed the Lord to shape them into His ministers.

A transition assumes that a church can visit a model church like Bethany, copy their structures, use their materials, and see the same success that they have. A transition focuses on "surface issues like skill training, communication of the new vision, planning and oversight, and lack of understanding."[3] I worked with a church who caught the vision for cell groups at a Bethany conference and they received much skill training from TOUCH consultants. This church of about 150 people had developed about eight cell groups. The leaders had been trained well and they were receiving weekly support from the senior pastor. Yet this church was forced to shut these groups down. The cells were a positive experience, but there were other issues eroding the foundation beneath the groups. Cell leader marriages were in trouble. Elders were not supporting the vision. The worship services were struggling because the church could not find the right worship leader. Finances were tight. And one leader rebelled and left the church with a group of dissenters to start another church (which failed).

Transformational change extends below the surface of structural change. This senior pastor realized this and pulled back from pushing the cell groups. The church created some interim small groups that met on the church campus. He identified a new group of elders whose values and vision lined up with his and began meeting with them every week. He prayed until God revealed the right worship leader. The pastor began to teach on the values and the vision so that the people would know where God was leading them. After about a year, this church restarted a few groups, much more slowly this time. Now, the groups are beginning to take off because the church has been transformed, not just because it has the "right" structure.

Transformation is the radical shift from one state of being to another, so significant that it requires a shift in culture, behavior, and mindset to implement successfully and sustain over time. In other words, transformation demands a shift in human awareness that completely alters the way the organization and its people see the world, [their ministry, the church and themselves.][4]

A cell pastor from the east coast shared honestly, "After about three years into cell groups, I became angry with the cell group experts. I did not want to read anything they said. They painted a picture of cell group grandeur. They promised that the new structure would make everything great." This church knew how to develop a strong cell group structure, because it started over 100 groups. Church leaders implemented all the right training. But cell leaders were burning out. Pastors could not support them well. This church had to learn the hard way that people take more time to transform their ways than leadership can take to enact a new structure.

A Transformation of Values

George Barna researched the values American Christians have abandoned: radical obedience, holistic stewardship, church loyalty, submission to authority, accountability, diversity, discipline, persecution, biblical knowledge, theological purity, salvation by grace alone, elder care, family spirituality, holiness, patience, and confession of sins.[5] Barna writes: "Perhaps the most significant revelation emerging from an examination of our values is to realize how extensively we have shaped our worldview and values around the indices of worldly success and acceptance."[6]

Some people have argued that once people step into the "biblical" model of cell groups, these values will return to the church. The implication is that the lack of cell groups in the church is the only problem with the church. But the evidence does not support such a conclusion. Cell groups work when people embrace the values that Barna lists as abandoned. If a cell group is filled with people who have the values of the world instead of the values of Christ, the group will be dominated by worldly values. One business consultant observes how personal change impacts organizational change. She writes:

Group behavior and organizational change cannot be separated from personal behavioral change. This is one of the hardest parts of any change effort, particularly at the executive level. As Leo Tolstoy wrote, 'Everyone thinks about changing the world, but no one thinks of changing himself.'[7]

It is not enough to change the church's organization, write a new vision statement, and train leaders. Individuals must embrace the change that will support the new structure. When a core group of cell members have embraced godly values, Christ's life will dominate the group and transform the values of other people.

Transformation Through Repentance

TAKE UP YOUR CROSS —DIE TO YOURSELF

Repentance is the foundation of a life in Christ. It is the way a person starts her walk with Him. And it is the way a person advances on the journey with Him. Repentance cannot be relegated to a "salvation prayer." Repentance is the way of life for a Christian. Isaiah 30:15 reads, "In repentance and rest is your salvation."

If Barna is correct and the church has embraced the values of the world rather than the values of God's Kingdom, the only alternative for the church is to seek God for spiritual renewal. This renewal will not come if the church is asking God to bless what it is already doing. It will only come as the church repents.

The cell group model is very innovative. At the same time, it is very traditional. It only works when it is built upon and by Jesus. If He is present, then cell groups are dynamic. If He is absent, then cell groups are only another good ministry idea.

Resurrection life (transformation) can only come through death. Cell groups join Christ in His transforming life as the cell members repent and turn away from their captivity to the values that dominate the culture. As they radically obey, freely give, show church loyalty, submit to authority, become accountable, embrace diversity, exhibit discipline, endure persecution, discover biblical truths, care for the elderly, have family spirituality, practice holiness and patience, and confess sins to one another, cell groups and cell group members will experience the transformative power of Christ.

Cell groups serve as a place for people to live as counter-cultural or alternative societies. Cell groups do not work when the people within them embrace the values of the dominant culture. Cell groups should call people out of the values and practices that the culture has established and "let the new order of God's reign be established in one's heart."[8]

A Comeback Congregation

When Randy Frazee assumed leadership of Pantego Bible Church in 1990, the church was going in the wrong direction. The attendance fell from 1300 to only 425 between 1985 and 1990. The church needed more than cell groups. It needed new life. In Frazee's book, *The Come-Back Congregation*, he states, "the remaining congregation was suffering from low corporate self-esteem. It was questionable whether the members believed that revitalization was possible.[9]

The strategy the church took included cell groups, but it did not begin with cell groups. First, Frazee initiated a change in the Sunday services, a move from choral programs to a worship focus. This involved a shift from a Music Director to a Worship Pastor. The next shift came as they restructured their Sunday school classes. He writes:

We decided to transform the adult Sunday school classes into biblical communities. They would not function simply as education centers, but as churches within a church. They would teach one another, encourage one another, and hold one another's hands during a crisis. We wanted these groups to become everything that the Body of Christ was intended to be. Even though the group would still gather on Sunday mornings, it would not be their sole opportunity for interaction. We wanted these people to get involved in one another's lives. Instead of discipling through traditional class structures, we wanted to achieve our developmental mission through a relational structure.

The first step was to change the name to match the purpose, hence the name "Community Groups." The second step was to identify a group of leaders in our congregation who could serve as Community Group Shepherds. These people, mostly couples, would become the pastors over congregations of fifty people. The next step was to write a manual that laid out the function of these groups and their leadership.[10]

After transforming the Sunday school classes, the church developed small groups that were connected to these classes. A Community Group of 50 has five small groups of ten. "This strategy would allow people to deepen their relationships with a group in which they are already familiar in the larger, Community Group setting."[11]

Pantego has come back from a discouraging situation. About 1,900 people worship together in corporate services. They have cell groups throughout the Dallas/Ft. Worth area. And they have just built a new facility on new property located on a major highway.

The Transforming Presence

Jesus said, "No one sews a patch of unshrunk cloth on an old garment, for the patch will pull away from the garment, making the tear worse. Neither do men pour new wine into old wineskins. If they do, the skins will burst, the wine will run out and the wineskins will be ruined. No, they pour new wine into new wineskins, and both are preserved" (Matthew 9:16-17).

These words have been used to argue that new structures (new wineskins) are needed in the church. While this interpretation is not wrong, it is incomplete. The key to understanding Jesus' message here is understanding the preceding verse. "Jesus answered, 'How can the guest of the bridegroom mourn while he is with them? The time will come when the bridegroom will be taken from them; then they will fast.'" Jesus used a parable to answer questions about the lack of fasting by his disciples. In the parable, Jesus is the bridegroom; His presence has inaugurated a reason for celebration, not mourning. When He stated that new patches cannot be put on old garments and new wine cannot be put in old wineskins, he was pointing to His presence, not to the new methods of ministry. Without the new wine of His presence, there is no need for a new wineskin.

Jesus wants to create new wineskins in the church, but new wineskins are dependent upon the presence of the new wine, Jesus. When He comes and pours His Spirit into the hearts of people, the new wineskins provide a container for Him. Cell groups are that new container today. But they are only needed if the new wine is flowing.[12]

Getting Over Slow Death

I shared about transformation through repentance with one pastor who had started cell groups after attending a cell church conference. His face lit up because it made sense to him. He said, "I have been thinking these very things." Some people reading this section will agree with this pastor because it will ring true in their hearts. Others will read it and skip right over it. They will conclude that their churches only need cell group transitions, not transformations through repentance. They will rush through Stage 4 and press on to Stage 5, because they want to know how to get cell groups started.

The topic of repentance does not seem nearly as exciting as practical instruction on how to lead a growing cell group ministry. The natural tendency is to invest leadership energy on developmental change or transitional change so that a church can start groups as quickly as possible. One change expert refers to transformational change as deep change. He argues that if leaders do not embrace deep change, they are embracing a slow death. He puts it this way:

> We actually seem to prefer slow death. Slow death is the devil we know, so we prefer it to the devil we do not know....Deep change requires discipline, courage, and motivation. We would rather experience the pain of slow death than the threat of changing ourselves.[13]

The church finds itself caught in an incessant trap of tweaking current programs to make them better, advertising to attract more people, exchanging one program for another, all the while losing more and more ground, and becoming less and less effective as the church. While the church has more training, more money, more books, more theological education, it cannot seem to stem the tide toward this "slow death."

We do not need a new innovation to break the pattern of the "slow death." The journey of repentance will lead a church to discover new ways to "be the church," new ways of participating with God in His Life. This kind of change impacts every aspect of a person's life. Transformation gets personal because it deals with the personal beliefs, assumptions, and values that comprise a person's identity. The transformation journey seeks to change those things in order to line them up with Kingdom values. This journey has much in common with the journey Abram began in Genesis 12:1-4: "The Lord said to Abram, 'Leave your country, your people and your father's household and go to the land I will show you....So Abram left, as the Lord had told him."

God did not call Abram to develop a better religion, or to transition religion by replacing the old with the new. He called Abram to a journey of life transformation, to repent of the ways that he knew in Ur. The journey of the church into cell groups is no different.

SECTION 4.2 Prepare Individuals for Cell Group Life

One large church embraced the cell group vision completely. The pastor taught on cell groups and trained the leaders. But the church was known for its musical heritage, its creative ministries, and for not requiring church members to commit to anything specific. As the cell group structure was implemented, the church members balked. They did not understand the vision, they felt controlled, and they wanted their old church ways back. While this church now has almost 100 cell groups, its cell group start-up had several hiccups along the way because individuals were not prepared for the journey.

When starting the first cell groups, it is crucial that the vision team develop a clear strategy for preparing individuals to enter into cell group life. Such preparation helps people shift their images of church and embrace the repentance that leads to transformation. This preparation happens on three levels.

- Preparing the Crowd
- Preparing Cell Group Members
- Preparing the First Cell Group Leaders

Such a three level preparation strategy resembles the way Jesus prepared three distinct groups of people before He went to the cross.

Jesus' Preparation Strategy

During His three and a half years of ministry, Jesus did not minister to everyone the same way. In fact, He ministered in different ways to three different groups of people. First, He ministered to the crowds through parables, healings, and teachings like the Sermon on the Mount. The focus of His ministry to the crowd was to teach them the broad principles of life in His Kingdom.

On the second level, He taught those people who followed Him more closely but were not members of His inner circle. Luke 10 records the story of Jesus sending out 72 people who returned saying to Jesus, "Lord, even the demons submit to us in your name." He was preparing this group to participate in His church at a different level than the vast crowds. The preparation at this level went beyond the broad principles, as Jesus taught them techniques for ministry in His Kingdom. They learned how to pray for the sick, how to cast out demons, and how to share the good news.

The third level of Christ's ministry focused upon His future leaders, the disciples. He prioritized his ministry to ensure that leaders would be prepared to pastor the people after his ascent. Robert Coleman has been arguing this point since the 1960s. In his best-selling book, *The Master Plan of Evangelism*, he writes,

Jesus was not trying to impress the crowd, but to usher in a kingdom. This meant that he needed people who could lead the multitudes. What good would it have been for his ultimate objective to arouse the masses to follow him if these people had no subsequent supervision or instruction in the Way?…For this reason, unless Jesus' converts were given competent men of God to lead them on and protect them in the truth they would soon fall into confusion and despair, and the last state would be worse than the first. Thus, before the world could ever be permanently helped, people would have to be raised up who could lead the multitudes in the things of God.[14]

In these men, Jesus invested His richest insights regarding life in the Kingdom. His focus was on mentoring them in the ways of His Kingdom. Through this mentoring they were prepared to be the leaders for the church Jesus was inaugurating.

In a cell group transformation, the crowd needs preparation. This will most often occur within some of the old structures that have been used for years. The first cell group members should be prepared and invited to embrace repentance and transform their values to line up with those of the Kingdom of God. And finally, the cell group leaders will require preparation through mentoring.

Preparing the Crowd

Jesus did not reveal His intentions to the crowds that followed him. He knew they could not handle the reality that God's plan of salvation included a trip to Jerusalem and death on a cross. The crowd believed the Messiah would come to reestablish Israel and would rule as a Davidic king. They expected Him to throw off foreign oppression and return Israel to its former glory. The crowd did not understand the costs of following Jesus (Luke 10:57-62; 14:25-35), how He could heal on the Sabbath (Luke 13:10-17), why He would spend time with tax collectors and "sinners" (Luke 15:1-2), or why He would take time to spend with a reprobate like Zacchaeus (Luke 19:1-9).

Jesus knew He could not completely reveal His message of life in the Kingdom of God because the crowd did not have the maturity to understand it. He limited His message to the crowds to broad principles like those found in the Sermon on the Mount and the parables. Through creative repetition of these principles, He painted a picture of life in His Kingdom that would one day make sense to the crowds.

Likewise, pastors are called to stand before the crowds and teach them the principles about life in the Kingdom. Such teaching should focus on the biblical principles about life in community, the values of Upward, Inward, Outward, and Forward, and the call to reach the lost.

The vision is not shared with church members in Stage 4 by announcing visions of cell group grandeur, explaining how the cell group structure works, or how big the church will grow through cell groups. I heard one pastor share his vision for 200 cell groups within three years, and how everyone in the crowd would be leading a cell group. The crowd only saw cell groups as a structure. Many felt that the pastor was using them to build his church, which was not his intention at all.

The average person in the crowd does not care how much the church will grow, how many cell groups will be started over the next year, or how he can be used in ministry. This is a sad but true reality, because the crowd has yet to see the picture of what it means to participate in Jesus' ministry. They only see themselves as spectators, as people who receive ministry. The crowd needs to hear the call to be a different kind of church, to be a different kind of people: a people of prayer, a people of unity, a people of love.

The goal of crowd preparation is to lay the foundation of the principles of Kingdom living. To accomplish this, the crowd needs a place where people can receive ministry and take steps into life in God's kingdom.

Crowd ministry should not require the primary energy of the leadership and the organization of the church. This means the crowd should not be the central focus of the senior pastor's and the pastoral team's ministry. Such a focus will require a major shift in the job description of most pastors, because historically the crowds have been the ministry focus.

Crowd preparation begins where the crowd is located today. This location is set within the current system of church that holds the crowd together. Crowd preparation should begin in Sunday school classes if that is the current system. If a church has an associated group system, then the crowd preparation should begin in those groups. There are several ways to prepare the crowds in Kingdom principles.

Preaching the Values of Upward, Inward, Outward, and Forward in the celebration gatherings. Pastors should use sermons to paint a picture of what the church should look like, to cast the vision of what the people of the church are called to do, and to invite people into deeper levels of life in God. Many pastors make the mistake of preaching about the cell group structure before enough leaders are prepared to start groups for the crowd. This is a time to preach values, not to reveal all the pieces of the vision.

Calling the crowd together for special prayer gatherings. Because cell groups flourish in the atmosphere of prayer, calling people to prayer will always point people in the right direction. Prayer gatherings do not work well when they replace normal services on Sunday or Wednesday nights, because so many people are in the rut of attending church services on those nights. This kind of prayer should be sacrificial and out of the ordinary in nature. Prayer should focus on the church, the lost, the city, and the nation.

Beginning focused teaching courses that use break-out small groups. Examples of this kind of material abound. Ralph W. Neighbour, Jr. developed *Life Basic Training* to help "sit-and-soak" Christians understand their calling as servants of God. *Experiencing God* by Henry Blackaby will equip people to understand how God speaks and how to get involved with what God is doing. These are just two examples of materials that will prepare the values of the church and require little or no preparation by church leadership.

Dealing with unhealthy patterns in the corporate body. Unhealthy patterns include corporate strife, division created by previous disagreements, hurt due to past sin by leadership, or any other historical events that maintain a hold on the people of the church. These patterns might come in the form of disunity, strife, racism, prayerlessness, etc.

One church kept experiencing a great deal of frustration and could not move forward in its vision. It was doing all the right things, but a key group of people kept balking at the pastor's initiative. Through much discussion, the elders identified two groups of people in the church: the old guard who felt like they were a part of the original church, and a newer group of people who had joined the church en-masse after leaving another large church. This newer group did not feel like they belonged because they did not have the denominational heritage of the old guard. After the elders identified the problem, they called the entire church to fasting and prayer. The church building was open all day for people to pray. At the end of the second day, a special prayer and repentance service was called and the group renounced the division of the past and affirmed the call to unity. After this time of corporate repentance, the church really entered into biblical community. Neal Anderson and Charles Mylander have developed a comprehensive process for leading a church into corporate repentance in their book, *Setting Your Church Free*.[15]

Preparing Cell Group Members

When Jesus ministered from town to town, there was a group of people that followed Him more closely. They were not part of the inner circle, but they were closer to Him than the crowd. Jesus prepared these people by showing them the ways in which to minister. As these people followed, they saw how He ministered, they heard His teaching on the Kingdom of God, and they discovered how He was breaking with the traditions of the religious leaders of the time. Then Jesus sent them out as His emissaries to do for others what they had seen Him do. All of this was part of the preparation process. These people were not His primary leaders, but they needed training in His ministry techniques in order for the church to get off the ground.

Most church leaders recognize the importance of preparing cell group leaders, but few understand the need to prepare cell group members before they enter cell groups. Pastors often think, "I have eight leaders who are ready for cell leader training. I will train them and then start eight groups. That means 80 people in cell groups. Wow! This is easy." These groups will consist of one committed leader and 8-10 uncommitted attendees. It is hard to expect the group members to contribute to a vision they do not know or understand. Most of these groups will prove anemic and leaders will grow frustrated.

New and young Christians are great in cell groups. They bring life and are hungry to grow. Older Christians who are steeped in a spirit of religion often breed a slow death to cell group life. People who are schooled in the traditional church must go through a transformation of their understanding of life in the church. Without such a transformation, they will bring the stench of legalism, superiority, and dominance.

When a church is starting cell groups, the key is to start strong groups with committed people. Cell group members who do not know the vision or who question the validity of the vision often undermine the cell group leader. When Bethany World Prayer Center began its groups, it could have started many more than 54 groups. But church leaders chose to start groups in which all of the members possessed values that would contribute to the success of the groups, not just the cell leaders.

Cell group member preparation is a process of leading people to repentance, moving away from the old ways of doing church and toward the values of UIOF. They need training in the techniques of ministry that make cell groups work. They need to understand the basics of the vision, how to participate in a cell group discussion, and how to minister relationally. There are many practical strategies for preparing cell group members.

Create a discussion group about the cell group vision. This works especially well in smaller churches or new church plants. This group is not a cell group, but a group where up to 12 people can discuss the vision of cell groups, how they work, and what it means to participate in them. The book *Life in His Body* by David Finnell is a very simple guide that includes discussion questions at the end of each chapter.

Create a prayer ministry training opportunity. Try something like the Gideon's Army of Bethany World Prayer Center. Train the participants to pray, and after a season of committed prayer, train them in cell ministry. Bethany used the *Intercession as a Lifestyle* video series to train the Army to pray.[16]

Develop short-term prayer and praise groups. These groups of four to six people commit to meet with one another every week for three months. In their meetings, they will pray for one another, pray for three lost friends, and pray for the vision of the church. After participating in these prayer and praise groups, potential cell members will attend a brief presentation about the cell group vision and then join groups.

Use Alpha to reach people and experience dynamic small group life. Alpha is known around the world as a great evangelism tool. It also teaches people how to interact in small groups and grounds people in the basics of the Christian faith. Cell groups can easily be developed from these Alpha small groups when the course is completed.[17]

Prepare people in current small groups for a transformation into cell groups. For those churches who already have small groups, the best strategy might be to transform those groups into holistic cell groups (i.e., groups with a focus on UIOF). Of course, the small group leaders will need training. The small group members will also need to understand the difference between the old type of small group and the new holistic cell group focus. The book *Upward, Inward, Outward, Forward* by Jim Egli will prepare small group members for this change.

Establish a cell group preparation class. This strategy has been used across North America. This class meets weekly for up to eight weeks and introduces the vision of cell groups, addresses the values that make cell groups work, and provides practical ways to contribute cell group life.

Transform a regular church service, usually a Sunday or Wednesday night, into a time to share the vision and the values of cell group ministry. For the last 45 minutes of the time together, group leaders will facilitate small group discussions about the topic that was presented.

Use Sunday school classes to prepare members for holistic cell group life. Churches with well-organized adult Sunday school classes can prepare people by slightly changing the way the classes are taught. Instead of organizing classes in larger groups, people should be organized into table groups with a table leader. A head teacher will introduce the topic and then the table leaders will facilitate discussion with those in the table groups. Eventually, these groups can be transformed into cell groups. Serendipity has developed four volumes in its *Small Group Plus Series* to help Sunday school classes experience the dynamics of small group life.[18]

Take potential members through an Encounter God Retreat. Jim Egli developed *Encounter God* to help cell group members enter into the God-promised freedom from sin that so many Christians fail to experience. It is helpful to prepare the first cell group members through an Encounter God Retreat before they enter into groups.

Preparing the First Cell Group Leaders

Jesus set aside most of His time to spend with a small group of key leaders. He focused his energy upon them, mentoring them and showing them how to live the life of the Way. To the crowds He told parables; to His disciples He explained their meaning. To the crowds He gave food; to His disciples He gave Himself. In the Gospel of Mark, 51% of Jesus' words are addressed to the disciples. This means that 49% of Jesus' words were divided between the crowds, the Pharisees, and the "sinners" and other on-lookers of His ministry. Jesus knew that if He was going to build a church, He had to invest his energy in showing His future leaders how to live, lead, and pray. He taught them in secret the meaning of the Kingdom of God. He demonstrated His power over nature on the Sea of Galilee. He taught them about faith, about prayer, about endurance. These experiences with Jesus transformed rough-edged fishermen, a tax collector, a zealot and others into one of the greatest leadership teams ever.

Carl George says in his book *Prepare Your Church for the Future*, "In my experience, no church has successfully launched a cell system without averaging three turnovers of leadership. In other words, pastors typically flounder twice with each cell-system start-up before they discern and train the right person for it."[19] Most churches adopt the trial and error approach to choosing the first cell group leaders. This results in false starts. Most pastors do not have permission to choose the wrong leaders two or three times. They need to see success much earlier.

Jesus knew that He had to mentor His leaders from the ground up. He had to teach them His leadership ways. Just because someone has been a leader in traditional forms of church ministry does not automatically qualify him to be a leader in a cell group. Many of these leaders have become more dependent on man-made programs or curriculum than on the Spirit of God. Some have discovered how to teach a Sunday school class or serve as a deacon without living in holiness. Such leaders may have been effective in the traditional church, but they will find cell leadership difficult if not impossible. Therefore, the first cell group leaders must evaluate their hearts to see what God is doing. The following areas are especially crucial:

Hidden sin. Good leaders in the old ways of doing church often find themselves struggling with hidden sin when they begin leading cell groups. In the past, the hidden sin was not overpowering. But when they assume leadership and care for people in a cell group, the enemy starts aiming his guns. Areas that were hidden before behind programmed ministry are suddenly revealed when people enter the relational ministry of cell groups. Satan knows that he can take down not only the leader but an entire group when the hidden sin becomes uncontrollable.

Rebellion. There is enough rebellion within the rank-in-file of the church. Cell group leaders must be on board with their pastor and be willing to work through issues rather than undercutting his authority.

Unforgiveness. Many church leaders are walking-wounded because they have not forgiven people from their past. They may carry hurt from the words of a previous pastor. They might shoulder bitterness due to a poor relationship with a mother or father. Such feelings lead to strongholds and make room for the enemy to gain control.

Marital strife. Healthy marriages are crucial for healthy cell group ministry because cell group leadership is about relationships. When married leaders have unhealthy home lives, it is very difficult to minister relationally to others.

As pastors develop leaders for cell groups, they will usually start small because they can only work with a few at a time. One pastor might develop three new leaders. Then these three can work with three more each. As more leaders are developed, the system can be completed.

Churches have used many different strategies for developing the first cell group leaders. Here are a few of them.

Mentoring by the senior pastor. In reality the best way, if not the only way, to develop cell leaders is to mentor them. Training courses are crucial, but without mentoring they are empty. Cell leaders will care for cell members with the same care that they receive from their pastors. If the cell leaders feel loved, supported, mentored, and prayed for, they will be much more likely to do the same for the people in their groups. If they do not receive these things from their pastors, they will not have much to give their group members.

Not focusing on how many groups the church can start. The vision team should focus on how many potential leaders are ready and willing to lead groups. These leaders should come from the primary influencers of the church. If these primary influencers are not ready to discover what it means to lead a cell group, then it is probably not the time to begin the change to the cell group structure. Some churches must navigate their ships down the entire Mississippi River before finally gaining access to the open sea where a straight course can be set.

Determining if the primary influencers are ready to enter into cell group life. To prepare first-tier leaders for cell group life, it is important to get to know the leaders on a deeper level. TOUCH Outreach Ministries and the Cell Group People have developed two tools that are especially helpful: the *Journey Guide for Growing Christians* and the *Journey Guide for Cell Group Leaders*. These 16-page booklets will help people assess where they are with the Lord as individuals. It will help the pastor understand the strengths and weaknesses of his potential leaders and know how to minister to them. These tools will also establish the values of transparency and personal ministry that happen in effective cell group ministry.

Participating in a spiritual freedom encounter. There are many good resources that help people address hindrances to spiritual freedom. TOUCH Outreach Ministries provides a resource that has proven effective for leading people into personal freedom called *Encounter God* by Jim Egli.

Praying over influencers who seem unready. If there are some influencers who are not ready to participate in or lead a cell group, the vision team must pray that God will have His way.

Inviting the influencers who are ready to a recruitment retreat, where the vision and the values will be fully discussed and planned. At such a retreat, the vision of cell groups will be explained and people will be invited to participate in the first cell group. An example of a recruitment retreat is available for download from <www.cellgrouppeople.com>.

Section 3.3 highlighted the observation that churches with leaders who are ready to embrace the interpersonal ministry that fits cell group ministry are much more likely to see success with cell groups. When a church develops a preparation strategy to transform the ministry patterns of key leaders, along with the cell group members and the crowd, it will be able to set a course for starting strong groups in Stage 5 that are much more likely to succeed.

SECTION 4.3 Prepare the Corporate Body for Cell Groups

Imagine a ship with a captain who gives orders to sail in one direction, a helmsman who chooses to steer in a different direction, and a mutinous crew who all seek their own gain rather than the safe and effective transit of the ship. For a ship to move toward its destination, the crew must be prepared to work together as a unit under one vision. In the same way, the corporate life of a church must be prepared to sail toward the cell group vision in unity.

As I listened to the stories of churches, I heard four scenarios of corporate church life that undermined or at least de-energized the journey toward cell groups. If you can identify with any of these experiences, then corporate life preparation will prove to be a crucial step in your church's journey toward cells.

—Pastor Dwight finds himself so overwhelmed with the daily activities of being a pastor that he has not had time to hear God's vision for the church, much less lead it. He already works 60-hour weeks, he hasn't had a date with his wife in three months, and he continually explains to his two boys why he must miss their baseball games.

—Pastor Tim catches a vision to move toward cells. He sits down with the board, but board members are focused on adding a new wing to the church building. The Sunday school director is concerned with staffing a demanding Sunday school. The youth pastor is new, and besides, no youth pastor has stayed more than two years. Everyone is going in a different direction, as there are more bosses than workers.

—Pastor Chris is an excellent preacher. The 95 people who attend his church hear God's word every Sunday. But he is left with a nagging question: Do people experience the presence of God in weekly worship or are they just going through the motions?

—Pastor Andrew is a strong leader. He has implemented new ideas and people are excited with the recent growth. Worship is first-rate and the teaching is excellent. At the same time, he is concerned about the overall spiritual vitality of the people. Leaders work hard at their responsibilities but there is little time for prayer. In fact, when prayer is mentioned, little enthusiasm is expressed. The church has become a church of doers and spectators who lack passion for intimacy with God.

When churches try to plant cell groups in these situations, they eventually see that the soil will not provide the nutrition that the cell groups need to germinate and grow. As was stated in Stage 3, cell groups are much more likely to flourish when churches have four things in place:

- Permission given to the pastor to lead instead of being bogged down with administrative duties.
- Worship services where people are inspired by the presence of God.
- A passion for God expressed through prayer.
- Primary church leaders ready to embrace the interpersonal model of ministry that cell groups require.

Section 4.2 addressed how to prepare the primary leaders of the church for the interpersonal model of cell group ministry. This section will address the other three areas.

Permission for the Pastor to Lead and Equip

Transformation is impossible without a transformation "point person." Every time God led His people into repentance, He used a person. God called Moses to bring the Israelites out of slavery. God spoke to Gideon on the threshing floor. David was anointed as King by Samuel. Frazee states, "If revitalization and revising is to occur, a point person must emerge."[20]

The problem is that most pastors do not have the permission from their churches to act as a "point person." Imagine the average church of 100 people. The pastor has served there for fewer than five years. His weekly job activities include preaching in three different services, teaching a Sunday school class, organizing weekly visitation, making hospital visits, counseling with the hurting, sitting in on committee meetings, managing the upkeep of the church building, overseeing the volunteers who lead worship, the nursery, and the Sunday school, and dealing with any disruptions during the week. In such a scenario, the pastor might have a vision to develop cell groups, but he does not have permission to lead a new vision. He has permission to run the old system.

The last section highlighted how Jesus had an intentional strategy to minister to three groups of people: the crowds, the followers, and the leaders. It is impossible to adopt such a strategy if the pastor does not have a significant level of permission from the church to operate according to that strategy. There are some practical things pastors can do to increase this level of permission.

Build credits to lead the transformation.

Van Ducote of Northwood Christian Center in Mississippi had gained the trust of his people before introducing the major change of cell groups. The church had carried a large debt load and he had led the church out from under it. Bishop Robert Davis of Long Reach Church of God in Maryland had led the church for over 10 years and had grown it to over 1,000 members. Randy Frazee had proven himself as a volunteer leader at Pantego before being invited to lead the church. Don Finto, who pastored Belmont Church over 20 years, up through the mid-nineties, led the church into using musical instruments—as they were associated with the brotherhood of Churches of Christ—into spiritual renewal. All of these pastors possessed leadership credits with the people before they embarked upon the cell group journey.

Not every pastor has this luxury. Many carry a high leadership debt load that hinders their ability to serve as the transformation point person. Pastors accrue debts through things like initiating new programs with little follow-through, making promises that are not kept, scolding the people for not being committed, excluding church members from participating in ministry, high turn-over of pastoral staff members, and always asking for money. If previous pastors have had contemptuous relationships, didn't stay long enough to carry out the vision, or had been involved in something immoral, the position of the "pastor" carries a debt load that subsequent pastors must pay off.

Credits are accrued when pastors lead the church into positive results: financial debts are paid off, new ministry ideas are developed and produce fruit, the pastor shows a commitment to stay longer than five years, people feel encouraged while at the same time challenged through the sermons, and people sense the presence of God upon His leadership.

Pastors must observe their leadership bank account as they lead people into transformation. Pastors with a high leadership debt load need to not only transform the life of the church but also to transform the view of the pastor.

Create room to develop leaders.

Traditional forms of ministry establish a pattern in which the pastor "works" for the church and has little time to develop leaders. In a way, this is very similar to the role of a chaplain. Bill Easum puts it this way:

> Most of today's pastors function as chaplains—going about taking care of people, visiting shut-ins and hospitals, serving communion, and mouthing archaic rituals understood by a decreasing number of people. This shouldn't be. These ministries are important, but they are not the responsibility of the pastor. That's not biblical. These ministries are the responsibility of all the people of God.[21]

The chaplain system requires that a pastor be a caregiver to a congregation, rather than equipper of a congregation of caregivers. Pastors find themselves ministering to hurting people who do nothing with what they receive. They have no one to pass it on to. If a pastor's schedule is full of responding to emergencies, going to the hospital, performing weddings and funerals, counseling couples with broken marriages, where is the room to mentor the cell group leaders? The problem lies in the fact that all of these activities are important and if the pastor does not do them, then he feels that he is not doing his job. But according to the pattern that Jesus established, if the pastor is not raising up leaders, he is not doing his job.

The biggest change must take place in the minds of the pastors. Easum states, "Most of our seminaries teach us to be theologians, chaplains, and managers instead of spiritual leaders. Pastors right out of seminary often become associate pastors and are taught how to manage or chaplain by the senior pastor. Many leaders of today have been shut down or turned off by the present way of 'doing' church."[22] Pastors need to leave the paradigm of chaplaincy that they have inherited and catch a vision for ministry that will awaken their giftings and turn them on to caring for God's people.

Pastors must quit giving their best ministry to people other than the leaders. Church leaders that care for people—often trying not to bother the busy pastor—should receive the primary focus of the pastor. When the pastor begins to mentor, invest, and pour his life and vision into a few key leaders, they in turn have something to pour into those in the crowd who need ministry.

Stay the course.

Leading people through transformation is not an easy process. Many pastors have confessed they felt like going back to the old ways of church or moving on to another church. Getting through these hard times requires tenacity and maybe even some hard-headed tendencies. The journey into transformation is not a short one for most churches. Church members do not need a pastor who will get them started and then move on when it gets tough. When a church enters into years seven and eight of the transformation, it begins to see the fruit of the hard work. It takes that long for values to shift.

Embrace brokenness.

Almost every pastor that I interviewed talked about hitting a wall of discouragement as he struggled to transform his church. Pastors questioned their ability to lead; they wondered whether they heard God; they even doubted that God was near. The best cell groups around the world arose out of the seedbed of brokenness. The vision for cells in Korea was birthed on a sickbed with the Holy Spirit revealing through Scriptures how Yonggi Cho could make cell groups work. Dr. Ralph Neighbour, Jr. shares how he wanted to give up when his original experiments with cells were resisted. Laurence Khong birthed his cell vision after a time of being fired from his former church. Billy Joe Daugherty was burned out and confused when he first started doing cells.

The same pastors also confess the joy that came out of this brokenness. It led them to seek God in prayer, to depend upon the Spirit, and see creative ways to accomplish the vision.

Permission-Giving Organizational Structure

A pastor of a mid-sized traditional church caught the vision for cell groups. He began a cell and grew it by reaching out to nonbelievers. He convinced the staff and deacons that the cell group vision would work. They trained leaders and expanded the number to ten groups. The visible or external structure of the cells were going well. New leaders were being developed, and new Christians were reached. But the church hit a wall. They could not get the cell groups going full steam. The pastor was so bogged down with organizational duties that he could not do the things required to advance the groups forward. William Easum claims that the success of cell group ministry depends on three things:

- Members who are willing to release to the staff control of the day-to-day decisions of running the congregation.
- Members who are willing to receive pastoral care from other members rather than always expecting it from the staff.
- Pastors who are willing to spend the majority of their time training members for ministry, and then getting out of their way so they can actually be the ministers of the church.[23]

This church had internal structures in place that stood in the way of these things happening. Therefore, the groups stalled. The structure was permission-withholding rather than permission-giving. The church could have expanded its cell groups if leaders and church members had addressed the structures that held them captive. Peter Senge writes:

> Structures of which we are unaware hold us prisoner. Conversely, learning to see the structures within which we operate begins a process of freeing ourselves from previously unseen forces and ultimately mastering the ability to work with them and change them.[24]

Churches, especially traditional ones, must learn to see the hidden structures that run the church. If a pastor tries to plant cell groups in unprepared soil, the hidden rocks and bugs will quickly stifle them right after they get going. These structures usually come in three forms: competing visions, controlling polity, and committee structure.

Competing Visions.

The traditional church leadership model promotes competing visions. The youth minister has his vision and goals, the children's minister his, the education minister has his. On top of this, the deacon board has its own ideas about what should happen, and one rich, powerful person sways his influence in another direction. "The lack of alignment among leaders is the most common cause of failure for major change efforts."[25]

Unity of staff and key leaders around one vision given by God is a basic requirement for developing an effective cell group system. Since most churches find themselves in a system where leaders are on different pages, what can be done?

First, the senior pastor should dialogue with the staff and the key leaders about his vision. Those who enter into this dialogue positively should be identified as team players. Those who resist it are probably stuck in the old mindset. The senior pastor should invite the team players to contribute to the vision in concrete ways. Some may already be on the vision team (Stage 2). Others will contribute to the implementation of the vision at specific levels, i.e. youth, singles, etc. Then, the senior pastor should help these staff pastors and key leaders discover their own personal visions and determine the ways he can help them realize their God inspired dreams. Finally, the senior pastor should commit to mentoring the staff and key leaders, thereby creating a team. As he shares his desire to mentor, he may share that he is in the process of learning how to focus his ministry and not feel the need to respond to every problem that arises.

Some senior pastors have shared that some of their staff pastors could not make the shift from the traditional church system to the cell group system. The relational nature of team ministry in the cell group system threatened many staff pastors. In such situations, the staff pastor left. If a key leader is not in favor of the cell system, it will prove impossible for him or her to remain on staff.

This issue is a little more difficult to deal with when a key lay leader disagrees with the cell vision. In some churches, the key leaders end up going to different churches to avoid conflict. In other churches, the leader continued to lead in the old forms of ministry, while new leaders were raised up through cell groups. In quite a few cases, the senior pastor chose to go to a different church or plant a new church so that he could focus on cell groups.

Church Polity Issues.

Because the New Testament describes the leadership of the early church without prescribing it, 20 theologians can sit in a room arguing for a different kind of church government with scriptures to back it up. Therefore, it is not my intention to make a biblical argument for a specific type of church government or polity.

Historically, there have been three broad types of church government: episcopal rule, where primary authority is placed in a bishop with clergy below him; presbyter rule, where a board of elders make decisions on behalf of the church; and congregational rule, where autonomous congregations operate by making decisions through majority vote. Each system has strengths and weaknesses. I have observed how the weaknesses of these systems have been exploited as churches tried to begin cell groups.

In the episcopal system, local pastors have district overseers, and these overseeing officers have the authority to transfer pastors from one church to another. Don Tillman consulted with one church in California. At the end of the leadership retreat, the pastor pulled him aside. He told Don that he was being transferred in two months. Don explained that the training probably did more harm than good. To successfully navigate such a journey of change, his congregation would need a leader who could stay the course with them the entire distance. The episcopal system often promotes the chaplain mentality of pastoring and undermines leadership.

In the presbyterian system, elders can be very controlling and feel threatened by the thought of changing the system. They are afraid that they might lose their power. If the elders are against cell groups or refuse to participate in them, a senior pastor will find it virtually impossible to develop groups.

In the congregational system, the church might approve of the venture to cell groups via majority vote, but they can just as easily revoke the vote at the next congregational meeting. In one church, the old guard did not like the changes the church was undergoing with the new Christians entering through cell groups. The congregational system allowed them to vote cells out even though the groups were working and the congregation had approved of them a few years before.

From my observations, I have found three principles consistent in churches that have made cell groups work:

1. The senior pastor carries the vision for the church. While he is not a dictator, the congregation does not dictate his job to him. He leads and the church governmental system allows him to lead.

2. The senior pastor works as a team member with a group of elders. These elders are involved in the cell ministry and should be cell leaders. They are not simply decision makers who separate themselves from the ministry of the groups.

3. The team of elders, which includes the senior pastor, works at gaining the trust of the people by increasing credits and decreasing debits. They see their role as equipping people for ministry and setting them free to do this ministry. The people affirm the ways the elders are leading them.

Do these three points elevate one of the three polity systems over the other? This I do not know. Cell groups have worked in all three forms of government. Some churches have found it necessary to change their by-laws or church constitutions so the system could work more effectively. Others have been able to practice the above principles without changing the by-laws officially.

Committee Structure.

Many churches operate with an extensive committee system. Each year, multiple committees are elected; these may include finance, nominating, calendar, facilities, and any number of others. The role of a committee is to make decisions about how the church should operate in certain areas. Finance committees set annual budgets, nominating committees recruit volunteers to fill ministry vacancies, facilities committees decide how the church building(s) and grounds are maintained. These committees are responsible for making decisions, but often they are not responsible for carrying out those decisions.

Some have sought to change the committee system by calling committees "teams" and requiring the team members to implement the decisions they make. While this is a step in the right direction, the result remains much the same. A committee by any other name is still a committee.

Committee members usually feel like they are involved in the ministry of the church. This type of ministry could be called "administry" because the committee system tends to focus on administration that is not necessary. The bulk of the "ministry" in many churches is not really ministry at all. Those who are involved in people-touching ministry are typically controlled by those in committees, and they often find their efforts misunderstood and resisted.

In the most effective cell group churches, administration lies in the hands of a pastoral leadership team, and ministry is being carried out by the whole congregation. The pastoral team takes care of the administrative decisions, budget, hiring and firing, recruiting volunteers, etc. The people of the church are released into the ministry of the church.

Recently, a church leader with lots of committee experience asked me, "How does the administration get done in the cell church?" I asked, "What committees do you have?" He responded, "The finance committee who oversees the budget. The event committee which coordinates all of the major church-wide events. The vision committee who determines if ministry ideas fit the stated vision of the church. The house and properties committee that oversees and maintains the buildings. The personnel committee that recruits people to serve in various positions."

I responded, "The leaders of the church should set the budget which should be reviewed annually by a board of trustees which meets once per year for such an occasion. Events should be coordinated by short-term teams who have a passion for a specific event, not by a group who is stuck on a committee always having to oversee the next big event. The senior pastor is the vision carrier and the leaders around him should help him focus the vision. Building maintenance can be coordinated by the church secretary, and much of the work can be hired out or short-term teams can be developed. Finally, the senior pastor and other key leaders should be in charge of developing and recruiting leaders to serve in various positions."

One might argue that such a structure will work in a large church, but not in a small church. It is true that the scale will alter things somewhat. In small churches, the pastoral team might consist of a few key volunteers who help the pastor carry out the administrative duties. But because the church is smaller, the administrative load should also be smaller. One small church had committees for everything. They found that most of these committees—the bulletin board committee for example—were unnecessary. To accomplish the essential tasks, one volunteer coordinator was appointed. If more help was needed, this coordinator could seek short-term volunteers.

Church members often like the committee system because it gives them a sense of control. Pastors play into this thinking by organizing committees consisting of members who are not involved in people-touching ministry. These people are given permission to make crucial decisions or recommendations for the church. Because most of them do not have a clear picture of the church's vision, these committees focus on minutia, on details that may or may not actually contribute to the vision accomplishment.

The change from a church with an ad-ministry system to a church with a ministry system must be approached with great delicacy. If committee members perceive a loss of control, trouble often brews. Here are a few helpful tips:

• The pastoral staff and/or the vision team should review the committee structure to determine the committees that serve no purpose. Some of them can be dismantled; others should be committed to attrition because they will die away when they are not given any attention. Do not dismantle every ineffective committee at once. This will cause a knee-jerk reaction opposing the pastoral leadership.

- Those involved in the ineffective committees should be refocused through the cell member preparation strategy the vision team adopts. Taking something away without replacing it is often traumatic, even for adults.
- Re-engineer all remaining committees so that they are in unity with the leadership of the church. These remaining committees should be structured so that they are empowered to carry out the decisions they make.
- Pray and act according to God's timing. This process may take more time than desired. Going too fast is the number one mistake church leaders make when trying to change structures.

Inspiring Corporate Worship Experiences

The churches that have had the most success in starting strong cell groups already had vibrant corporate gatherings where people experienced the presence of God. The large group experience feeds life into the cell group start up. When first starting groups, so much energy is required because the learning curve is so high. If corporate worship is boring and people do not expect to meet God, people will not have the energy to make cell groups work. The cell group members and leaders draw life from the large group worship so that they can minister in the groups.

The key to a life-flowing experience in large group worship services is not found in the style of music, as the styles are many. The key is found in the answer to this question: do people experience the presence of God to the point that they leave corporate gatherings inspired? While worship is a crucial factor in the creation of an inspiring large group service, singing songs does not equal the presence of God. I have attended churches where the latest worship songs were sung and people sat down unmoved. I have visited other churches where people sensed the presence of God while singing those same songs. People need an encounter with God, not a few songs typed out on a screen.

Inspiring corporate meetings include more than worship. They provide an atmosphere where people catch the vision of the church. Rick Warren has said that people need to hear the vision every 26 days or they will forget it.[26] Every week, Pastor Van Ducote of Northwood Christian Center stands before his congregation and proclaims the vision to win souls and make disciples. Then he shares how the church has the goal to equip every believer to become a leader of others.

Of course, the large group worship services should be a place where the people hear the Word of God taught. I have yet to find a church that developed strong cell groups who did not place a high value on teaching and preaching.

While developing a strategy for starting cell groups, churches must also evaluate their weekly worship services and pray about ways to improve them. Some churches are already strong in this area, but many, if not most, are lacking. Maybe the church has practiced the same routine so long that God is no longer expected to show up. Maybe the worship leader no longer has a passion to lead the congregation in worship. Maybe the senior pastor is a gifted overseer but not a gifted teacher and is just boring.

Passion for God
Expressed Through Prayer

The most effective cell-based churches around the world are praying churches. Cell groups without prayer are like water bottles with no water. After Joel Comiskey traveled the globe to understand the basic principles that make cell groups work, he wrote:

Cell churches contain the power, the current of the Holy Spirit. They don't automatically produce that current. If your church is choking the life of the Spirit of God, don't expect cells to remedy your problem. You must first invite God to fix the basic problem and clean the rusty pipes that impede His flow. He uses the cell system, but He winces at being used by it.[27]

Model churches invite the power of God through prayer. Bethany World Prayer Center changed its name because of its conviction that prayer had to be the focus. The International Charismatic Mission in Bogota, Colombia holds five prayer meetings every morning beginning at 5 A.M. Over 1,000 people each day ascend to Prayer Mountain in Korea from Yoido Full Gospel Church to cry out to their Lord.

Churches that have seen the most success at making cell groups work had already developed a seedbed of prayer before they started groups. It is much easier to lead people into change when they have a deep hunger for more of God. Larry Stockstill populated his first groups with his prayer warriors. He explains why:

I have learned that the strongest disciples are those who long for the presence of God. Though you must occasionally endure some who are unbalanced, it is reasonable to say that your prayer warriors are the committed core of the church. They are also the most sensitive to the changing direction of the Holy Spirit in a church and most aware of the spiritual warfare necessary to birth something that is a major threat to Satan's kingdom. Therefore, they will be the least resistant to change and the most resistant to demonic efforts to thwart the fledgling effort. Teaching your prayer core the principles of intercession and spiritual warfare equips them to be the leaders and reapers of the cell dynamic.[28]

The stronger the prayer effort, the more quickly a church can develop cell groups. If the key leaders in the church are not prayer warriors, it is time to lead them to pray. Even Pastor Cho's people were not always prayer models. He reports, "At YFGC, our people learned to pray in this manner. At first it was not easy, but as I led the way, they followed. We began with early morning prayer at 4:30 A.M. We added an all-night prayer meeting Friday nights from 10:00 P.M. to 4:40 A.M. Our people came to one or both prayer meetings."[29] One pastor organized his most committed people into prayer triads while preparing to launch cell groups. These short-term groups (3-6 months) were to meet weekly to pray for the church, one another, and at least one nonbelieving friend.

Passion for God will feed cell groups and then the cell groups will feed that passion. On top of making the journey to cell groups a lot easier, it might very well change the complexion of your entire church.

Levers

Develop a strategy to prepare the values of the first cell group members.

Develop a strategy to prepare the first cell group leaders in both the values of the Great Commandment and Great Commission and in the vision of cell groups.

Identify resources that will be needed to prepare the members and leaders.

Identify areas of the corporate life of the church that must be addressed. Pray over these areas. Listen to God's voice, and wait upon His strategy for dealing with them. Consider:
- The role of the senior pastor
- Competing visions within the church
- Controlling polity or church government
- Committee structure
- Corporate worship experience
- Corporate commitment to prayer

Vision Team Questions

(Most likely the discussion of these issues must be broken up into multiple sessions.)

1. What is the difference between developmental change, transitional change, and transformational change?
2. What does it mean for a church not only to change the structure but to see the people transformed?
3. What role does repentance play in transformation?
4. What are some key areas in your church where transformation is needed?
5. Brainstorm some ways to prepare the values of the first cell group members before they enter into cell groups.
6. Brainstorm some ways to prepare the vision and the values of the first cell group leaders before they begin leading groups.
7. With the permission of the senior pastor, explore this question: How does the traditional understanding of the "role" of the pastor need to be changed? Make sure that no one accuses the person, but instead evaluates the role.
8. Identify competing visions within the church and how these competing visions might block cell group development.
9. Identify polity or church government issues that might impede God moving through the church with His vision.
10. How do committees bog down the ministry flow in the church?
11. Evaluate the health of the corporate worship services. The senior pastor should share his vision for corporate worship and teaching.
12. Evaluate the passion for God expressed through commitment to prayer.

STAGE 5
Launch
the First Group(s)
with Kingdom-seekers

Stage 5 is the point on the journey when the ship raises its sails and begins to advance with as much energy as it can muster. The officers have navigated around the impeding hazards that kept the ship moored in its old sailing territory. The crew members have prepared themselves for traveling into unknown places. The excitement level is high. The expectations are boundless.

Now it is the time to answer the question that almost every pastor asks: "How do we start the first cell groups?" After preparing the church through Stages 1-4, the first cell groups will have an opportunity to produce good fruit.

Essential to starting fruitful groups is starting strong groups. When churches launch their cell groups with weak groups, with leaders who are not ready and cell members who are not committed, the vision stalls quickly. But when strong groups are started, they produce fruit and propel the church forward into subsequent stages.

Stage 5 delineates how to launch strong first groups. A church can do this by populating the initial groups with Kingdom-seeking people. It is not enough for the first leaders to be Kingdom-seekers. There must be a core group of members within each initial cell group who are committed to the vision of cell groups and to living out the values of Upward, Inward, Outward, and Forward.

"Launching Strong," (Section 5.1), explains why cell members should be Kingdom-seekers and then provides key questions that the vision team must address as it launches the first group.

"Launching Strategies" (Section 5.2), illustrates some practical ways that churches have successfully launched their first groups.

SECTION 5.1 Launching Strong

A large successful church in the eastern United States started 45 cell groups. Four years later, the church had only 60 groups. The pastor confessed that most of the groups the church started did not have the strength to expand and multiply. It didn't matter what curriculum the groups used or how much the pastors supported the leaders; the groups were stuck in mediocrity.

A small church in the midwest started with one prototype cell group. After four months, the prototype leaders started three groups. Four months later, the church started two more groups. After five years of cell ministry, the church now has 20 groups.

As I interviewed pastors, I always asked this question: "If a pastor came to you seeking advice on how to start groups what would you tell them?" Over and over again, pastors would say something like, "Be patient; go slowly. I learned this lesson the hard way."

For more than ten years, cell group trainers and consultants have taught that the best strategy for starting cell groups is a deliberate and "slow" strategy. When cell groups first became popular and church leaders began attending cell seminars, people asked cell church visionaries like Yonggi Cho and Dale Galloway how to get started. They would respond, "Start one group yourself and grow from there." Yet most pastors have chosen not to listen to this advice. They count how many leaders they have in the church, train them as fast as they can, and place each person in charge of a group, inviting all who desire to join.

This is a "quick win" strategy. It looks good in the short run, but the cell groups often fizzle out after a few years. One reason this strategy fails is that each leader has a different idea about what should happen in a group. For instance, one leader has 20 years of experience as a Sunday school teacher and he emphasizes exposition of the Scripture. Another leader loves to worship and therefore leads the group each week in 40 minutes of singing to the Lord. Still another leader is very hospitable, so she prepares elaborate meals each week and the meetings last over three hours. And yet another leader led small groups at a previous church that were very controlling in nature, so he feels the need to "reveal God's will" to people in his group, even if what he shares is absurd.

Each leader does what is right in his or her own eyes. One might teach that tithing is not a biblical requirement. Another might allow a pastor-bashing conversation to occur because he wants people to be honest. Yet another might gather a group of people who are faithful attendees of different churches. This is the reason why some pastors confess, "Yeah, we tried cell groups, and started a lot of churches we didn't mean to. Now those people are gone."

Instead of starting as many groups as possible with whoever wants to lead and whoever wants to join, a church must start with strong groups with leaders who are hand-picked and cell members who are sold out to God.

Principles for Starting Cell Groups

Strength comes from strength. Strong groups birth strong groups. If a church starts strong groups, it is much more likely to start more strong groups. If a church starts weak groups, it is absurd to think that the next groups will be different. Here are three principles to help start strong groups:

It is easier to speed up than it is to slow down or restart. Imagine a pastor who starts with one group of ten people that will meet for four months to learn how the cell group works. After two months, he realizes that four of the ten people are ready to lead groups. The other six people are ready to help these four. His original plan was to start two groups after four months, but now he sees that he can start four. These four will soon become five or six groups. In a little over a year, he will have gone from one to six strong groups.

Now imagine another pastor who thinks that he has four leaders who are ready for cell leadership, but they are untested. He decides to begin with four groups straight away. After two months, he realizes that he has two mediocre groups and two weak groups that need to be closed. He is spinning his wheels trying to get on the right track. He knows that he needs to start over, but he is afraid that it will look like he is going backwards.

The first cell group or cell groups must consist of strong cell group members, not just strong cell group leaders. Imagine another scenario: a church has six couples who are strong leaders, committed to the vision of the church, and committed to prayer. The pastor trains these leaders in cell ministry and asks them to recruit people for their groups. This strategy leads to groups that will be composed of people who have mixed levels of commitment to the Lord. Some will be controlled by a spirit of religion. Others will have personal hang-ups that keep them from living victorious lives. Still others will get frustrated because the cell group does not meet their needs. In such a situation, it is very difficult for a cell leader to be effective. Not only is he or she leading a cell group for the first time, but the group consists of people who are marginally committed to God, sometimes committed to the church, and self-servingly committed to the cell group. The result is lone-ranger leadership of a maintenance group that will do little for the Lord.

However, if these six incredible couples work together to begin one or two groups, the groups are much more likely to be effective. First, the couples will learn more quickly because they will have other leaders to provide feedback, discuss experiences, and support one another in the group. Second, these couples will share the load and model team leadership and community for their cell group members.

Focus on those who want to do cell groups. Not everyone will support the adoption of cell groups. It is impossible to convince everyone of a new idea before it is initiated. This means that the first groups should only include those who express a desire to participate. These people will have the energy to contribute to the process, while those forced to participate will drain the groups. Those who resist the move toward cell groups need not be argued with. The cell groups should speak for themselves. As one pastor stated, "Some people did not want to change. They were given space and time to see the cells in action without removing them from their positions in the church. They were convinced by the genuineness of the ministry and outreach of the cells."

How many groups can you start?

I could list 50 reasons for the slow start strategy, yet almost every pastor will still ignore these reasons, thinking that his church is unique. Although a few churches have successfully launched with several cell groups, these are the exceptions rather than the rule. The number of cell groups that a church can start is directly related to the number of cell members who have been prepared to be cell members, the number of cell group leaders who have been prepared to lead groups, and the number of cell coaches who have been prepared to coach these groups. How do you know how many members, leaders, and coaches are prepared? Simply by asking a few hard questions.

Cell group members must be Kingdom-seekers.

The best way to launch is with sold-out, God-seeking cell members. It is not enough to have sold-out leaders. Bethany World Prayer Center started its first groups with its prayer warriors, not "sit-and soak" Christians. Nominal Christians are wet towels on cell group life. They have little understanding or interest in living out the "one-anothers" of Christian life. They treat cell meetings just like any other church meeting. When they do attend the group meetings, they often hide behind religious jargon or "correct" answers. They demonstrate little passion to see nonbelievers transformed through an encounter with Christ.

Kingdom-seekers understand the calling to love one another in the cell group. They are committed to life in the cell group. They are open to transparency and they want to see people come to Christ. Kingdom-focused people may not know how to do all the stuff of cell groups, but they are open to learning how.

Kingdom-seeking members are faithful, available, and teachable. The questions on the next page will help determine if a person is ready to participate in the first cell group(s). When selecting those people to join the first cell groups, focus on people who exhibit leadership characteristics. If the new cell members are unable to become future leaders, the first groups will prove too weak to generate new groups.

Faithful

- Has this person done anything to undermine the authority of the pastor (or other staff members)?
- Does this person understand AND AGREE WITH the philosophy and vision of ministry, and does this person support it with consistent attendance and stewardship?
- Has this person undertaken other ministries and followed through to their success?
- Does this person have a heart for God and the fruit of the Spirit that is evidence of His active presence and life?

Available

- Does this person have areas of ministry he or she is involved in that will prevent him or her from effective cell group life?
- Are you able to release this person from current ministry responsibilities to have him or her serve as an initial cell group member?
- Do work or other outside commitments limit this person from being effective in ministry?

Teachable

- Does this person respond positively when someone challenges his or her thought pattern?
- Does this person work well as part of a team?
- Does this person respond positively to and respect authority?

Cell group leaders must be Kingdom-mentored.

The commitment to cell leadership is a high calling, especially at the launch point. Marginal leaders are destined for mediocrity when trying to start groups. The first cell leaders must be 100% committed to the leadership of the church, 100% committed to the vision of cell groups, and 100% committed to seeing people enter the Kingdom of God through cell group life.

This kind of commitment only comes through relationships with those in leadership, usually with the senior pastor. These first cell group leaders must be open to mentoring and training. They must be willing to have someone speak into their lives and help them develop as people and as leaders. Committed cell group leaders are trustworthy, submitted, and trained. Here are some questions to determine how many Kingdom-mentored cell group leaders a church has:

Trustworthy
- Is this the kind of person you want other cell members to emulate?
- Is this person fulfilling responsibilities in his or her person life, family, and job?
- Has this person proven faithful in other leadership responsibilities?

Submitted
- Does this person honor those in leadership?
- Does this person see himself or herself as part of a bigger vision that God has given the church?
- Has this person responded positively when he or she has disagreed with leadership?

Trained
- Has this person been trained in cell ministry?
- Does this person understand the goal of the cell groups and is he or she committed to accomplishing that goal?
- Has this person proven effective in relational ministry in other settings?

The first cell group leaders should be the cream of the crop. Most churches, because they are small, will discover that they only have one or two of these leaders, and one of them will be the pastor.

Cell group coaches must be Kingdom-centered.

Only large churches looking to launch more than five groups should consider these questions. For every three to five groups, there must be a coach. These coaches are not only committed to the cell group vision, but their lives model what it means to be a cell group leader. They know how to minister to people relationally. They have an abundant amount of time to support the leaders and the groups they oversee. At the point of launching groups, these initial coaches will be staff pastors.

Kingdom-centered coaches are prepared, available, and focused. Here are a few questions to determine the number of coaches that are ready:

Prepared

- Is this person experienced and fruitful in effective small group ministry?
- Has this person been exposed to other churches with effective small group ministries?
- Has this person been taught the principles of cell ministry that are effective to your church?

Available

- Does this person have the time to mentor 3-5 cell leaders?
- Can this person visit one or more cell groups per week?
- Is this person accessible for cell leaders to approach and seek help?

Focused

- Is this person passionately focused on the cell group ministry vision?
- Is this person called and committed to the ministry and vision of your church?
- Does this person have the lifestyle values that you want cell leaders and cell members to emulate?

Kingdom-centered people are rare. Good coaches are developed through the experience of cell groups. It is very difficult to coach another person in something that the coach has not experienced. This is the reason that the only people who would qualify as coaches at the launch point are those with extensive small group experience at another church or pastors who practice relational ministry.

If a church has 10 people prepared to join a group, two leaders ready to lead a group, and no coaches, it can start one group. Some would be tempted to start two groups, but this would be a mistake because it would water down the membership. This first cell group is called a simple prototype cell group and is discussed in the next section.

If a church has 50 people prepared to be cell members, seven prepared to lead a group, and one prepared to coach, it should start about four groups. The leaders should double up to provide strength, and the groups will quickly multiply.

If a church has 100 people prepared to be cell members, 20 prepared to lead, and four coaches, it can take a risk and start 10 groups. It will take a lot of work to make sure that these groups are going in the right direction. Some of the groups may fall on their faces, but a reliance on God and the passion to do relational ministry will make it work.

Training the First Cell Group Leaders

Good

The only way to train a cell group leader is through mentoring. Cell leaders require training in the techniques of leading a group, including how to lead a cell group meeting, how to ask good questions, how to delegate responsibility, how to reach out to new people, etc. Such training can be easily provided through retreats, seminars, books, or classroom courses. But techniques will not complete the training because cell leaders must receive spiritual DNA that they can pass on to their cell group members.

DNA is passed from father and mother to son and daughter. The same is true about cell group leadership. It is caught more than it is taught. It is passed from spiritual mothers and fathers to spiritual sons and daughters. This DNA cannot be passed down through sermons, classrooms, books, or even through technique training. DNA comes only through relational mentoring. Mentoring is the spiritual impartation of God's life from one person to the next. Spiritual DNA is passed down by spending time together, praying together, sharing vision, and discussing problems.

When starting groups, pastors spend much time teaching key leaders on why cell groups are important. They will have a day of technique training on cell leadership. But most stop there. They fail to impart the spiritual DNA to the leaders, making them spiritual sons and daughters. As a result, cell leaders know what they are supposed to do and know how to do it, but they don't have the ability (the spiritual DNA) to get it done.

Pastors ask cell leaders to develop their groups into spiritual families, with the cell leader serving as a spiritual parent to those in the group. But cell leaders can only give out what they receive. If they are being parented themselves, they can provide the same to their group. If they are only receiving principles and techniques, this is all they can give to their groups. Cell group leaders need spiritual mothers or fathers more than they need books or a training class, as important as those are.

For this reason, pastors find that they can only start one group to ensure that they impart the right kind of life into their future leaders.

The Composition of the First Groups

Cell group composition comes in one of two forms: heterogeneous or homogeneous. The former refers to groups that consist of people of mixed gender, various age groups, and different interests. The latter refers to groups that are comprised of people who are of common gender, common age, or common interest.

Intergenerational cell groups are a type of heterogeneous groups because they include the entire family. The advantage of these groups is that they enhance the sense of family in the church by allowing those without family to participate with other people who become their family. Displaced singles find surrogate parents. Children find aunts and uncles. Couples find other couples with whom to share their lives. The heterogeneous cell often becomes a closer family to the cell members than their real families are. Another advantage is that the heterogeneous cell keeps the family together, a growing issue with the division between husbands and wives who tend to be going 77 different directions 24 hours a day.

Heterogeneous cell groups are most often organized geographically. They typically seek to reach out to people within a certain geographic area. For example, a cell group might target a specific subdivision or a certain small suburb.

Homogeneous cell groups include men's groups, women's groups, couples' groups, youth groups, singles' groups, single mothers' groups, etc. The advantages to homogeneous groups are three-fold. First, they tend to be more evangelistic. It is easier to reach out to people who have common points of interest. Second, it is easier to relate to other members of the group and therefore people develop friendships more easily. Third, the groups do not have to wrestle with how children will participate in the cell groups.

Homogeneous groups can be organized geographically, but usually they tend to be organized into networks. There might be a men's network, a women's network, a couples' network, a youth network, etc.

Some churches have a clear vision for heterogeneous, intergenerational cell groups because they place a high value on the entire family being together.[1] Other churches only have homogeneous groups because they have realized that most people relate to others around common interests.

When first launching groups, it is easier when they are all either heterogeneous or homogeneous. After leaders start to discover the DNA of cell group ministry, they can start groups based around the vision of the cell group leaders. For instance, if a woman wants to reach other women, then she should begin a women's group. Or is a couple wants to reach out to families, they might like to lead an intergenerational group. Diversity can develop after the basics are understood.

Cell Group Content

Dr. Ralph Neighbour developed a common pattern for cell group meetings that is being used around the world. It includes four basic parts. It opens with the Welcome, which is an icebreaker question and should last no more than 10 minutes. Then it moves to Worship, where a group will sing a few songs and pray together. After this comes the Word, which is a time of Bible discussion and prayer ministry for one another. The final part is the Witness, a brief time where the group members share how they are ministering to nonbelieving friends and praying for these people.

These 4 Ws provide a great pattern to get started with the first group or groups. But it is crucial for the vision team to determine what the cell groups will discuss during the Word portion of the meeting. There are four common options:

- Each group discusses what the leader chooses or what it agrees as a group to discuss.
- Each group can choose its topic of discussion but must seek approval from the cell group pastor.
- Most groups discuss a standard lesson provided by the pastor, while some groups vary depending upon the needs of the group.
- All groups discuss the lesson provided by the pastoral staff.

The last option seems very legalistic, while the first seems very freeing. At the same time, the churches that have proven most effective with cell groups have adopted the fourth option. The reasons this method is effective: it aids in the reproduction of cell leaders (its easier to teach someone to facilitate an already-designed meeting agenda than to teach them to do the designing); it frees the cell leader from having to develop his or her own lessons; it allows the cell leader to focus on caring for the group; it ensures that the group is discussing a topic the church agrees with; it promotes the development of spiritual DNA within the cell leaders; and most importantly, it helps keep the church flowing together in unity.

Most churches that have adopted the fourth option develop cell discussion guides based on the biblical text of the pastor's Sunday sermon. When they do this, the group members have the opportunity to process the message and then apply it to their lives. Notice that the discussion does not focus on the sermon, but on the biblical text of the sermon. This leads people to interact with the Word of God.

Critics of the fourth option have called it a Sunday Sermon Cell. Many feel that Americans require options and therefore the church should provide a variety of groups depending upon the interest of the individuals. If cell groups only offers discussion of a Sunday sermon, then such an experience is probably less than exciting. But the discussion guide is provided so that group members can apply the Word of God to their lives, not so they can get the right answers to a set of questions. When the focus is on Christ and what he is doing in the group, it is impossible for the group to be boring.

When launching cell groups, a uniform cell lesson seems to work best. It takes the pressure off cell leaders to be innovative and helps steer the groups in the right direction. One Houston church of about 250 people has started groups using cell group lessons based upon the pastor's sermons. The questions are written not to rehash what the pastor taught but to apply the message to life. But the cell lesson is not the only component to the evening. In fact, when asked about the meeting, the lesson is not what the cell group leaders and members talk about first. Instead, they talk about people sharing, about someone revealing a need, or about people praying for each other. The uniform lesson keeps all of the groups on the same page, but each group applies the same lesson differently. The Spirit continually does new things to meet individual needs.

SECTION 5.2 Launching Strategies

Sherman Bible Church in North Texas launched five cell groups led by five very committed and competent leaders. Christian Fellowship Church in Benton, Kentucky started 16 cell groups. The people in these groups had been meeting for six months as break-out groups during their Sunday evening services. Northwood Christian Center in Mississippi started with four cell groups that had been meeting as table groups during their Sunday school classes. The Vineyard of Champaign, Illinois already had kinship groups. The leaders were trained to lead holistic small groups and supported through the change in group emphasis.

There is no perfect way to launch the first cell groups. In fact, when a church depends upon a magical strategy to get groups started, it misses the point. Launching must be bathed in prayer, listening for God's strategy, not man's.

Options for Launching the First Group(s)

In Section 4.2, I listed various ways of preparing the first cell group members for cell group participation. Churches that have successfully launched cell groups tied their launch strategy directly to their preparation strategy. The preparation flowed into the launch. This is wise because it reduces the shock and increases the comfort that people feel when they first join a group. They at least have some knowledge of what they are supposed to do. There are several different methods for launching groups.

Prototyping. This is the wisest approach. It is also the slowest approach (more later in this section).

Transforming the current small groups. Churches that already have good small groups often are able to change them into holistic cell groups. Usually these groups already possess the Upward and Inward components, but need to add Outward and Forward. One pastor shared that adding these is really about leading group members out of selfishness and into seeing the way God wants them to minister.

Starting cell groups with praying people. Prayer groups can be transformed into cell groups after leaders receive training.

Using Alpha groups. The small groups used in Alpha can continue to meet after Alpha concludes. The leaders of these groups will need more training to lead the new cell groups. Jim Egli is experimenting with an eight-week follow-up course to Alpha which aims to transform Alpha groups into cell groups.

Using table groups in Sunday school. After Sunday school classes have experienced body life through table-groups, the table-group leaders should be trained in cell group leadership and then transition the table groups to meet in homes.

Using break-out groups in a large group service. After groups have been meeting for 11-13 weeks during a weekly service (i.e. Sunday night), the leaders of these groups can move the groups into a home. Some churches shut down the service, replacing it with the new cell groups.

Using department cell groups. Some departments (i.e. youth, college, young married couples) are very open to change and are hungry to do ministry. Some churches have trained leaders within a department to lead cell groups and have launched the first groups within that department only. The strategy was not broadcast to the entire congregation. The goal is to see fruit within one department, to test it out, and to show others how to do it down the road.

Starting cells with committed people. One church was desperate to see something happen. The pastor saw that he had a group of about five leaders who had experienced small group body life in previous ministries, and they were extremely committed to prayer. They launched five groups. The pastors met with these leaders every week to minister to them and make sure they were on the right track. This approach is riskier, but it can work.

As the speed of implementation increases, the risk level rises. Those churches that fall on the side of the life-giving churches will have a little more freedom to take some risks, while those churches on the life-depleted side of the spectrum should take a more cautious route.

The Cell Group Prototype

New Life Christian Fellowship in Chesapeake, Virginia, had 200 members when it first began cell groups in 1993. It launched with a prototype, one cell group consisting of the deacons and elders. This group of about 15 people met from January through September, and in October these 15 started eight new groups. Seven of the eight were successful. Today, there are six congregations which multiplied from the original, with over 150 cell groups.

The prototype process allows a group to test and refine the model so that it can be easily reproduced. Robert Quinn, one of the most respected change consultants, writes, "The most potent lever for change is modeling the change process for other individuals. This requires that the people at the top themselves engage in the deep change process."[2] In the prototype group, the top pastors set the standard for others to follow. Some refer to the prototype as a pilot group or turbo group.

There are four purposes for a prototype.[3] First, it serves as a learning tool. It seeks to answer the questions "Will it work?", "How well does it meet needs?", and "What must be adapted to make it work?" The biggest question that it answers is, "What do the cell leader and the cell members do in a cell group to make it work?" The best place to learn how to minister in the cell is by watching as someone else models how to do it.

Second, the prototype communicates the vision of cell groups. Most people have to see a new idea in action before they understand what it looks like, how it works, or if they even like it. Key leaders need to experience the positive impact of cell ministry before they can communicate it to others.

Third, the prototype allows time for integration. Most small groups in North America emphasize one of the four values of Upward, Inward, Outward, and Forward at the expense of the other three. Without a pattern of integration for people to copy, future cell groups will continue to emphasize one of these values and fail to integrate all four into the life of the group.

Fourth, the prototype provides time for leaders to develop competence in leading cell groups.

Developing Leadership Competence

Key church leaders will typically be cell group members in the prototype. These people usually operate according to the old ministry patterns established in the church. Some will come with ideas that cell groups should focus on deep Bible study. Some will think that cell group leaders should preach to members. Everyone will bring false expectations to this first group.

The first cell group members are a part of the prototype cell group so that they can learn how to lead a group in a few months. They will learn new ways of ministry and receive honest feedback on how they are ministering. They will discover things that work and things that don't. This learning process will contribute to their leadership competence.

Developing leadership competence begins with incompetence. The prototype group members don't realize that they are incompetent, but after a few weeks they begin to consciously identify areas where they need to work. I realized this early on in my cell journey. I received cell leader training and knew how to lead meetings. But when it was my turn to lead the meeting, people seemed bored. We were just going through the motions. I grew frustrated. This frustration drove me to prayer and a lot of discussion with other leaders.

After conscious incompetence comes conscious competence. I discussed my weaknesses with other leaders and then began to improve. I asked better questions, was sensitive to the Holy Spirit, and involved more people in discussion. I focused on these things until I developed them into unconscious competence. Now I don't have to work on these areas much. When I am prayerful, God uses these skills that I developed.

The process of developing competence looks something like this:

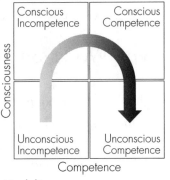

Fig 5.1 Competency Model[4]

The prototype cell group members go through this process together. Every week is a time of discovery, which will result in a pattern cell group. A pattern cell is the cell group model that will be reproduced in subsequent groups. It contains the DNA that the church wants replicated in future groups. The prototype group should answer these questions to make sure that they have the pattern cell group defined:

> - What will happen in the cell?
> - What should be happening in the cell group meetings?
> - What does prayer look like in a cell group context?
> - What does community and body life look like?
> - What does evangelism look like in a cell group?
> - What does edification look like?
> - What does equipping look like?
> - What does leadership development look like?

To help develop this pattern, the prototype cell group members should be trained in cell group leadership, which occurs at a separate time from the prototype group meeting. For instance, if the prototype meets on Thursday night, the training could occur on Sunday nights. This frees the prototype meeting to focus on living in the cell group, because the training time will allow the group members to discuss what is working and not working.

How a Prototype Works-Simple System

Simple prototyping begins when the senior pastor chooses up to twelve people to participate in a prototype group. These people will form a group that will meet for about four months as a cell group, seeking to learn and practice all of the values of UIOF. Simultaneously, they will receive training in the techniques of group leadership and meet several goals:[5]

- To gain a knowledge and understanding of cell values.
- To ensure that everyone practices leading each of the different parts of a cell group meeting twice.
- To provide feedback on each person's leadership of the meeting.
- To allow everyone to experience edification, both in the meeting and outside the meeting.
- To understand the need to create and cast vision for the group.
- To experience a group as it develops through the stages of group life.
- To practice relational evangelism.

In the prototype, the group members should play the "game" of cell groups. The prototype is like a scrimmage game where the "players," the prototype members, get to try out what they are learning about cell groups. It is tempting to use the prototype to analyze the cell groups, to talk about theory of the cell group strategy, or to discuss visions and dreams about the church. Such discussions are important but should be done outside of the prototype group meeting, through the weekly cell leader training sessions, one-on-one meetings, and phone conversations.

Note that this game includes relational evangelism. If future groups are going to reach out to their nonbelieving friends, family members, and co-workers, the first prototype group members must set the precedent. They should establish relationships with nonbelievers, pray for them as a group, and seek to reach out to them just like future groups will. The only difference will be that the new Christians will not come directly into the prototype group but will be ministered to in one-on-one type meetings.

After the first prototype has sufficiently met its goals (usually in four months time), the prototype members will start three groups. Typically, the senior pastor will continue to lead one of these groups because he is setting an example for others. This second set of groups will be composed of potential cell group leaders who will meet for approximately four months. After these groups have met for four months, the second-generation prototype members will work together to start the first generation of cell groups. The model might look something like this:

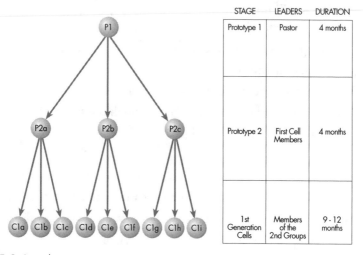

STAGE	LEADERS	DURATION
Prototype 1	Pastor	4 months
Prototype 2	First Cell Members	4 months
1st Generation Cells	Members of the 2nd Groups	9 - 12 months

Fig 5.2 Simple Prototyping

Practical Steps for a Simple Prototype

- Identify the first group of potential leaders. This group should be 12 people or fewer.
- Introduce the cell group vision to them. You can do this at a retreat or you can meet weekly and discuss a book like *Life in His Body* by David Finnell or *Reap the Harvest* by Joel Comiskey.
- Assess each potential leader. Using a tool such as *Journey Guide for Cell Group Leaders*, meet with each one individually for an interview.
- Invite those who are ready to be a part of an initial Prototype Group. This will be a 12 to 16 week group that will experience all of the various components that comprise cell group life. See prototyping cell lessons available at www.cellgrouppeople.com.
- Meet at a separate time for cell leadership training. An example of such training is *Cell Group Leader Training*, which includes eight sessions to train leaders in the basic skills necessary to lead a group.

- Go on a retreat that will help members experience spiritual victory. This is usually done after the prototype group has met for eight weeks. *Encounter God* is an example of such a retreat.
- Start three Prototype-2 groups. After 16 weeks of experiencing cell group life in the Prototype Group, the second-generation groups.
- Take all the Prototype-2 group members on an Encounter God Retreat. This should take place after the groups have been meeting for about five weeks. Those who went on the first Encounter God Retreat will help you facilitate.
- Recruit potential leaders from those Prototype-2 Groups. Lead them through a *Journey Guide for Cell Group Leaders* Interview.
- Train these potential leaders using the *Cell Group Leader Training*.
- Train all cell group members in relationship evangelism. Watch to see who actually embraces the call to love the lost.
- After these groups have been meeting for about three months, lead the cell group members through the *Upward, Inward, Outward, Forward Strategic Planning and Team Building Workshop*.

How a Prototype Works-
Complex System

Even if a church launches with 10 cell groups, it will still go through a prototyping process. When a church starts with 10 groups, these groups will have 10 different DNA codes. Most likely, only three or four of these groups will possess a DNA code that is close to what is desired. These three or four groups should be used to test the various elements of the cell group and to answer the pattern cell group questions.

In this approach, the three or four cells will possess different strengths and weaknesses. One cell group holds really good cell meetings. Another discovers how to do relationship evangelism. And still another group practices incredible body life. When this occurs, the pastors should facilitate cross-pollination so that all the groups can share their strengths with one another. The process might look something like this:

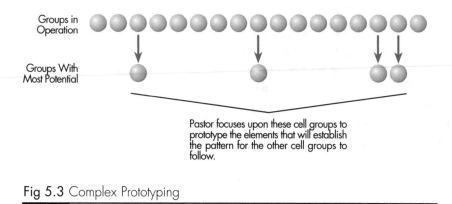

Pastor focuses upon these cell groups to prototype the elements that will establish the pattern for the other cell groups to follow.

Fig 5.3 Complex Prototyping

The pastors should focus on these three or four cell groups, instead of spreading out their energy over all of the groups. It is tempting to focus energy on the groups that are struggling while allowing the groups that have potential to develop on their own. But pastors should focus their mentoring on their best leaders, set the pattern for what should happen in a group, and then begin to multiply that pattern. The pattern cannot be discovered in weak cell groups, and if the pastor focuses his energy on those groups, he will never set the pattern for others to follow.

How a Prototype Works– Parallel System

One pastor shared that his church already has groups and he is trying to transition them into holistic cell groups. Because he is finding that the small groups are resisting the change, he is starting a prototype cell group with potential leaders (using *Leading from the Heart* by Michael Mack) to start new groups. This prototype group runs parallel to the old small groups. He plans to develop a new DNA code, with the hope that the older groups will see the new groups and make some changes down the road.

Launching Youth Cell Groups

Many churches have used youth cell groups as a place to start cell groups. At International Charismatic Mission in Colombia, all new ideas are tested out on the youth cell groups before they are incorporated into the rest of the church. One Arkansas church has grown from six to over 300 through youth cell groups, while the adults are still trying to get groups off the ground. Youth are generally the most flexible people in the church. They are surrounded by lost people every day and they are highly social. Therefore, transforming the youth ministry into a cell group ministry often proves to be one of the easiest ways to launch groups.

The key piece to changing the youth ministry is the presence of a youth minister who has a vision for youth cell groups. When this person is in place, he or she should move forward with youth cells as soon as possible. The principles for starting youth cells follow the same stages that have been outlined thus far. The difference lies in the speed in which youth cells can take off. Because youth are much more flexible, launching can happen much more quickly. Here are a few guidelines for getting started:

- The youth minister should share the cell vision with adult volunteers and determine who feels called to develop youth cells.
- The youth minister should train adult volunteers to lead cell groups.
- With adult volunteers, the youth minister should identify the youth that God has His hand upon and begin to mentor them. Youth are very flexible in their schedules and can often meet weekly outside of normal youth ministry activities. If the youth pastor will begin to pour his or her life into these potential leaders, they will begin to blossom in ministry.
- Both the adult volunteers and the youth leaders should participate in an Encounter God retreat.
- The youth leaders should go through cell leadership training.
- As they grow as interns in the adult-led youth cells, the youth leaders should be released more and more until they are ready to lead their own groups.
- At this point, the adult volunteers become hosts to the youth-led cells that meet in homes and coaches of the youth leaders.

Some churches use young adults to lead the cell groups. Others focus on raising up youth to lead the youth. One youth pastor started his youth cell groups by identifying eight youth who demonstrated leadership potential. He invited them to participate in a weekly meeting at his home. He and his wife began to pour their energy into these eight young people. They taught them how to lead, showed them how to pray, and shared their lives with them. This group of eight has led to the development of over 30 youth cell group leaders.

Each church must ask God about the strategy that He has ordained. The vision team should spend time in prayer, seeking God's wisdom about the many options available. Some churches will even develop new launching strategies by combining elements from others or starting from scratch. No matter what your church chooses, the key is to start slowly and deliberately. If God provides excited and well-trained people, you can always speed things up. It is much harder to slow down or backtrack.

Levers

Identify the number of Kingdom-seeking cell members.
Key Resource:
—*Journey Guide for Growing Christians*

Identify the number of Kingdom-mentored cell leaders.
Key Resource:
—*Journey Guide for Cell Group Leaders*

Identify the number of Kingdom-centered cell coaches.

Develop a launch strategy that coincides with the preparation strategy developed in Stage 4.

Train the first cell group leaders.
Key Resource:
—*Cell Group Leader Training*

Prototype the cell group, whether through a simple or complex system.
Key Resource:
—*Prototype Booklet* by Laurence Singlehurst
—*Leading from the Heart* by Michael Mack

When there is a youth cell group champion, begin youth cells.
Key Resources:
—*Youth Cells and Youth Ministry* by Brian Sauder and Sarah Moler
—*Youth Equipping Resources* by Ted Stump

Vision Team Questions

1. What is the likely result of starting weak groups?
2. Why is it important to start fewer but stronger groups?
3. Why is it so difficult to take the slower strategy?
4. The team should dialogue about the questions in Section 5.1.
5. Based on the answers about the number of Kingdom-seekers, Kingdom-mentored leaders, Kingdom-centered coaches, how many strong groups can be started?
6. What is the result of the prototyping process?
7. Brainstorm ways to launch strong groups.

STAGE 6
Generate
Cell Group Momentum

When a ship has navigated the shallow waters and entered into open sea, it is ready to raise the sails and let the winds carry it forward. Although the winds are responsible for the forward motion, the crew cannot expect to progress toward its destination without doing everything possible to catch more wind. This requires constructing sails, raising them, caring for them while raised, and mending them when torn.

The question most churches ask at this stage of the journey is, "How do we experience dynamic cell group community and not just cell group meetings?" It is very easy to develop a cell group program, but the experience of spiritual community is a work of the Holy Spirit, the wind of God. A cell group program results in meetings that people feel obligated to attend every week. Spiritual community creates an atmosphere where people do not need to be convinced to attend. Most of the time, cell groups need some help from pastoral leaders to develop this spiritual community. This support will result in momentum that will produce new leaders and new groups. This stage contains the following sections:

"Generate Momentum Through Spiritual Community" (Section 6.1), addresses how momentum results from short-term wins. Cell groups have short-term wins when they experience spiritual community rather than unspiritual or fleshly relationships. Spiritual community results in personal victories, new believers, and new cell groups.

"Strategies for Generating Spiritual Community" (Section 6.2), demonstrates what cell groups need from their church to overcome the inertia that groups often encounter.

"Generate Momentum by Developing Leaders" (Section 6.3), provides practical strategies for ways to develop new cell group leaders, the best way to generate momentum.

"Generate Momentum by Coaching and Supporting Leaders" (Section 6.4), explains the importance of developing cell group coaches and explains how to develop a coaching system.

SECTION 6.1 Generate Momentum Through Spiritual Community

One midwestern church concentrated its vision completely on cell group development. The pastor focused on leading the vision, the staff poured its energy into the cell strategy, and the church even brought in consultants to train members. Structurally, this church did many things right. Even so, the cell groups at this church lack energy, the leaders are frustrated, and the groups have not grown. Many church members look at the cells and ask, "Why should we join one? They aren't any fun." Some creative lay leaders have even developed competing ministries that drain resources from the cell groups, including a women's ministry and a men's ministry, both with small group components.

While this church is doing cell groups "by the book," the groups have not provided experiences that the people find attractive. The groups meet the basic definition of a cell group: the groups have no more than 15 people, meet weekly off-campus, seek to evangelize and disciple people, and have the goal of multiplication. But the groups lack life and fail to produce much-needed momentum.

To produce momentum, cell groups need to experience short-term wins. It is not enough to do cells according to the right program, nor is it enough to talk about the cell group vision and what the church should look like. One church in central Florida realized this. When this church started groups in 1999, the pastors focused less on getting the structure perfect and more on developing the key leaders. The groups have reached out to the hurting, and their two initial groups have turned into 10 groups.

Life produces momentum. Programs do not. Without momentum, the cell group journey will stop short of the final destination. If the ship is not making steady progress toward its destination, the crew will become disenchanted and try to turn the ship back toward old, familiar territory.

Short-term Wins

The Florida church mentioned above did not set out to become the biggest church in the city. The pastors just focused on doing cell groups well and producing the fruit necessary to build momentum. The momentum came as the groups experienced short-term wins. John Kotter puts it this way:

> Major change takes time, sometimes lots of time. Zealous believers will often stay the course no matter what happens. Most of the rest of us expect to see convincing evidence that all the effort is paying off. Nonbelievers have even higher standards of proof. They want to see clear data indicating that the changes are working and that the change process isn't absorbing so many resources in the short term as to endanger the organization.[1]

Pastors with a vision for cell groups are "zealous believers" who will stay the course no matter what happens. They are motivated by big-picture dreams about such things as a "biblical vision of the church," the "expansion of cell groups across the city," and turning "every cell member into a cell leader." The leaders and followers in the church are not motivated by these big-picture dreams. The average person only wants to see the dream working. He is a doer of the vision, not a visionary who sees the ultimate destination. Therefore, he needs to realize small victories in order to keep advancing toward that ultimate vision. This advancement comes in the form of short-term wins. As the graph below illustrates, no long-term vision is attainable without short-term wins.[2]

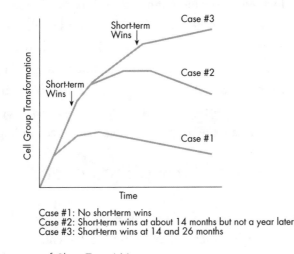

Case #1: No short-term wins
Case #2: Short-term wins at about 14 months but not a year later
Case #3: Short-term wins at 14 and 26 months

Fig 6.1 The Impact of Short-Term Wins

Some pastors have failed to understand the power of short-term wins because they can only see the ideal of a full-blown, working cell-based church. One church posted a goal on their walls of 2000 cell groups by the year 2000. When I saw this goal in 1994, they had about 40 groups. The pastor is a visionary and thought that such a goal would challenge the people to reach out to others. He felt that it would communicate the priority of the cell group vision. But the leadership was so focused on the ultimate goal that they missed the practical steps that it takes to advance toward that goal.

In pursuit of the full-blown cell church ideal, some churches limit themselves to only one kind of group, an intergenerational, heterogeneous small group that meets in a home to discuss the Bible. In other words, they do not include men's groups, women's groups, groups that meet at the workplace, coffee shops, or elsewhere as cell groups. They claim that the church should have no programs at all because everything must be done through the cell groups. They require participation in cell groups, whether or not people find them attractive. They have focused on the ideal of being a cell-based church so much that they do not understand the life that makes groups work.

Change experts assert that, "The half-life of a change project is six months; that is, if you are not showing measurable results in six months, expect your support to halve and the barriers to double."[3] If pastors fail to lead people into short-term wins within six months, they will find it very difficult to create the momentum needed to keep sailing.

Cell Group Promotion

Many pastors have tried to produce short-term wins by promoting cell groups through preaching, explaining to the church that cell group membership is crucial to the church's vision, and telling people that they are not really part of the church unless they join a cell group. Jim Egli and Dwight Marable have performed extensive research on the causes of cell group growth. They have found:

> ...that a strong emphasis on small group ministry from the pastor, church, and its printed publications did not contribute to an increase in any of the small group factors. Apparently, helping small groups to be vibrant and growing depends upon practical support, not mere pronouncements about their importance. In other words, pastors need to walk the walk and

not just talk the talk when it comes to encouraging cell groups and their leaders.[4]

An old saying about barbeque restaurants in the South goes, "If the food is good, you don't need to advertise." The same applies to cell groups. For the first year of cell group development, they should not be promoted publicly. The experience of the groups will speak much louder than any sermon on cells, any printed piece promoting cell participation, or any PowerPoint™ presentation explaining the vision. If the taste of cell groups is good, people will come. Other ways of promoting cells are helpful and should be employed, but the primary emphasis should lie on creating short-term wins that arise out of the groups themselves.

Short-term Cell Group Wins

"Wins" in the minds of the cell group leaders and members come in the form of tangible benefits that people experience within the cell groups. These "wins" come in three forms. First, cell members and leaders experience a win when they see personal victories in the lives of cell group members. A marriage is restored, a cell member confides a secret for the first time, a woman is able to forgive her dad of unmentionable wrongs, a man cries for the first time in front of other people. When things like this occur, it is hard to argue with the power of cell groups.

Cell groups experience a second type of short-term win when they see a nonbeliever receive Christ. In the cell group church that Don Tillman pastored, a young man shared how he had been afraid to share a deep secret because he did not want to experience rejection. When he shared that he was infected with HIV, the group surrounded him and prayed for him with tears, hugs, and love. The climate in the room became electric. Two individuals were visiting the group that night for the first time. One stood up, said, "This is weird," and left. The other began to cry and to share some very personal issues of her own. Through more tears, prayers, and hugs, this woman received Christ into her life and experienced a very deep healing. After such an experience, no one in the group would dare miss the next group meeting, much less argue against the power of cell group life.

The third type of short-term win comes in the form of new groups. In early cell group literature, authors often argued that cells should multiply every six months. Some read this and assumed that cell groups would automatically multiply every six months simply because 10 people met in homes once per week. But new groups don't just happen. New groups require new leaders. Without a new leader, it is impossible to have a new group. With new leaders, new groups are spawned and excitement rises. I visited one church in New York City in the early 1990s that understood the short-term win found in birthing a new group. The cell pastor stood before the congregation and called forward the cell group leaders of the multiplying group. They each shared a brief testimony and then the church as a whole prayed for the new group.

Spiritual Community Required

The short-term wins of personal victories, new Christians, and new groups generate momentum. Such experiences are the result of spiritual relationships, or spiritual community, as Larry Crabb calls it.

In a spiritual community, people reach deep places in each other's hearts that are not often or easily reached. They discover places beneath the awkwardness of wanting to embrace and cry and share opinions. They openly express love and reveal fear, even though they feel so unaccustomed to that level of intimacy.[5]

When John starts a new group with Jeremy and Heidi, Ken and Sarah, and others the group will not immediately enter into this spiritual community that Crabb proposes. They will not have a magical experience during the first meeting that will bond them together. Instead they will go through a process, a five-stage development process into spiritual community. These stages are Forming, Storming, Norming, Performing, and Reforming. Each group moves through the stages in unique ways, but the pattern is the same.

This process begins when people gather in superficial relationships, protecting their self-interests and questioning everything that happens. This is the Forming Stage of group development. At this stage, everything is new and exciting, but there are also many questions and apprehensions. The new leader, John, has high hopes and dreams. Jeremy and Heidi are looking forward to making friends with other couples like Ken and Sarah.

After the group forms, it will enter the Storming Stage, the period when people begin to see reality. They learn about each other, what they like and do not like. Sarah talks too much. Jeremy has an annoying laugh. John dominates. Ken lies sometimes. Cell members also see things about themselves that God wants to change, and they question whether or not they want to. Tom realizes that he rebels against authority. God shows Sandra that she is controlled by anger. John and Debbie learn just how bad their marriage really is. In some groups, this stage looks like chaos. In others, it is a quiet discomfort with one another.

When people are willing to work through the storm and die to their personal self-interests, they enter the Norming Stage. At this point, the members accept each other, work to meet each other's needs and support one another. Sarah and Heidi support Debbie as she works through her marriage troubles. Jeremy and Ken play sports with John, then go out for coffee to talk about the troubles he faces. John works with Tom on his rebellion issues. The group has become a family; it has found its identity because it has worked through the struggles of the Storm. This is the stage where the group begins to experience the power of spiritual community.

Following Norming is the Performing Stage, where the group seeks to intentionally minister to those outside the group. Sandra invites her parents. Tom brings a friend from work. Sarah asks her neighbor to come, and even though she chooses not to, the group prays for her. While the group is always open, at this point it makes plans to care for the lost and invite those who do not know Jesus to the groups.

The final stage of development is the Reforming Stage, as a new leader is commissioned to lead a new group. Jeremy has helped John with the cell group, leading worship and the word sections. He sought training, and now he will start a new group, taking Ken and Sarah as the core. Together, they will work to build a family cell.

The development of spiritual community can be impeded, thereby hindering short-term wins, when cell members pass through the Forming Stage and begin to experience the beginnings of the Storm. Because these cell members are experiencing a cell group for the first time, they are not quite sure how to handle the emotions they have about the group, the thoughts they have about other people, or the personality differences they experience with other people. They see Storming as either sinful, requiring too much effort, or requiring too much vulnerability. They balk at anything that looks like conflict and retreat emotionally from the group. They might continue to attend the group meetings every week because they are "committed" Christians, but they walk into the meetings with big yellow smiley-face masks hiding how they feel inside. They substitute man-made relationships for spiritual ones.

Larry Crabb identifies five types of man-made relationships that happen in small groups.[6]

> **Congenial Relationships** occur when group members practice being "nice" with one another even though it is clear that conflict is lurking beneath the pleasant surface. Nice is not the same thing as polite in this case. Polite is "speaking the truth in love." Nice is ignoring the truth to avoid conflict.

> **Cooperative Relationships** occur when the members work together but the work becomes so much the focus that people hide behind it. Some groups hide behind "Bible study," some behind the goal of "growing the group." These are not bad things, but if people fail to be honest in the name of cooperation, the group will get stuck.

> **Consoling Relationships** occur when members try to help one another "feel better" rather than addressing underlying issues. Jane confides in Jennifer, another cell member, that the cell leader speaks to her in a condescending tone. Jennifer feels sorry for Jane. She does not challenge Jane to talk directly with the cell leader, but tells her what she wants to hear, thereby reinforcing the wall of division.

> Cell groups encounter **Counseling Relationships** when members seek to analyze the hidden source of each person's behavior. Such analysis often blames sinful actions on personality, parents, rejection, sexual problems, and much more. Instead of depending upon the Spirit to set people free, the group focuses more and more on a person's problems, which never leads to repentance.

> **Conforming Relationships** focus on the performance of group members who are judged on their ability to act according to certain expectations. The cell group becomes a place where people cannot be real with one another; it is a place to "get it right" and straighten up. This creates a very condemning atmosphere where intimacy is rejected, truth becomes a lie, and people feel like they never measure up.

Forming

Storming

Norming

Performing

Reforming

When a cell group embraces one of these five relationships, it will not press through the Storming stage. When groups embrace man-made relationships and fail to enter into spiritual community, they try to produce short-term wins through programmic community. In man-made, programmic cells, all of the structures are in place, leaders are properly trained, and groups meet according to the proven patterns found in other churches. Yet the participants in those groups have failed to make the shift from the programmic emphasis required when starting cell groups to the spiritual relationships that make them work.

When I started leading my first cell group, I expected to be the best cell leader our church had seen. I had been trained by teachers who were sought out around the world, I worked for one of the cell group pioneers, and I had read all of the books. I was committed to making it work and I knew how to do it. But my group floundered after about six months. I joined up with another leader and worked to grow his cell group. I noticed that he did not have as much knowledge as I did, but the cell group was a lot more fun. People flocked to it and the Spirit seemed to flow in ways I never saw in my group. I realized that I was depending on a cell group program and not the Spirit flowing through me.

Too many churches have man-made cell groups that are not seeing any personal victories, new believers, or new groups started. Cell groups are full of struggling people who are not seeing personal victory. Cell leaders have given up on growing by reaching nonbelievers through cells. And some groups grow to 20 people with no one ready to lead a new group. Pastors try to fix this by tweaking the organization, unaware that the problem is spiritual rather than organizational. The man-made, programmic cell group experience will not produce short-term wins. As a result, the ship will either drift in open sea with man-made groups or return back to the old ways.

For many people, the concept of spiritual community will require a major shift in the basic idea of church life because members are accustomed to hiding behind programs, curriculum, or ritual. The old system did not require transparency, vulnerability, repentance, confrontation, or truth telling. Pastors and leaders must help these people enter into spiritual relationships that will create momentum in the group before the old ways can take over again.

The experience of spiritual community is powerful. It produces short-term wins. But these short-term wins are only experienced when groups are willing to go through the Storming Stage. God's "wins" are done God's way, the way of death to self, to pride, and to lying. 1 John 1:6-7 says, "If we claim to have fellowship with him yet walk in the darkness, we lie and do not live by the truth. But if we walk in the light, as he is in the light, we have fellowship with one another, and the blood of Jesus, his Son, purifies us from all sin." When group members walk through the storm together, God shines his light into their lives, opening the door to fellowship and forgiveness.

Jesus' Model for Spiritual Community

While sharing the values of Upward, Inward, Outward, Forward with Pastor Scott Hagan and the staff of Grand Rapids 1st Assembly, Pastor Hagan scribbled notes on a piece of paper. After my presentation, He held up a piece of paper that looked something like this:

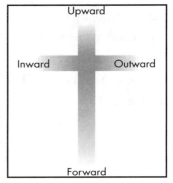

He said, "I have been looking for a way to share the vision on a napkin and I think I have found it." He explained further what he meant. "Jesus lived out these values on the cross as he had four different kinds of relationships with four different individuals or groups."

Jesus related Upward to God as He prayed on the cross. Jesus related Inward with the thief on the right who said, "Jesus, remember me when you come into your kingdom." Jesus immediately included him in the family of God. Jesus related Outward to those who rejected Him, including the thief on the left who mocked Him and the soldiers who beat Him. He said, "Father, forgive them, for they do not know what they are doing." Finally, Jesus related Forward with future leaders who sat at the foot of the cross: Jesus' mother, Mary Clopas, Mary Magdalene, and John the Beloved. Jesus set the model of Upward, Inward Outward, Forward.

Jesus modeled spiritual community through Upward, Inward, Outward, Forward throughout His ministry. Sometimes people make cell groups harder work than necessary. Cell groups that work minister the way Jesus ministered.

Upward—Relational Prayers. If there is anything that can be said about Jesus' prayers, it is that they were not pious, formal prayers. They were honest. Such prayers usually offend those with lots of religious knowledge or training. Jesus modeled a way of relating to God that stood against the patterns of prayer established by the religious leaders of His time. He boldly entered into the throne room of God. He showed the early church how to bring real needs before a real God as He prayed such things as, "Abba, Father, everything is possible for you. Take this cup from me. Yet not what I will, but what you will" (Mark 14:36). Jesus demonstrated how to love God without pretense.

Too many cell groups stall out because they do not understand how to be real in prayer. Cell group prayer falters when it becomes ritualistic. Most churches have ritual prayers behind which people hide. Some groups still pray in the King James form of "thees" and "thous." Some limit prayer to the request time at the end of the meeting, and members share requests for sick aunts who live in England or other people outside the group. Some groups even ask people to lift their hands if they have unspoken requests.

Cell groups work when real people bring real and personal needs to the group so that the group can lift them up before God. The focus of the cell group is to see God move in and through the lives of the people attending the group. This requires desperate honesty before God and one another. Relational prayers practice James 5:16: "Therefore confess your sins to each other and pray for each other so that you may be healed. The prayer of a righteous man is powerful and effective."

Inward—Relational Ministry. Jesus did not stand at a distance, lift himself up on a platform, or demand special privileges. He included people, especially His disciples, into His life. He said, "'Who is my mother, and who are my brothers?' Pointing to his disciples, he said, 'Here are my mother and my brothers. For whoever does the will of my Father in heaven is my brother and sister and mother.'" Jesus tore down the walls of hierarchy and power and treated those around Him with respect, love, and care.

Cell groups that practice family relationships and commitment to one another have powerful experiences together. Cell groups that reject Jesus' strategy of family only have meetings. Often these meetings have good discussions, with good biblical answers to all the questions. But the group's members do not trust one another to share what they think, how they feel, or what is going on in the hidden parts of their lives. Jesus shared His life with the disciples. They knew one another intimately. Jesus invaded personal space and dealt with real issues. His ministry was personal, not philosophical.

Outward—Relational Evangelism. Jesus related to prostitutes, tax collectors, the poor, and the rejected; simply put, sinners and outcasts. He said, "It is not the healthy who need a doctor, but the sick…For I have not come to call the righteous, but sinners" (Matthew 9:12-13). He did not preach to them at special events; he ate with them, went to their parties, and became their friend. He did not treat them as outsiders. He loved them as friends.

Many churches have a "bunker mentality" with regard to relationships with nonbelievers. Church members feel like they must protect themselves from their influence, rather than influencing them. When cell groups import this bunker mentality, group members will find the meeting a very boring experience. But cell groups who love the lost, embracing them as friends, never find a group boring. At a recent cell group meeting, a former Marine confessed, "I don't know if there is a God, a heaven or a hell. I just know my life is messed up and I've gotta do something." I was so happy when other group members did not pressure him to pray the sinner's prayer or accept Christ. They know that he will see the truth as Jesus lives through the group. We are praying for the day when he is open to receiving Jesus.

Forward—Relational Mentoring. Jesus' relational strategy even applied to the way in which he discipled those around him. Mentoring was a way of life for Jesus. His disciples were with Him, watching Him pray for the sick, listening to His revolutionary words, taking note of how people responded to His love, trying to grasp His prayers. Jesus knew that the only way the church would take off is if a few people got infected with the kind of life He led. He did not just seek to transform how they ministered; he sought to transform how they lived.

Most cell group structures encourage cell leaders to mentor cell group interns or assistants. The goal is to raise up future leaders as the intern learns how to lead a group from the cell leader. Cell leaders stuck in programmic, man-made relationships see their relationships with interns as duties to be fulfilled. Jesus saw His relationship with those He mentored as friendship. Jesus' method of mentoring was not limited to ministry activities. When a cell leader embraces spiritual mentoring, she seeks to impart spiritual direction into the life of the intern, desiring to see her become totally whole, both as a leader and in her personal life.

Leaders of spiritual cell groups follow the model set by Jesus and are committed to the basic practices that result in short-term wins:

• They pray honestly.
• They love the people in the group.
• They embrace the lost.
• They mentor others in the same practices.

A few years ago, Jeremy joined our group after moving to Houston from a Bible college. He was skeptical of cell group life, but we told him that after a few months, he would not want to go back to the programmic way of doing church. He questioned our arrogance. After a year, he moved away. He tried to find another church, and one day he said, "I thought you guys were crazy when you told me that I could not return to the old style of church. Now I know I cannot be a part of another church that doesn't experience spiritual relationships in cell groups." Even though our church was not perfect, Jeremy had experienced enough short-term wins in the cell group to know the power of cell group life.

SECTION 6.2 Strategies for Generating Spiritual Community

Spiritual community does not come naturally to most churches. For 1,700 years, the church has depended solely on the large group worship experience. Because spiritual community is unnecessary to the large group wing, the church has built up centuries of inertia. Most pastors and leaders deal with the causes of inertia before entering cell groups, but most cell group members do not. Instead, many bring with them a long heritage of doing church in ways that hinder the development of spiritual relationships.

Common Sources of Spiritual Inertia in Cell Groups

The clergy-laity dichotomy. Clergy is a word that is derived from the New Testament Greek word *kleros*, which means 'lot' or 'inheritance." Paul uses it in Colossians 1:12: "giving thanks to the Father, who has qualified you to share in the inheritance (*kleros*) of the saints in the kingdom of light." In the third century, the church developed a class of people called the clergy, who were thought to possess a special "inheritance" that allowed them to minister to those who had not received this inheritance. This idea could not be further from New Testament truth. The inheritance Paul speaks of belongs to all members of the church of God, not just to special people who have been called to lead the church.[7]

The greater the elevation of the clergy over the laity, based on the New Testament word *laos*, which means all the people of God including church leaders, the harder it will be for the people to enter into ministry. In most churches, the people do not see themselves as having an inheritance. They only see themselves receiving from those who possess it. The pastor might make the shift from a person who does the ministry to the equipper of others for ministry, but church members will often resist such a shift. For instance, most Christians who have been part of the church for any length of time will be offended if the pastor does not visit them in the hospital even though a cell group leader and three or four cell group members come by and pray.

The Sacred Place. For most people, the term "church" applies to the building. They do not understand that the Spirit of God will show up wherever two or three are gathered together in His name. Many people feel that the ministry that happens in a cell group is not quite as good, not quite as anointed, not quite as blessed by God as the ministry that happens in a building that is used on Sunday mornings for worship. This feeling is not often expressed or even realized, but it certainly shows up in the way church members approach ministry.

Program Competition. Randall Neighbour consulted with a church in the midwestern part of the United States. He returned frustrated, feeling like he had wasted his time. The church had kept all of its old programs and simply added cell groups to the list. Church leaders held worship services five nights per week and then expected group attendance on top of that. Church members were worn out. They had no time to develop relationships with one another or with any nonbelievers who might want to come to the groups. I have seen other churches require cell leaders to participate in committee leadership, choir practices, children's programs, and long business meetings. Such competition between cell group commitment and program commitment will sap the life out of a group. When people are required to give time and energy to the old as well as the new, the old will always win.

Time. Many church leaders ask, "Do people in America have enough time to commit to a weekly cell group?" Some have used this question to argue that cell groups will not work in America. Time is certainly a legitimate concern. Kids have soccer, band, art, and countless activities; dad works 60 hours per week; mom carts the kids to the endless list of extracurricular activities, all after working eight hours a day. To add a weekly cell group on top of this frenetic pace of life seems almost impossible.

Overcoming Inertia

Cell groups work best as a part of a two-winged system. Both wings can work together to propel the church forward. The large-group wing works best with a fully functioning small-group wing. Likewise, cell groups do not realize their full potential without help of the large group. As the spiritual atmosphere rises in the large group, momentum is created in the cell groups. If the large group is struggling, the cell groups will eventually hit a wall.

The ministry of the large group is much more than a weekly worship service. The large group should feed the life of the cells by providing vision and spiritual energy. Without this input, cell groups will find it very difficult to overcome the inertia that comes with the old ways of doing church. The battle against inertia can be won only by applying more energy to the new direction than the amount applied to the old direction. Churches do this as they help cell groups practice the values of UIOF. The church cannot assume that cell groups will advance in these four areas by themselves, especially in early stages of cell group development.

Upward-
Develop an Atmosphere of Prayer

If a church is not a praying church, it is foolish to expect the cell groups to be praying cell groups. Even more so, if the senior pastor is not a praying pastor, his church will not be a praying church. Cell group members are not likely to enter into Spirit-led prayer by themselves. Corporate prayer life must lead and feed the prayer life in the cell groups. Gene Getz states that, in the New Testament church,

> ...prayer experiences did not seem to be only 'periods of prayer,' or a 'time,' or an 'evening,' or a 'day' set aside for prayer, though it certainly included this....More frequently, however, prayer seemed to be interwoven into a variety of experiences believers participated in as they met together to be edified. And as they prayed, they prayed for each other's needs. They prayed for those carrying the gospel to others, and they prayed for all men.[8]

Most pastors have taught sermons that sound similar to what Gene Getz writes, yet their churches have failed to create an atmosphere of prayer. A church embraces a lifestyle of prayer when church members have opportunities to follow their spiritual leaders in prayer. This means much more than creating "prayer meetings" that often turn into more talking about prayer than actual praying. It means creating opportunities where people are led into the throne room of God to pray and intercede.

Churches that take off with cell groups base their lives on prayer. From Prayer Mountain in Korea to 5:00 A.M. prayer meetings in Colombia to the prayer deliverance teams in the Ivory Coast, prayer is an essential element to success. These three countries have huge churches with a heavy corporate emphasis on prayer.

But the power of prayer is not limited to non-Western cultures. When Rob Campbell started a cell group church in Wimberley, Texas, he saw the importance of building groups through prayer. He invited one of his key leaders, Cecilia Belvin, to spearhead the church's prayer effort and serve as the Pastor of Prayer. She leads a Prayer Ministry Team consisting of people who feel a special calling to spend regular, extended time in prayer. Every Monday night, this team meets for three and a half hours to pray for the specific needs (usually a list of over 50) in the church body. This team serves as a catalyst for prayer in the rest of the church. The team meeting does not replace the corporate prayer, but rather stimulates it.[9]

There are many different ways to facilitate prayer corporately: establishing congregation-wide times of prayer, calling cell groups to periodic "nights" of prayer and worship, inviting the church to a corporate fast, and setting up a prayer room. On the cell group level, leaders must provide various ways for the groups to enter into Spirit-led prayer. For instance, the church can develop three or four agendas for a cell group half-night of prayer. Cell leaders can receive training on how to facilitate the Lord's Supper in the cell group. A cell group lesson can be written on fasting and then the group can fast together for a breakthrough. The ideas are endless and many resources have been developed which provide practical ways to facilitate prayer.[10]

More than any prayer techniques, churches need a fresh touch from God. Jim Cymbala, pastor of Brooklyn Tabernacle, wrote in his book *Fresh Power*, "[T]he answer won't come from another seminar....We have too many mere technicians who are only stressing methodology, and they are increasingly invading the church. The answer is not in any human methodology. The answer is in the power of the Holy Spirit. The answer is in the grace of God."[11] The Spirit of God must stir up a hunger for God within the leadership. From this stirring, He will create a wave of desire for Him in the rest of the congregation.

Inward-
Facilitate the "One Anothers"

Randy Frazee pastors upwardly mobile commuters who have little time for relationships and naturally treat church as another activity in their busy lives. In his book, *The Connecting Church*, he reports that "Americans are among the loneliest people in the world."[12] Frazee argues that just because church people join small groups, they will not necessarily experience the community that is so lacking in North American life. Robert Wuthnow, a Princeton researcher, has observed that

> ...small groups mainly provide occasions for individuals to focus on themselves in the presence of others. The social contract binding members together asserts only the weakest of obligations. Come if you have time. Talk if you feel like it. Respect everyone's opinion. Never criticize. Leave quietly if you become dissatisfied.[13]

Such an experience contradicts what the Bible teaches about small group relationships: "encourage one another "(1 Thessalonians 5:11), "love one another" (1 Peter 1:22), "forgive one another" (Colossians 3:13), "confess sins to one another" (James 5:16), "serve one another" (Galatians 5:13), "offer hospitality to one another" (1 Peter 4:9), "teach and admonish one another" (Colossians 3:16). Frazee writes, "Christian community is not an occasional group getting together led by small group leaders; it is at its core a familial structure."[14]

Many cell group leaders limit their ministry to getting people to show up, rather than moving toward becoming a spiritual family. Cell members attend but simply go through the motions. To help cell leaders develop to openness of a family with their cell members, the church leaders must take a risk and create a community or family atmosphere in the church as a whole.

In the largest churches in the world, a person can walk in and sit among the thousands of people and at the same time feel that he or she somehow belongs. Victory Christian Center is one of the largest churches in North America with more than 13,000 members, yet church leaders have created an atmosphere that welcomes people. The pastors and cell group leaders are genuinely glad to see people. Churches like Victory Christian Center have created a place where the people minister through the "one anothers."

This community atmosphere does not spontaneously happen. Instead, it develops at the top and works its way down throughout a church. Ben Wong, senior pastor of Shepherd Community Church in Hong Kong, was one of the early pioneers in cell group life. He first tried to legislate accountability relationships where people would care for one another outside of the cell meetings. Church members only saw it as another program, and the effort soon flopped. He realized that he, as the senior pastor, had to set an example. He began mentoring his staff pastors one-on-one every week. Then he told them to do the same with their key leaders. These leaders then started mentoring their key cell group members. Then those key members started mentoring other cell group members. While some churches have developed successful accountability systems without going to such extremes, such systems only work in the long run when the pastors are involved. Faith Promise Church in Knoxville, Tennessee recognizes this. Every pastor and every elder is not just involved in leading a group; each is required to mentor at least one potential leader on a weekly basis.

Mentoring within a cell group gives life to the group. It facilitates ministry outside official meetings and takes the pressure off the cell leaders to do everything. Immature Christians are linked with more mature Christians who can show them the way. Ralph W. Neighbour wrote a practical how to-guide called *Mentoring Another Christian* to help cell members understand how to minister to newer believers.

Another practical way to facilitate "one another" relationships in cell groups originated with Neil Cole in his book *Cultivating a Life for God*. Cole developed gender specific sub-groups of two or three people (when a fourth is added, the sub-group multiplies) which meet weekly for about an hour. He calls these Life Transformation Groups (LTG). During the hour, a group of men or a group of women will share their responses to a set of accountability questions, discuss what they are learning from the Bible, and strategically pray for specific people who need the Lord. There is no curriculum or training for such a sub-group. Cole states, "Many of the New Testament 'one anothers' are functioning at the LTG level, which releases the cell leader and pastor from being the chief caregiver."[15]

Through the use of accountability relationships, mentoring relationships, or life transformation groups, cell group leaders are freed from having to be the "priest" who does all of the ministry to a facilitator and overseer of body-life ministry that the entire group does.

Another way that the corporate church can help cell leaders facilitate "family" in their groups is to help them "waste time" together.[16] A woman's group might have a "facial night." A men's group might play golf together. A college group might take a day trip to the lake. A family group might have a cookout. Cell groups that are not having fun will not experience the "one anothers." Groups often need permission from the church leadership to have fun. Some of the best leaders in a church are very driven, goal-oriented, and focused people. If pastors do not encourage these leaders to have fun in their groups, the groups' meetings will often become dry and boring.

Outward-
Stimulate Relational Evangelism

At a recent TOUCH training conference for pastors, our team surveyed the participants, asking them to identify the biggest obstacles they have encountered in their cell groups. Evangelism was mentioned as one of the top three obstacles in almost every case. At the same time, researchers have consistently found that cell groups are one of the most effective means for reaching nonbelievers. George Hunter III writes, "My own interviews in churches have revealed that people who do engage in witness and inviting are very likely to be involved in a small group where people share their experiences and discuss the faith...One such man reports, 'I can invite my neighbor to church, or to the empty chair in my group, or to a group for people with his problem!'"[17] How are some churches able to grow their groups through evangelism, while others are stuck looking at the same people week after week?

Jesus prayed, "May they [believers] be brought to complete unity to let the world know that you sent me and have loved them even as you have loved me" (John 17:23) The experience of biblical unity will represent the Gospel of Jesus to nonbelievers. Maybe the problem with the lack of evangelism in the church has less to do with the methods that have been adopted and more to do with the life that the church lives. As Ghandi once said, "I might have become a Christian if I had seen one." The task of evangelism is about sharing the Good News, and that comes when a nonbeliever sees the Good News as a priority in the lives of people living in basic Christian community. Howard Snyder puts it this way:

This is why the New Testament says very little about evangelism. It puts the emphasis on authentic Christian community, the reconciled life together that comes from being mutually joined to Christ and mutually growing up into him.

The implication is clear: If the church is genuinely a reconciled and reconciling community, the Lord will add to its number those who are being saved.[18]

Cell group evangelism, at its core, is basically relationship evangelism. If the people in a church do not value relating to nonbelievers, putting these people in cell groups will not suddenly change their minds. Relationship evangelism must be stimulated by the leaders who are overseeing the groups. Here are some practical things church leaders can do to stimulate evangelism in the cell groups:

Model Relationship Evangelism.

Cell group members and cell group leaders will emulate the commitment to evangelism they observe in their leaders. George Barna writes in his book, *Evangelism that Works,*

When it comes to the focus of the organization, the people who serve there tend to take on many of the core personality traits of the leaders toward fulfilling the mandate of the organization. If this is true, and most churches seem to lack fervor and focus for evangelism, is it reasonable to conclude that it may be because of the lack of zeal most pastors have for identifying, befriending, loving, and evangelizing non-Christian people.[19]

When the Vineyard of Champaign, Illinois first looked at the cell group vision, Happy Lehman, the senior pastor, led his staff through Dr. Ralph Neighbour's *Life Basic Training.* In this training, Dr. Neighbour highlights the fact that being a son of God also means being a servant of God who seeks out those who do not belong to God. The staff members quickly realized that their time was so filled with "ministry" commitments that they did not have any time to be God's servants who ministered to nonbelievers. First they had to repent—a process that constituted changing their weekly schedules—before they were able to encourage the rest of the church to enter into relationship evangelism.

Cast a Practical Vision for Evangelism.

Wayne McDill states, "Evangelism will be effective...in direct proportion to its dependence on the establishment and cultivation of meaningful relationships."[20] While such statements are true, the average cell group member has no idea how relationship evangelism works. Jay Firebaugh, pastor of Clearpoint Church in Houston, Texas explains the vision for relationship evangelism with five easy points. He will stand up before his church and have church members repeat after him so that they can remember how it works.

- Target one.
- Pray.
- Pray Together.
- Work on the relationship.
- Do fun things.

Every group member is told to target one person. That cell member will then spend time praying for this person, seeking God as to how to minister to her. The cell group will pray together for all of the people that have been targeted. Each member will work on the relationship with the nonbeliever, and then the group will plan fun things that the nonbelievers would be willing to do.

Train cell group leaders to lead cell groups in prayer for nonbelievers.

As discussed in Stage 5, a common pattern for leading a cell group meeting is the Welcome, Worship, Word, and Witness pattern. In this last portion of the meeting, the group members discuss the people they are praying for, how they are working on the relationships, and actually pray for nonbelievers. In most cell group meetings, this part is ignored. Cell leaders often find it awkward to spend time praying for people who do not know the Lord.

Therefore, leaders need training in how to facilitate such a time. Some use the concept of the empty chair, where the group prays for different people who could fill an empty chair sitting in the circle. Others create a poster and list the names of those the group is praying for. TOUCH Outreach Ministries has developed such a poster called *The Blessing List* which fully explains how to develop a list and guide a group into prayer.

Van Ducote shared how his groups have taken off evangelistically. When I asked what they were doing differently, he said that they have trained every cell group member to pray for three people for 30 days. Individual cell group members commit to pray at a certain time each day —lunch is a common time—and they pray during the cell group meetings for these people. After 30 days, they invite these people to a cell group meeting, a men's or women's meeting, or a worship service. Not only are the people responding, but God is supernaturally drawing them. During one cell meeting while the group was praying for their people, one of the people they had just prayed for knocked on the door of the home where the group was meeting.

Train cell group members in relationship evangelism.

Many cell group members do not understand how cell group evangelism works. They think that cell groups are for Christians and that nonbelievers will mess things up because they have not decided to accept Christ. In reality, cell groups are about creating a place where people can discover who Christ is. Rick Richardson writes in his book *Evangelism Outside the Box*, "Most people today do not 'decide' to believe. In community they 'discover' that they believe, and then they decide to affirm that publicly and follow Christ intentionally."[21]

Section 6.3 discusses the importance of developing a discipleship process that will help cell members move from being new Christians to the point of cell leadership training. Part of this process should include training in how to minister to nonbelievers and how to share Christ with them. Many great tools exist for this purpose, including Dr. Neighbour's *Touching Hearts* and Jim Egli's *Relating Jesus*.

Provide practical ideas for reaching out to nonbelievers.

Steve Sjogren has developed a creative pattern for ministry called servant evangelism that can easily be used in cell groups. He defines it as "demonstrating the kindness of God by offering to do some humble act of service with no strings attached." Examples of service include setting up a table at a local mall for free gift-wrapping, giving away soft drinks on a hot day, feeding parking meters, raking leaves, and many more.

One church trained its groups in servant evangelism and the creativity started to fly. One cell member worked for a trucking company. Group members borrowed one of the trucks and invited people to stock it with food for needy people. The idea became contagious and nine other groups joined in the project. Because most of them did not know how to share their faith, the groups had to take time to learn how. On the day they took the truck to give away food to the needy, they had two stipulations. First, they asked people if they could share the love of Jesus before they gave away the food. Second, they asked the staff pastors to come and observe, but they could not say anything or take a leadership role. This project was completely cell group initiated.

Sjogren has written a book full of ideas called *101 Ways to Reach Your Community* and even more ideas are listed on his website, <www.servantevangelism.com>. Sjogren says that this approach is low risk, and high grace.

Cell Group Strategic Planning

Many times the best ideas for developing Upward, Inward, Outward, and Forward will come from the group members themselves. They just have never had a context in which to contribute their ideas. Jim Egli developed a workshop called *Upward, Inward, Outward, Forward,* which provides such a context. This tool opens with a brief cell group evaluation that identifies strengths and weaknesses. It then facilitates discussion around practical ways to improve the dynamics that make groups work. Cell group members will brainstorm ideas, make a plan for implementation, and assign responsibility.

Through this process, the cell group leader will often recognize a cell group member who can serve in the short-term as a ministry captain. Cell leaders look for a person to spearhead the Upward movement, someone who can serve as Inward captain to help develop deeper fellowship, and someone who can champion the Outward effort by always keeping a focus on reaching out. Saddleback Church first developed this idea around their five purposes: Worship, Ministry, Fellowship, Discipleship and Evangelism. (Note: Warren's five purposes address the same values as UIOF, with ministry and fellowship combined into Inward). Faith Promise Church adapted this idea. Each cell group looks for a captain or a champion for each area. Every week the champion has responsibilities in the cell group meeting. For instance, the evangelism champion will lead the Witness part of the meeting or the Worship champion will lead the Worship portion. Such responsibilities lighten the load of the cell leader, raise the level of vision ownership, and provide opportunities for cell members to prove themselves before they enter cell group leader training.

SECTION 6.3 Generate Momentum by Developing New Leaders

Stephen did not attend church with his wife Rose and their three children. He was dedicated to his work and his workout regimen. Rose prayed for him diligently, and after several months, he finally gave his life to the Lord. Stephen and Rose joined a cell group when their church first started them. Stephen quickly became an intern. Shortly thereafter, he started a group on his own. Stephen has proven to be a very effective leader and mentor to his group members.

The best way to generate momentum is to start new groups. New groups are dependent upon new leaders. Cell groups are a natural breeding ground for leaders. Stephen went from new Christian to cell leader in less than two years. This rarely happens in the traditional church. Some churches around the world have a goal to help people launch a cell group less than one year after receiving the Lord.

Yet many churches have not been able to develop new cell group leaders like Stephen. The groups grew, but no one was ready to take on the leadership of a new group. In order to generate leadership momentum, churches must intentionally mentor cell members. They must develop a clear path that will guide a person from new believer to effective cell group leader.

Forward-
An Equipping Journey

CONDUCT - CHARACTER - CORE

Every believer is on a journey. Different people are at different places on their journeys. A few are hungry for God, seek Him in new ways, and want to explore new facets of life in Him. Some have walked far with God and hold leadership positions, but they have grown content with their positions and are sitting on nice park benches. The largest group of people are those who started the journey with God, but they either became frustrated with their progress or distracted by other options. Now they really do not know how to progress in their journey with Him.

Attendance, even leadership, is not the final goal. Paul writes that we should "want to know Christ and the power of his resurrection and the fellowship of sharing in his sufferings, becoming like him in his death, and so, somehow to attain the resurrection from the dead" (Philippians 3:10-11). Paul follows this verse by stating that he has not obtained this goal, but that he is pressing on to "win the prize for which God has called me heavenward in Christ Jesus."

Just as churches journey toward God's calling, so do the individuals within churches. For a church to reach its goal, it must help the people reach theirs. The ultimate goal will not be achieved until the fulfillment of the Kingdom of God when Christ returns. At that point, the church will be transformed into His spotless bride, but this does not mean that Christians have His permission to sit on their laurels waiting for the ultimate consummation. The church should set a goal to help every member along their journey toward maturity in Christ. Alan Roxburgh, church consultant and co-author of *Missional Church*, illustrates this journey this way:

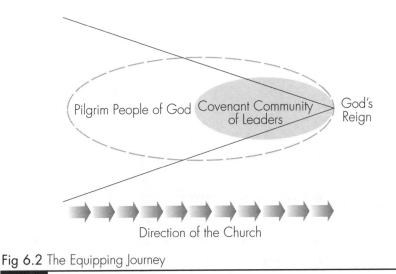

Fig 6.2 The Equipping Journey

The ultimate goal of the people of God is to shape their lives around the values and commitments of God's reign. As the dotted line illustrates, entrance into the journey is open to all. Anyone can enter into this journey with Christ. Roxburgh writes, "People are constantly being invited to move toward and into a covenant, disciple community. This kind of…church is open to all who may want to be on this journey. It has a permeability that is open to others since it seeks to draw others alongside and minister to people at every level on the way."[22]

The community of covenant leaders is formed by a group of people who are also traveling on the journey, but they have crossed a clear line into a certain set of leadership practices or disciplines of God's Kingdom. Everyone is invited to participate in a process of equipping so that they too can enter into this covenant community of leaders. This is what happens in the equipping journey that a church should develop. Along this journey there are several stages:

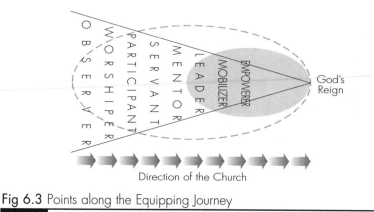

God's
Reign

Direction of the Church

Fig 6.3 Points along the Equipping Journey

This diagram demonstrates the movement of a person from a nonbeliever who is observing what God is doing to belief expressed through worship to full participation, to servanthood, and on into the mentoring of a younger Christian. The circle signifies a leadership community that is set apart to oversee and mentor those who are progressing on the equipping journey. The leader is a cell leader. The mobilizer is a cell group coach. And the empowerer is a pastor who has been called to oversee cell ministry.

Observers need experiences where they can see the reality of Christ in action. This will come through worship services, cell group activities, harvest events, Alpha courses, and many other places.

Worshippers are new or immature Christians who need to discover the basics of faith, who Christ is, and how they can take the first steps into obedience. New believers material, like *Beginning the Journey* by Ralph W. Neighbour, Jr. and Jim Egli works well here.

Participants have committed to cell group life. They need to be set free from the sin, condemnation, and thoughts that plague them from their pasts. Almost every effective cell-based church has developed an Encounter Retreat to facilitate this experience of freedom. After this retreat, churches provide follow-up training on the meaning of living out Christian values.

Servants are cell group members who need training on how to hear God, how to minister to other Christians in prayer, and how to reach out to nonbelievers.

Mentors require training in how to provide spiritual guidance to a younger Christian.

Leaders need cell group leader training, followed by an internship under a cell group leader. The training aspect is essential, but it does not fully equip a person for leading a cell group. The mentoring that comes in the form of an internship under a cell group leader provides the best preparation for leading a group.

Mobilizers mobilize other leaders. Mobilizers are cell group coaches who oversee one to three cell groups. (This is also the role of a Group of 12 leader. See Joel Comiskey's book *From 12 to 3* for more details.) The cell coach plays the role of mentor, overseer, and friend to cell group leaders that have been developed out of his or her group. Because the role of the cell coach is so crucial, the church must have a plan for equipping coaches to perform their role effectively.

Empowerers are people who feel called to become a part of pastoral oversight in a staff position. While most will not sense a calling to enter into a full-time ministry role, the church must provide training and mentoring for those who have the potential and calling to become empowerers.

Some churches have taken this equipping journey process and created a set of classes like Christianity 101, Discipleship 201, Ministry 301, and Leadership 401. While the intent and the content of these classes is usually excellent, church leaders often fall into the trap of parading people through the classes. They expect the graduates to mature but they only gain more head-knowledge about God. They expect new leaders from the 401 class, but the graduates do not seem ready. Such classes can help people know about God, about the church, about ministry, and about leadership, but they are limited in their ability to help people know God, commit to the church and embrace a life of ministry and leadership. Classes are good, but more is needed.

Cell Member Equipping

Pastors often ask, "If the cell group is not for Bible study, then where do people get their Bible training?" Excellent question. First, when cell groups apply the Scriptures to their lives on a weekly basis, they will learn a lot about the Scripture. Second, the church should develop a parallel cell member equipping process that will help train people in the Word, in personal development, in ministry skills, and in leadership.

Cell member equipping is holistic.

Most traditional training focuses on the cognitive development of the students. Cognitive training is based on that attainment of knowledge, and it focuses on principles. Such learning is dependent upon an expert who serves as a teacher. Cell member equipping is more holistic because it also addresses the other two domains: the psychomotor and the affective.

The psychomotor domain relates to training in techniques of ministry; this requires repetition and practice. Some psychomotor techniques that should be addressed include how to minister to one another in the cell group meetings, how to allow spiritual gifts to flow in the group, how to develop relationships with nonbelievers, how to lead someone to the Lord, how to lead a cell group meeting, and much more.

The affective domain relates to the formation of values. Values are not developed by listening to a talented teacher lecture on the Bible. Values are controlled by the will, not by the intellect. To change a person's will requires that a person process what he or she is learning. This processing opens the door to the work of the Holy Spirit.

Cell member equipping is progressive.

When taking college courses, each student enrolls in classes that he can handle. A freshman will take freshman chemistry, not organic chemistry or theoretical chemistry. He must learn the basics first. Cell member equipping should be the same way. New Christians need equipping in foundations of the faith. Growing Christians need help overcoming struggles with sin. Then they need to learn how to minister to one another and lead people to Christ. For over 20 years, Dr. Ralph Neighbour has taught this principle using 1 John 2:12-14, which recognizes three levels of spiritual development: children, young men, and fathers.

I write to you, dear children,
    Because your sins have been forgiven on account of his name.
I write to you, fathers,
    Because you have known him who is from the beginning.
I write to you, young men,
    Because you have overcome the evil one.
I write to you, dear children,
    Because you have known the Father.
I write to you, fathers,
    Because you have known him who is from the beginning.
I write to you, young men,
    Because you are strong,
    And the word of God lives in you,
    And you have overcome the evil one.

The children discussed here are immature believers. They know the Father but are not far along in the journey. At this first stage, the discipleship path brings new believers into an understanding of what it means to live in the Kingdom of God and raises their awareness of Satan's presence and motives on earth.

The second stage in this passage is that of Young Men. When believers have overcome the evil one, they will have won the battle over satanic strongholds and possess the Living Word within them. The discipleship path takes each believer through a mentor-led learning process and an encounter experience, providing the freedom to walk in Spirit and Truth.

The third stage in this passage refers to fathers. By virtue of the name, spiritual fathers have sired children and are described as having a long-term, deep knowledge of God. This discipleship path trains up believers to reach the lost through relational evangelism and to mentor these new believers through the journey they have already begun.[23]

Cell member equipping is uniform.

If a college student chooses to be a chemistry major, he will take the same basic chemistry courses as every other student in that major. There is one basic track. The same is true of cell member equipping. Churches develop one basic entry track. This helps people get on the same page by instilling the same language and values into every person. New Christians go through the equipping tool, course, or retreat designed for new Christians and then they progress to the next level. At that point, if specific needs must be addressed, the cell leaders and mentor can help them discover what is needed.

Cell member equipping prepares cell members for cell leader training.

The goal is to prepare every member for a ministry of leading others. While it is obvious that not every cell member will enter into leadership, the equipping process should be designed to guide people into the basic leadership training.

Cell member equipping contains common components.

The best cell group churches around the world train their cell group members in these basic elements, though they may look different in each church:

- Spiritual formation in the basics of the Christian faith.
- An Encounter event to facilitate freedom from strongholds.
- Development of Christian values and grounding in the Word of God.
- Personal ministry training (evangelism, spiritual gifts, etc.).

The Encounter event is proving to be one of the most important pieces. I have highlighted its importance in the preparation and start-up stage, but it should also be incorporated into the on-going training provided to every cell group member in the church. This event provides an opportunity for cell members to retreat from their hectic lives and allow God to touch the parts of their lives that keep them bound. Few cell members realize how past sins continue to plague their lives through guilt, condemnation, destructive habits, and poor relationships. When churches provide an opportunity for them to safely confess the sin and the pain of the past, God washes them clean and sets them free to step forward into new levels with God.

Cell member equipping uses a combination of these methods:

- One-on-one mentoring with personal study.
- Classroom teaching over a period of 4-11 weeks.
- Retreat events.

Cell member equipping is best started using materials others have created.

When starting cell groups, pastors should focus on supporting the cell groups and equipping the leaders. Some pastors have used their time instead to develop equipping materials. Writing good materials is a very time-consuming process and can prove very frustrating. Dr. Ralph Neighbour has long argued that churches need not reinvent the wheel, especially when there are tested cell member discipleship tracks available. The two most popular tracks are *Your Equipping Journey* Series by Dr. Neighbour and the *Encounter/School of Leadership* material developed by the International

Charismatic Mission. After a church has used such material for a few years, then the leadership will adapt them for its setting.

Equipping Cell Group Leaders

The advancement of cell groups directly depends upon the development of new leaders. Very few churches have a surplus of equipped leaders, and without them there is no future for expansion of cell groups. Therefore a church venturing into cell group life should remember this formula:

> Number of cell group leaders = Number of cell groups

If there are no new leaders, there are no new groups. There are churches with groups ready to burst, some with over 20 people. But they can do nothing because they don't have any leaders ready. Such an experience can be very de-energizing because cell members quit coming. They don't feel like they can talk with that many people.

Two parts comprise the equipping of cell group leaders. First, potential leaders require basic training in the technical aspects of leading a group. These topics include what a cell group is, how to facilitate a meeting, how to care for people, how to reach out to nonbelievers, and how to raise up and mentor future leaders. Cell leaders do not have the time or qualifications to train their interns or apprentices in these techniques; therefore an experienced pastor should facilitate this training through a weekly course or in a retreat setting. When a person completes cell group leader training, it is the equivalent of graduating from the eighth grade. Eighth grade graduates are usually not ready to work. They are ready to go to high school.

High school in this case is mentoring from a cell group leader, the second piece of cell leader equipping. As future leaders are mentored, they are released to do more and more ministry in the group. This process allows the future cell leaders to practice what they learned in training with someone who can back them up if they do it wrong. It also continues the affective learning process, as the cell leader serves as a spiritual mentor and guide to help the future leader enter into and discover what God is doing in his life. Cell groups depend upon relationships. Equipping cell group leaders is no different. The following illustration demonstrates the entire mentoring process.

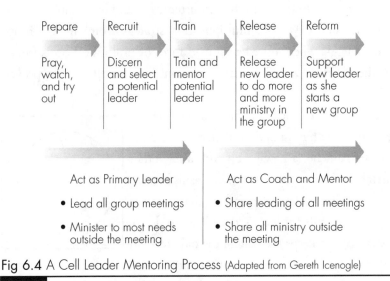

Fig **6.4** A Cell Leader Mentoring Process (Adapted from Gereth Icenogle)

When a group first starts, the cell group leader acts as the primary leader. As potential leaders go through the training, they begin to take on more and more responsibility in the leadership of the group. During this time the cell leader begins to delegate responsibility to the trainee (intern or apprentice) and then he begins to act as a coach and mentor.

Don Tillman and I developed an eight session equipping unit called *Cell Group Leader Training,* which provides flexible training options (weekly, biweekly, or retreat), adjustable content based on the needs of the future leaders and the time available, practicums for experimentation within the cell groups, and it covers the basic elements to get a future leader started.[24]

Multiplying Groups

After a leader is trained, mentored, and released to do more ministry, she can lead a new group. This is called group multiplication or reformation. There is no greater short-term win.

Group multiplication comes in many forms; there is no one right way to do it. The best approach is to listen to what God is doing in the groups and then develop a multiplication strategy from there. Groups seem to struggle when a predetermined form of multiplication is forced upon them. Here are five multiplication options that have proven effective:

New Leader Launch. In this strategy, the old leader remains with most of the cell members and the new leader launches a new group with a few other cell members. This approach is advantageous because it is vision driven. The cell members that start the new group feel called to do so, not forced to do so. This strategy also keeps the core of the old group in tact, thereby retaining a sense of community.

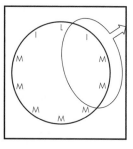

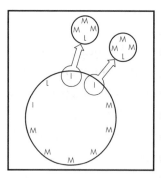

New Leader Plant. In this strategy, a new leader recruits three or four people who are not part of the original group to start a new group. This is a very exciting approach to launching groups. The greatest strength of this strategy is that it keeps the original cell group in tact, while at the same time sending out those who are ready to lead. It seems to work best after the cell group system is developed and more people understand the kind of ministry that makes cell groups work.

Old Leader Launch. In this approach, the leader of the original cell group launches a new group with two or three cell members and gives the original group to an intern, who is now a new leader. This strategy allows exceptional leaders who like to start new things to do what they like to do. It also helps a novice leader get a strong start with an established group.

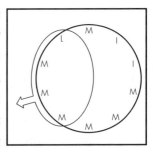

Organic Multiplication. In this approach, the new leader takes half of the group and the old leader takes half of the group. For many, this experience feels more like group "division" than group "multiplication. This is the downside. The upside for this approach is very high. It

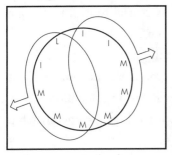

makes room in both groups for growth, whereas the other strategies only make room in one group. It provides the opportunity to start two new groups. This can be very exciting for group members because the emphasis is not on the multiplication of one group, but the birth of two new groups.

Group Reorganization. Reorganization comes in many forms. Two groups can work together to start a new group. Three groups might become five groups. A cell leader might step down for a season and a new leader step up.

Group multiplication is one of the goals of a healthy group. The key to every successful multiplication is hearing God's strategy and moving forward to do what He says to do.

Going Public with Cell Groups

As groups are developing in Stage 6, the vision team must determine when to "go public" with the cell group vision. Some churches have gone public too soon, which resulted in a waiting list because the cell group leaders were not ready. Others have waited too long, which caused the groups to lose momentum. While there are no hard and fast rules for going public, here are a few guidelines:

- A church should not go public with the groups during the first two rounds of prototyping.
- There must be enough leaders trained to handle the new cell group members from the congregation. This is crucial to avoid having a long waiting list of people wanting to join a cell group.
- After going public, the groups should still have room to reach out to nonbelievers. This means that the groups should not be filled with 13-15 church members, or they will end in stagnation.
- Church members should be prepared for cell group membership through the strategy adopted in Stage 4.

Such a public change in emphasis will likely bring out those who do not support cell groups. They will complain that their needs are not being met and that the church is forcing people into groups. There are three ways to steer clear of these complaints. First, the leadership team should not mandate cell group participation. Church members should join only if they want to do so.

Second, the leadership team should always remember that it is easier to attract flies with honey than vinegar. If good things are happening in the cell groups, then the cell leaders and members should share those things in the large-group worship. When the leadership focuses on producing good results, it is much harder to complain about what is happening.

Third, the leadership team should not dismantle old programs that people slow to change still love. For instance, one large traditional church kept its Sunday school intact while expanding the cell system. The

Sunday school ran itself, and its adherents loved it. All of the growth came through the cell groups and new members were attracted to the growth of the cells, not to the stagnation of the Sunday school. Going this route does encounter difficulty when it comes to producing enough leaders for two separate ministry approaches, however. Those in cell group leadership must keep in mind the fact that their future leaders are in the harvest. Continuing to reach into existing church leadership pools or trying to convince qualified leaders to come over to the cell group side will only produce more leadership shortages, ministry competition, and great frustration.

When the church arrives at Stage 6, it is time to focus. The cell group system must receive energy for the cell groups to move forward and gain the needed momentum. Church leaders must avoid distractions and always keep the cell groups at the top of their agenda. When they do this, the church will increase momentum and press on toward making cell groups work.

Assessing Cell Group Spirituality

When a church enters into stages 6 and 7, the pastor and the vision team are usually so close to the situation that they are unable to objectively assess the strengths and weaknesses of the groups. Those who are overly optimistic have blind spots to reality. Groups that are failing will cause the team to become overly pessimistic. Either way, it will prove very difficult to determine the root causes of the shortcomings. Therefore, assessment is necessary in stages 6 and 7. This assessment should measure two things: the corporate church factors that contribute to cell group health and growth and the cell group factors that contribute to growth. Jim Egli and Dwight Marable have collaborated to develop the most accurate assessment for cell groups available.[25]

In addition, evaluating the overall health of the church will prove quite helpful. Such an assessment will reveal other areas outside of the cell groups that are limiting the church. Many cell-based churches have used *Natural Church Development* regularly to get an accurate health update.

SECTION 6.4 Generate Momentum by Coaching and Supporting Leaders

I sat with a cell pastor over lunch. He had 20 cell groups that were stalled out. His senior pastor was frustrated with what was happening. I asked him, "How many coaches do you have?" He responded, "None. I directly work with all 20 leaders." It didn't take long to diagnose the problem.

Such a scenario is all too common. Churches train leaders and get people excited about joining the groups, but they didn't think ahead about how to support the leaders they trained. Before a church makes cell groups open to the public, the pastoral overseers and the vision team must determine how to coach their cell group leaders.

The Importance of Coaching

Jim Egli and Dwight Marable have completed extensive statistical research to determine the factors that result in group health and growth. Their findings pointed to one distinct conclusion that promotes cell group health and growth more than any other activity. They asked cell group leaders about the support they receive from a coach (supervisor) or a pastor. The statistical evidence is overwhelming. They report, "When leaders are personally encouraged by supervisors or pastors the group leaders have stronger prayer lives, the groups engage in more outreach to others, and new leaders are more actively identified and utilized."[26] The quality and quantity of coaching that a cell group leader receives directly impacts the life of the group.

Statistical evidence that proves the importance of coaching is not surprising. David Yonggi Cho concluded the same from his experience. He said, "The most important role in cell ministry is that of the section leader (coach)."[27] What was surprising is the fact that this one factor proved to be the most important factor, more important than cell leader training, more important than monthly support meetings, and more important than promoting cell groups publicly. Good coaching promotes healthy groups. Good coaching stimulates group growth. Good coaching positively impacts the prayer life of cell group leaders. Good coaching develops new cell group leaders which results in new groups. Good coaching produces cell group momentum.

When There Are No Coaches

If the positive evidence for developing coaches is not convincing, then the negative evidence is. Dave Earley, a pastor who has developed a church from one group to over 100 groups, states, "The lack of coaches is the reason why cell group experiments don't make it past the third year." Here are a few reasons why this is true.

The absence of coaches results in cell group leaders that promote unbiblical teaching. Cell leaders can teach information that is wrong. Cell group members might give advice that is unbiblical. In one group, a cell group member gave advice to another member to sue a Christian that owed him money. If the cell group leader does not have a coach with whom he can talk about the meeting, such issues will be left unaddressed.

The absence of coaches promotes patterns of group leadership that *2* **are not espoused by the pastor.** Group leaders often don't realize that what they are saying or how they are leading might be incorrect. Therefore they don't know what needs to change. One cell group was spending 45 minutes to one hour on praise reports and prayer requests every week. Without a coach, the group would have continued this pattern and would have stagnated.

The absence of coaches can result in cell group rebellion. Coaches *3* connect cell leaders to the vision of the church. Without this connection, leaders are often tempted to allow complaining about the pastors and the church to occur in meetings. Such discussions could lead to the group splitting off from the church and starting a separate house church. Because coaches are connected to the cell group leaders and visit the groups periodically, such temptations can be cut off.

The absence of coaches results in cell group leader burnout. *4* Leading a cell group is rewarding work, but it is work. Cell leaders gladly do the work of ministering to the group when they feel loved and supported. When they do not receive this love and support, they lose energy for their calling and often give up.

Coaching Structures

Churches have developed three basic structures for coaching. The first is the oldest and most common. It works this way: a successful cell group leader is promoted to the role of a coach, stepping down from the position of leading a cell group. He or she oversees from three to seven groups. In most churches, the limit is five groups.

The Groups of 12 model uses a different coaching pattern. A cell group leader becomes a coach when one of his cell group members starts a new group. The goal is to develop 12 new cell group leaders and oversee them. Even after becoming a coach, he will continue to lead a regular cell group.

The third coaching structure also allows a cell leader to continue leading a group while coaching other groups. In this structure, a leader only coaches up to three other cell group leaders that have multiplied out of his group. (This number can be higher if a person is willing and able to oversee more.)

The Role of a Coach

I stayed in the home of one coach who had been a very successful cell group leader. He was frustrated with his new role. He was unsure about his role. He felt that he was separated from the ministry of touching lives, because he was now a cell group middle manager. He felt that his role was to be an information pipeline, an enforcer of cell guidelines, and a paper-shuffler who gathers reports. Such a job holds little excitement.

The role of the coach begins with relationships, not with administration. Mike Shepherd has researched Evergreen Community Church in Burnsville, Minnesota, which has developed an exceptional coaching system. This church has grown from 120 people to 3400 people over the last 14 years. They have developed 160 groups and more than 50 coaches. Shepherd writes:

> Small group leaders are trained to lead by loving and serving their group members. Coaches are trained to lead by loving and serving their group leaders. Pastors have modeled to lead by loving and serving their coaches. There is a strong emphasis on relationally leading people verses leading them with information. They put 80 percent of their time into building relationships and 20 percent in providing information with those they lead.[28]

Len Woods, pastor of Community Life at Christ Community Church in Ruston, Louisiana, developed this acronym to explain the role of a successful coach:[29]

> **C**ultivates a personal passion for God and a contagious enthusiasm for His kingdom.
> **O**versees at least one other cell group leader. In some churches, coaches oversee up to three groups, while in others, they oversee as many as twelve groups.
> **A**dvances the church's cell group vision and strategy by regular communication and active implementation.
> **C**onsults weekly with those under his or her care, listening, advising, praying with, encouraging, training, troubleshooting, and supporting.
> **H**elps current small group leaders identify and train the next generation of leaders.

A coach is not just concerned about a cell leader's development as a leader. He is concerned about the cell leader's personal well being. He seeks to mentor his cell leaders in their personal and spiritual lives while helping them develop their leadership skills. This can only occur as trust is built through time spent together. In other words, a coach will become a friend to his cell leaders and support them in every aspect of their lives. This coaching usually happens through a combination of regular meetings, usually either biweekly or monthly, one-on-one discussions, and phone calls.

Through these relationships, the coach will help the cell group leader develop healthy leadership habits. Dave Earley has observed that growing groups have leaders that practice certain habits, while stagnant groups have leaders that leave out one or more of these habits. One of the jobs of the coach is to mentor his cell leaders in these eight habits:

1. Dream of leading a healthy, growing multiplying group.
2. Pray for group members daily.
3. Invite new people to visit the group weekly.
4. Contact group members regularly.
5. Prepare for the group meeting.
6. Mentor an apprentice leader.
7. Plan group fellowship activities.
8. Be committed to personal growth.

Earley's book, *8 Habits of Effective Small Group Leaders,* provides an excellent foundation for coaching content. A coach can help cell leaders determine which habit(s) they need to develop and then mentor them in those habits.

Finding Coaches

Some churches have appointed coaches because they have held leadership roles in the past even though they had little to no experience as a cell group leader. These leaders coach from theory, not practice. Such a pattern is self-defeating because a coach is not a professor who lectures from a classroom. A coach is a person who gets on the field and shows others how to lead. If the coach has never led, then it will prove impossible to show others how to do it.

Instead of appointing coaches, they should be discovered. The best cell coaches are found from the pool of current cell group leaders. They are those who have produced fruit as cell group leaders. Coaches should be people that other cell group leaders can respect because of who they are and what they have done. Dave and Bev Gowe were exemplary coaches at my former church. They had led groups. They knew how to pastor people. And they knew how to reach out to the unchurched.

When first starting groups, the senior pastor and/or staff pastors will serve as the first coaches. All of the pastors at Evergreen Community Church are committed to serving as coaches, even though the church has over 160 groups. They want to set the model for others. When group leaders produce fruit, they should be invited to help oversee new group leaders. For these new coaches to perform their job well, they will require some training.

Training Coaches

Training coaches begins with relationships. Coaching skills are caught from experienced coaches. At the same time, new coaches require initiation training on the practical aspects of their role. Some churches provide this training through a course which addresses topics like how to diagnose cell group problems, how to support and minister to cell group leaders, how to lead a cell leader meeting, and how to identify future cell leaders.

In addition, coaches need on-going support from their pastoral overseers. Coaches cannot serve if they are disconnected from those who pastor them. Evergreen takes their coaches away on a Friday night/Saturday retreat once every 90 days. Other churches gather the coaches together for a monthly support meeting. At such retreats or meetings, the goal should be to connect relationally, report and pray about what is happening in the groups, and restate the vision.

Ongoing Cell Leader Support Meetings

Jim Egli proposes that there are three basic pieces needed to support cell group leaders in their ministry. The first is cell leader training for new cell group leaders. The second is cell group coaching. The third is regular support meetings for current cell leaders.

Some churches gather their cell group leaders for regular support meetings only once per quarter. Other churches meet with their cell group leaders once per week. The former approach can work if the cell leaders have a very good coaching system established so that weekly support is provided by the cell coaches. The latter approach tends to work better in churches that are just starting cell groups and have fewer than twelve leaders.

The monthly meeting seems to be the most effective approach. It is frequent enough to keep the vision clearly before the leaders, but not too frequent to overwhelm them with meetings. To make a monthly meeting work, it must be designed in such a way that it meets the needs of the cell group leaders. These monthly gatherings should be designed to honor and energize the leaders who work on the front lines. Jim Egli has developed this pattern for his support meetings, which last about two and a half hours.

- *Dinner.* The church provides a meal for a nominal cost at the church building. Child care is also available.
- *Awards.* Every month he gives awards to cell leaders for things like the group leader who must drive the furthest, the group that has grown the most, the group who does the best job of filling out forms. And he always recognizes groups that multiply.
- *Announcements.* The cell pastor is the only one who is allowed to give announcements. Too many announcements will ruin the atmosphere and people will quit coming. All announcements and important events are placed on one piece of paper and the cell pastor calls attention to those that are the most important.
- *Words of Encouragement.* One of the pastors will take about 15-20 minutes to present the vision again and encourage the leaders to continue on.
- *Worship.* This turns the focus on God, lasting about 20 minutes.
- *Small groups with the coach.* For the last hour, the cell leaders will gather in small groups with their coaches. During this time, the cell

leaders explain what is happening in their groups, share personal needs, and pray for one another. Leaders express that this portion of the meeting is the most beneficial.

To make these meetings work, childcare must be provided and cell leaders must bring their interns and other future leaders. This increases participation and multiplies vision ownership. Some churches hold these meetings before a regular church service and do not include a meal.

Honoring Cell Group Leaders

Cell group leaders do the work of ministry. It is easy to take what they do for granted. The churches with the best cell groups have developed ways to honor their leaders and communicate their importance to the church. Some churches hold an annual appreciation banquet. Some hold annual retreats, all expenses paid. Some provide free gifts like books. Almost all of them recognize their leaders periodically in a worship service. While cell group leaders do not serve in order to be honored like this, it does encourage them to press on in their calling.

Coaching and supporting cell groups is about developing people. It is about helping leaders become the kind of leaders that God has called them to be. It is about helping new leaders discover their potential. It is about connecting leaders together into a leadership family. It is about praying for other leaders that God will increase them, move through them, and bless them. Such a ministry is not only exciting, but powerful.

Levers

Develop a cell member discipleship or equipping track.
Key Resources:
—*Leadership Explosion* by Joel Comiskey
—*Your Equipping Journey* by Ralph W. Neighbour, Jr.
—*Journey Guide* series of booklets

Develop an atmosphere of prayer.

Promote "one another" life outside of the group.
Key Resources:
—*The Safest Place on Earth* by Larry Crabb
—*The Connecting Church* by Randy Frazee

Stimulate relational evangelism within the groups.
Key Resources:
—*Relating Jesus* by Jim Egli
—*Touching Hearts* by Ralph W. Neighbour, Jr.

Hold a cell group member strategic planning workshop so that entire groups can develop a plan and take ownership for the life of the group.
Key Resource:
—*Upward, Inward, Outward, Forward* by Jim Egli

Develop new cell group leader training.
Key Resources:
—*Cell Group Leader Training* by Scott Boren and Don Tillman
—*How to Lead a Great Cell Group Meeting* by Joel Comiskey
—*8 Habits of Effective Small Group Leaders* by Dave Earley
—*Leading from the Heart* by Michael Mack

Develop cell group coaches.
  Key Resources:
    —*How to be a GREAT Cell Group* Coach by Joel Comiskey

    —*8 Habits of Effective Small Group Leaders* by Dave Earley

Develop energizing on-going support meetings for the cell group leaders.

Convert old small groups into cell groups.

Assess the strengths and weaknesses of the cell groups that have been developed.
  Key Resource:
    —*Cell Group Assessment* available at <www.missions.com>.

Vision Team Questions

1. How have the groups already experienced short-term wins?
2. What are some ways to celebrate these short-term wins?
3. What is the difference between a weekly cell group meeting and spiritual cell group community?
4. How can the team and/or the pastoral staff promote a greater Upward movement in prayer?
5. How can the team and/or pastoral staff stimulate Inward life through body life ministry?
6. How can the team and/or pastoral staff help groups develop their Outward movement through relational evangelism?
7. Why is it important to develop a discipleship or equipping track for people that will walk them from new believers to leaders?
8. What role does one-on-one mentoring play in such a process?
9. Why is the development of new leaders so important?
10. What means will be used to train and mentor new leaders?
11. Why is coaching cell group leaders so vital to cell group life?
12. How are leaders being coached at this point? What needs to be done to improve?
13. What kind of on-going support meetings are provided at this point? How should these be improved?

STAGE 7
Establish
the Hidden Systems
that Support Cells

A ship on the water is recognized by its visible trappings: the hull, the mast, the sails, etc. Yet beneath this visible exterior are many hidden mechanisms that make the ship work. Likewise, a church will have its visible exterior and its hidden support systems. When a church starts sailing toward the cell group destination, the focus lies on developing dynamic life in the cell groups. To advance these groups to the next stage of development, it is time to rethink the hidden support systems and adapt them to line up with the cell group vision.

In Stage 7, it is time to answer the question, "How do we establish cell groups as the base of the church?" In other words, this is the period when the church will look to restructure the church organization to support the cell groups properly. Churches that choose not to move into Stage 7, might continue developing groups, but they will not see the fruit that churches realize when they embrace the changes advised in Stage 7.

• "Establish Critical Mass" (Section 7.1). This section defines cell group critical mass and then identifies the components that must be developed for a church to reach critical mass. This section also addresses options for ways a cell-based church can carry out non-cell ministry functions without sapping energy from the cell groups.

• "Establish Pastoral Oversight" (Section 7.2). In order to develop an expanding network of cell groups, a church must staff the organization to provide the mentoring and pastoral support that cell leaders and cell members require. The role of the senior pastor is discussed and the role of the cell pastor is defined around a relational model rather than an administrative model. Finally, this section addresses how to cellularize the administration to support the cells.

• "Establish a Cell Group System Including Children" (Section 7.3). Everywhere I teach a conference, people ask questions about how to minister to the children in cell groups. There are many different approaches that churches have taken. This section introduces the best of them.

SECTION 7.1 Establish
a Critical Mass

Before a church can expand cells throughout the entire church or into different segments of society, it must develop a core of people who carry with them a deep conviction about the life in cell groups and who practice the kind of life that makes the cell groups work.

Bill Beckham has called this experience critical mass. The first critical mass was reached in the Jerusalem church of Acts 2. Beckham writes: "The 120 in the upper room were a critical mass because the presence of Christ came upon them, followed by His power, which resulted in His purpose as they streamed into the streets to witness of Christ. The Church continues to be birthed in the same way today."[1]

Critical mass in physics occurs at the point when there is a minimum amount of fissionable material present to produce a chain reaction. At critical mass, all of the elements are in place to create a self-sustaining multiplication of forces without help from the outside. Critical mass can also be applied to organizations. A business reaches critical mass when the financial, managerial, marketing, accounting, and personnel systems all line up under a clear business plan and thereby create self-sustaining growth without dependence upon outside forces.

One business change consultant stated, "If a level of critical mass is not achieved, you are in danger of building a house of cards."[2] Cell groups reach a point of critical mass when all of the elements are in place within the system to produce new cell groups in a natural and unforced way. When a church reaches cell group critical mass, an internal propulsion moves the groups forward, as opposed to the constant struggle early on to get groups going. Many churches have lots of groups—some with 50 or more—but they have yet to reach critical mass. There are three parts to cell group critical mass that the church leadership must assess as they move forward: conviction, subsystems, and spirituality.

Critical Mass Conviction

Conviction is based on vision. Vision stems from the heart of God. Without a word from God, church leaders will invariably compromise the vision because the cost to change will prove too high. Cell group critical mass is a result of a cell group vision that has captured the hearts of the church leaders to the point that they "must" do cell groups. Without this "must," other, potentially more glamorous ministries will take precedence over the groups.

But critical mass does not occur simply because the leaders are convinced that the church must have cell groups. A church reaches critical mass when enough people begin to operate under the vision of cells, practice cell techniques with competence, and walk in the Spirit of unity.

In many churches, getting the people to operate under one vision is quite a shift. Traditionally, they have operated with different visions and different techniques for doing ministry. Each person does what is right in his or her own eyes. This means that church leaders must disseminate the cell group vision to the point that enough people are internally motivated to live out the cell vision and propel it forward.

Each one does what is right in his own eyes

Clear vision is established, but people do not understand how to make it work

Critical Mass

Enough people are convinced and understand the technicalities of the vision and are walking in unity

Fig 7.1 Reaching Critical Mass

Critical mass does not require that every person walk in the direction of the vision, as the arrow on the right illustrates. It requires just enough people, including the key influencers of the church, to move the church in the right direction.

Critical Mass Sub-systems

Conviction of the cell vision is not enough. "Conviction is the thing that mobilizes [people], gets them to commit to a new context or new vision, but such catalytic energy is readily dissipated if leaders fail to channel it by building the right operational and management infrastructure [sub-systems], getting people to make decisions and not just talk about it, and then rousing [them] to operate at pace, with a sense of urgency—most times in complete rejection of the way [they] currently operate."[3]

Conviction must be supported by the proper sub-systems for the groups to work. These sub-systems are often unseen and therefore easy to ignore. Cell groups will not grow and multiply without the necessary support systems, just as ships cannot move along the ocean without the hundreds of unseen parts that hold them together and allow the sails to catch the wind. Stage 1 introduced the macro view of the cell based model, which illustrates how the major components of the system work together. But at this point, it is necessary to understand the sub-systems from a more detailed point of view. In order to reach critical mass, all of the sub-systems must be in place.

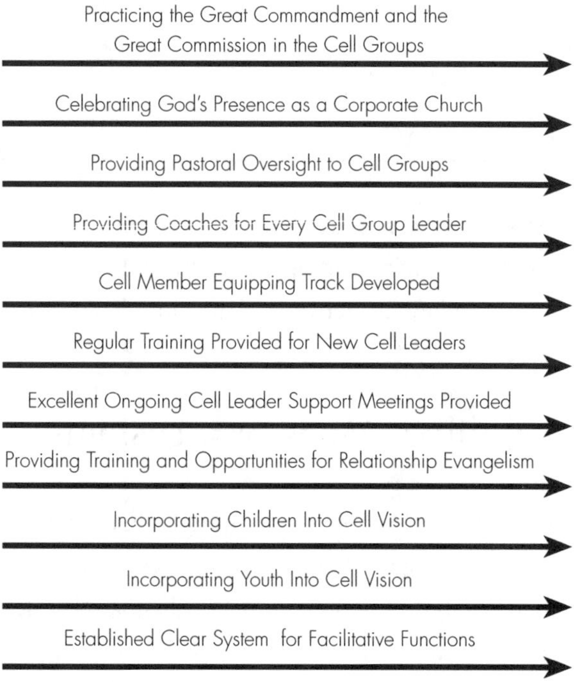

Practicing the Great Commandment and the
Great Commission in the Cell Groups
⟶

Celebrating God's Presence as a Corporate Church
⟶

Providing Pastoral Oversight to Cell Groups
⟶

Providing Coaches for Every Cell Group Leader
⟶

Cell Member Equipping Track Developed
⟶

Regular Training Provided for New Cell Leaders
⟶

Excellent On-going Cell Leader Support Meetings Provided
⟶

Providing Training and Opportunities for Relationship Evangelism
⟶

Incorporating Children Into Cell Vision
⟶

Incorporating Youth Into Cell Vision
⟶

Established Clear System for Facilitative Functions
⟶

Fig 7.2 Parallel Sub-systems

The most basic component is the practices of the cell groups themselves. These cell groups must not only believe in the cell group vision, but also they must be living out the values of Upward, Inward, Outward, and Forward. They must be doing the things that make cell groups work. Ten to 12 groups that are practicing UIOF are required to produce this component of critical mass.

Cell groups flourish when the church experiences the presence of God in corporate worship services. Without His presence moving and touching people in the larger group, all of the pressure lies on cell group leaders to facilitate the celebration of God's presence. Inspiring messages and celebrative worship invigorate groups for ministry.

The third component is group oversight. Cell groups that operate without pastoral care and oversight will flounder. Most of Section 7.2 is dedicated to this issue.

Fourth, churches must develop a working coaching system. Every cell leader must have a coach, the coaches must understand their job definition, and the church must develop a way to raise up new coaches.

The fifth component was addressed in Sections 6.2 and 6.3: equipping cell members and training new leaders. Churches with growing cell group systems have developed clear tracks for equipping every cell member for ministry. This takes the pressure off of the cell leaders to "teach" the cell members everything about the Christian faith.

The sixth component is evangelism. Because evangelism is one of the core elements of an effective cell group, it is not enough to populate groups with churched people. When this occurs, cell groups stagnate. Cell members need training in relational evangelism. Cell leaders need ideas for facilitating group evangelism. And the church should provide creative church-wide harvest events to which cell members can bring their lost friends.

Section 7.3 addresses the need to incorporate children into the cell vision. Section 5.2 provided basic instruction for starting youth cell groups. In order to reach critical mass, someone will need to lead the charge for both children and youth cell groups.

Facilitative Functions

Facilitative functions are the necessary elements of church life that do not directly fit into the ministry of cell groups. They include the organization of church-wide prayer events, oversight of corporate evangelism thrusts, provision of corporate children's ministry, care of the children in the nursery, and service as greeters or ushers during celebration. All of these functions must be addressed. When they are not, the cell groups will pay for it because the cell leaders will end up doing all of the work while the cell members stand by and watch, "receiving" ministry as they always have. There are three approaches to address these functions:

Small groups that focus on these functions. The "task group" strategy has been adopted by many churches in North America. Some churches have created usher groups, parking lot attendant groups, worship team groups, even children's worker groups. Such an approach is a step in the right direction, but there is one serious risk. In most groups of this type, the task becomes the focus. Although the group members might pray for one another 10 minutes before they usher, they lack a place to edify one another, hold one another accountable, reach out to nonbelievers, and raise up new leaders. Some churches believe that the groups can do these things without meeting separately. Research has yet to prove that this kind of group produces the same results as a holistic cell group. On the other hand, it is possible to create task groups that also operate as cell groups. They should meet once each week to seek God together, just like every other group. They should seek to reach out to nonbelievers, develop community, and raise up new leaders, as do all other groups. The tasks they are assigned to do must be done outside of the regular meeting.

Some churches have also developed worship cell groups. The cell group meetings are separate from the worship practices. These groups seek to reach out to nonbelievers and multiply just like other groups.

Cells that rotate responsibility. With this strategy, cell groups take on the different responsibilities of the corporate church on a rotating basis. A cell group might greet one Sunday in January, park cars one Sunday in February, serve in the nursery one Sunday in March, etc. In other words, the cell groups do everything. This system is advantageous in its simplicity. It tends to work very well when the church is small, although it can wear out a group when there are fewer than 10 groups in a church. As the church gets larger, the cells can continue to rotate some of these responsibilities— some larger churches use cell groups to minister at the altar during large group worship. However, some of these tasks, such as service in the nursery, require people who have the gifts and callings to perform them. Therefore, the rotation of cell groups sometimes asks people to do things that they don't do well or lack passion to do.

Short-term teams composed of cell group members. This strategy provides opportunities for cell members to serve the larger body within areas of their interests and giftings. For instance, some people will prove to be better greeters than others because they like to meet new people. Some people enjoy working in the nursery. Others like setting up the facilities for worship.

This strategy requires a leader for each support function, i.e. a nursery coordinator, usher coordinator, etc. This leader divides the function into four segments (Nursery: 1st Sunday, 2nd Sunday, 3rd Sunday, 4th Sunday). An individual with a spiritual gifting and interest in that area of service is recruited to serve each segment. No one can be a team member unless he or she participates in a cell group. Those who are recruited to serve repeat the recruitment pattern by dividing their assigned functions into segments (1st Sunday Nursery: Bed Babies, Toddlers, Younger Children, Older Children).

Facilitative functions are necessary for a church to operate properly. There are a few guidelines that will help a team develop these functions in a healthy way. First, these supportive functions should never compete with life in the cell groups. They are there to support the ministry, not become the only ministry. Second, participation in the cell and celebration is a prerequisite for serving in these functions. Ministry to the team members is just as important as the service they provide on these teams. Third, serving in these functions is a great way to help people grow in their leadership responsibilities before they enter into cell leadership training. When people prove faithful in these areas of service, they are opening doors to potential leadership opportunities. Fourth, the church leadership should reevaluate these functions on a regular basis to determine if a need remains. It is crucial to protect the system from bureaucracy that leads to more and more administration just to keep the system going. Finally, leaders of the various functions should always be looking for people they can train to take their place so that they can advance into new areas of ministry.

Critical Mass Spirituality

Conviction provides the motivation for developing cell groups. The infrastructure provides the necessary support for the groups. When churches stop at conviction and infrastructure, they miss the hidden dynamics that pull the people together into a unified body of believers. It is possible to "do" cell groups with all of the proper mechanical components of the infrastructure in place but never realize the dynamics of Holy Spirit life that produces critical mass. In other words, biblical structure without a biblical flow of God's Spirit results in a very dead structure.

If the Upper Room was the place of critical mass for the Jerusalem church, then we must seek to understand what happened in the Upper Room if the churches today want to enter the same experience. The issue at stake in Acts 2 is much more than numbers, although 120 people is a large enough group to contain all the necessary elements of critical mass.

The question is: what did they practice in that Upper Room in order to prepare themselves for critical mass?

> **Prayer.** "They all joined together constantly in prayer,…" The disciples and others felt an urgency to find out what God was doing. They did not return to their former vocations as they did after Christ's crucifixion. They entered the vocation of prayer.

> **Unity.** "They were all together in one place." The church that lacks unity is not a church prepared for the Holy Spirit. He does not pour Himself into selfish people who do not want to serve others. The disciples and other key leaders had been through three and a half years of humility training so that they could walk in unity with other believers.

> **Obedience.** Jesus told them, "Do not leave Jerusalem, but wait for the gift my Father promised." Luke does not record any resistance to Jesus' instruction. The core of the early church was ready to do what Jesus said, no matter how strange it might sound. This obedience resulted in evangelism, more evangelism than could have been possible if they had not obeyed.

> **Order.** The leaders led. The disciples led the prayer. Peter, not an anonymous follower, led the process of choosing a twelfth disciple. The new leader, Matthias, was chosen by leadership, not by a vote.

Prayer relates to the value of Upward, Unity relates to Inward, Obedience relates to Outward, and Order relates to Forward. When these four spiritual dynamics were in place with the 120 people in the Upper Room, the church reached critical mass.

Producing Critical Mass Spirituality

Most pastors know how to create critical mass conviction and critical mass infrastructure: cast the vision, organize the vision, implement the vision. But critical mass spirituality is another thing altogether. It is impossible to organize the Holy Spirit to change people. It is like trying to organize the wind (John 3:8). The Spirit of God will not be controlled that way. In addition, the human spirit must receive what God does; a leader cannot force-feed God into people. How then does a pastor lead people into critical mass spirituality?

For the answer to this question, I must return to a topic that has been addressed already in this book. Many readers have already taken the point to heart. To those readers, please forgive the repetition. Many other readers have given mental assent to the point, but have yet to see how crucial it is to the entire cell group system.

To understand how to produce critical mass spirituality, Paul's words in Philippians 3:17 prove helpful, "Join with others in following my example, brothers, and take note of those who live according to the pattern we gave you." Paul developed a theology of ministry that seems rather radical to many and even prideful to some. In 1 Corinthians 11:1, he said, "Follow me as I follow Christ." His theology of ministry was founded upon the principle "I will show you how to live in Christ." He knew that his words were pointless if his life did not set the standard.

Paul's theology of ministry was not unique. Jesus Himself established this ministry pattern. Jesus did not set his disciples and other followers in a classroom and explain to them the meaning of the Kingdom of God. Instead, He demonstrated the Kingdom of God and invited them to follow Him into that same life. Jesus spent His energy on showing people how to live, revealing the action of true prayer, and divulging the reality of obedience to God. Jesus knew that the Kingdom of God would be caught as people were infected with the life that He shared. Jim Egli puts it this way:

Seldom do we see Jesus by himself in the Gospels. When he preached, healed, taught, debated opponents, or delivered demoniacs, he was almost always accompanied by his disciples. In this way, Jesus was constantly modeling ministry skills and teaching by demonstration. The disciples learned by observation and could later ask Jesus follow-up questions during more relaxed moments.[4]

Moses passed on to Joshua what he received from God. Eli invested in Samuel. Elisha received a "double portion" following Elijah. The Word of God seems to place a high emphasis upon passing spiritual blessings from one generation to the next. The stories of the Patriarchs make this especially clear. The blessing was passed from father to son, Abraham to Isaac, Isaac to Jacob, Jacob to Manasseh and Ephraim. The blessings of God flow from one generation to another.

Over 20 years ago, Robert Coleman wrote *The Master Plan of Evangelism*, a book that analyzes how Jesus' ministry developed into critical mass and eventually expanded all over the world. In the epilogue, Coleman states,

> We should not expect a great number to begin with, nor should we desire it. The best work is always done with a few. Better to give a year or so to one or two people who learn what it means to conquer for Christ than to spend a lifetime with a congregation just keeping the program going.[5]

Coleman's book has sold over two million copies. He is respected all over the world. But 20 years later, most pastors have yet to practice what Coleman encourages, and as a result, most pastors find themselves running programs without any long-term success.

Paul wrote "Even though you have ten thousand guardians in Christ, you do not have many fathers, for in Christ Jesus I became your father through the gospel" (1 Corinthians 5:15). The Greek word for "guardian" refers to a trusted slave who would walk a child to and from school and oversee his or her conduct.[6] Guardians in Christ are many, and they are needed because they provide guidance and instruction. But spiritual fathers are few, because few will expend the energy, time, and resources to impart life into another person.

Larry Kreider lists seven things spiritual parents do in his excellent book *The Cry for Spiritual Fathers and Mothers*.

Parents have been with Jesus. They know the source of their spiritual strength. They do not wait for people to come to them for parenting. They seek God for those whom they should parent. Then they act upon what God has said.

Parents model parenthood. Parenting happens in real life. It does not happen in a classroom or in Sunday services. It occurs in the daily problems and victories, trials and joys of family, work, play, and ministry.

Parents set an example. Sons imitate fathers. Daughters imitate mothers. Spiritual parents reproduce a pattern of life in Christ for others to follow.

Parents give children a sense of significance. Spiritual parents pass down spiritual blessings. Sons and daughters long for blessing from their parents more than anything else. Spiritual parents see value in their sons or daughters as God sees their value, even when the evidence might contradict it.

Parents see the potential. Spiritual parents envision what their sons and daughters can become, even when the children do not yet see it. Parents provide hope and sow into that hope, helping their children become what God intends them to be.

Parents are available. Spiritual parenting is an unselfish act. It takes time, sometimes lots of it. It takes listening, sometimes to hard things. It takes energy, sometimes at the expense of personal pleasure.

Parents impart. They intentionally pass on what God has given them. They seek to multiply themselves in their sons and daughters. They do not hold on to ministry in fear that their own significance will diminish if someone else proves competent in ministry.

Critical mass spirituality begins at the top, just as it did with Jesus. The flow of God's anointing flows down from leadership onto those who are being led. It never flows up. In order to reach critical mass, the people in the 10-15 cell groups need to be fathered or mothered into the dynamics of Prayer, Unity, Obedience, and Order. Cell group leaders cannot provide this to their cell members unless they receive it first from their leader, the pastor.

SECTION 7.2 Establish Pastoral Oversight

On a ship, a captain must set up oversight systems to make sure that everyone does his or her job. The larger the ship, the more formal the oversight. A captain knows that his crew needs accountability, direction, encouragement, and vision to stay the course. Likewise, spiritual mothering and fathering will not occur in the church unless there is a system that facilitates it. There must be clear interconnectivity between pastors and leaders in order for the front-line cell groups to work properly.

Traditional Pastoral Oversight

In his helpful book *Staff Your Church for Growth*, Gary MacIntosh states his conclusions after 50 years of research: "Declining churches order their priorities in this manner: facilities, programs, and staff. On the other hand, growing churches order their priorities in this manner: staff, programs, facilities."[7] In the traditional church, staff is added according to specialized tasks that must be accomplished. McIntosh lists six task-oriented roles that churches use to organize staff: Finding People, Keeping People, Celebrating with People, Overseeing People, and Caring for People.

As a church grows, the pastor will seek to add an associate pastor to oversee one of these six areas. Wise pastors hire people who possess strengths that complement their weaknesses. For instance, if the pastor is strong at finding people, he might hire someone who is good at overseeing people. Or if he is strong in celebrating with people, he might hire someone who is strong in educating people.

The larger a church grows, the more staff it will need to oversee church members. Usually, larger churches will add staff who specialize in overseeing particular relational groupings within the church, such as a children's pastor, a youth pastor, and an adult education pastor. McIntosh illustrates it this way:

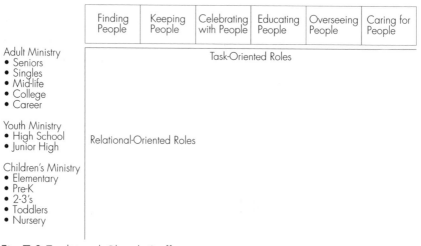

Fig 7.3 Traditional Church Staffing

In this system, relational-oriented roles are combined with task roles, as an adult education pastor might also play the role of "finding people," or a children's minister might focus on "educating people."

Research performed on churches organized around the above roles has found that churches usually hire one staff pastor for every 150 members. Based on this ratio, a staff pastor is responsible for the spiritual oversight of 150 people. While there are volunteer leaders within those 150 people, the staff pastor is expected to meet the spiritual needs of these members, administrate the programs that people participate in, and make sure that they are satisfied.

As a result, many staff pastors feel like Moses must have felt when the people "stood around him from morning till evening" and he was responsible for ministering to all of them and trying to meet their needs. Moses' father-in-law, Jethro, told him, "What you are doing is not good. You and these people who come to you will only wear yourselves out. The work is too heavy for you; you cannot handle it alone" (Exodus 18:13-18).

Four levels of leadership

Jethro gave some practical advice to Moses that day: "But select capable men from all the people—men who fear God, trustworthy men who hate dishonest gain—and appoint them as officials over thousands, hundreds, fifties and tens" (Exodus 18:21). Jethro was a wise man because he realized that one person cannot minister properly to a large group of people; sub-groupings are necessary.

Cell group oversight systems have been based upon Jethro's instructions since the days that Pastor Yonggi Cho began his first cell groups. From this, two basic oversight systems have developed. The first is called the 5x5 system, a term coined by Dr. Ralph Neighbour. In this system, a cell coach oversees up to five cell groups. A cell pastor oversees up to five cell coaches (or up to 25 cell groups). In larger churches, a district pastor oversees up to five staff pastors (or 125 groups). While the numbers do not exactly correspond with those Jethro lined out, the four basic levels are the same.

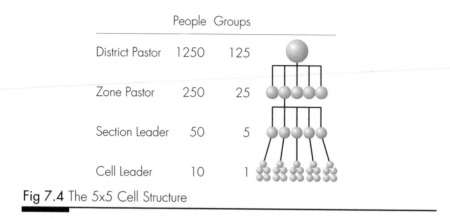

	People	Groups
District Pastor	1250	125
Zone Pastor	250	25
Section Leader	50	5
Cell Leader	10	1

Fig 7.4 The 5x5 Cell Structure

The second oversight system is called Groups of 12. This system has the same four basic levels of oversight, but the numbers differ. A G-12 leader plays the same role as a cell coach but oversees up to 12 group leaders. Every G-12 leader is a member of a group led by someone who oversees him or her. This overseer has the same role as the cell pastor in the 5x5, he just oversees up to 144 groups. In very large G-12 churches, there are key leaders who oversee top-level Groups of 12 and thus oversee networks of over 1000 groups.

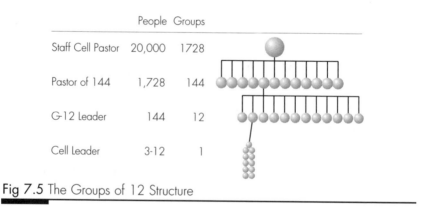

	People	Groups
Staff Cell Pastor	20,000	1728
Pastor of 144	1,728	144
G-12 Leader	144	12
Cell Leader	3-12	1

Fig 7.5 The Groups of 12 Structure

The first system is often called the Jethro model and the second the Jesus model. Some have argued that the Jethro model is an Old

Testament model that belongs to the old covenant, and that Jesus initiated a new model with the new covenant. Such an argument lacks the support of the New Testament. The New Testament highlights the fact that the new covenant replaces the old covenant, but it does not make any reference to a new structure replacing an old structure. What exists instead is a biblical principle of levels of leadership that pervade both the Old and New Testaments.

Even Jesus developed leaders on four distinct levels. First he ministered to the 12 disciples, then he trained the 72 to prepare them for ministry. The 120 were developed for leadership as they waited upon the Holy Spirit in the Upper Room. Finally, the church operated as a unit in the thousands after the day of Pentecost.

It is quite easy for church leaders to fixate upon specific models of cell oversight, trying to find a magical formula for growth. Large model churches have developed elaborate systems of oversight that look very attractive to much smaller churches. Small churches seeking to adopt elaborate structures are like small sail boats compared to aircraft carriers. Both are ships and operate according to the same principles, but the aircraft carrier is much more complex because of its size. Smaller churches do not need to develop a system to oversee 1000 cell groups. They just need to understand the four roles of leadership that underlie all effective oversight systems. These roles are vision and direction, cell pastoring, cell coaching, and cell leadership.[8]

	ROLE	TITLE	QUALIFICATIONS
	Vision Direction	Senior Leader & Team	Elder
	Cell Pastoring	Pastoral Overseer	1 Timothy 3:1-7
	Cell Coaching	Cell Coach	Deacon
	Cell Implementation	Cell Leader	1 Timothy 3:8-13

Fig 7.6 Four Roles of Leadership

When a church first starts groups, the senior pastor might perform all four of these roles. But as the church develops five to twelve groups, other coaches are necessary. As the number of groups grows from 12 to 25 in number, it is time to start thinking about developing someone who can operate as a cell pastor. The senior pastor should continue to focus his energy on the role of vision and direction no matter what the church's size.

G-12.3

Joel Comiskey has applied these roles to develop a flexible and organic model that draws from the best of the Groups of 12 Model and the 5x5. He calls it the G-12.3. One of the keys to this model is the G-12 principle that a cell leader can coach other cell leaders that are birthed out of his or her group. This makes sense because the old cell leader has a relationship with the new cell leader. Because of this relational history, the coaching is less mechanical and more relational.

Pastors have experimented and found that effective cell leaders like to remain in the fray by leading a cell group. Joel Comiskey has found that an experienced cell leader can also coach up to three groups as a volunteer. Staff pastors, on the other hand, can oversee up to twelve. Such a system might look like this:

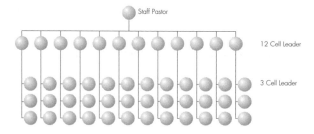

A senior pastor or staff pastor might start the first group and then serve as the cell coach for up to 12 cell group leaders. As these cell group leaders start multiplying groups, the new leaders can either become part of the pastor's Group of 12 or one of the cell leader's Groups of 3. Such a system allows for 51 cell groups under a staff pastor. As a cell leader advances in his leadership abilities, he might join the staff and develop his own Group of 12.

Church Visionary Role

Billy Joe Daugherty is the pastor of the 13,000-member Victory Christian Center in Tulsa, Oklahoma. His vision has not only stimulated the development of hundreds of groups, but also a school, a ministry training center, a network of churches, and missionaries around the world. The vision keeps expanding. Before meeting Pastor Daugherty I had met a few pastors of large churches; most were less than inviting. To be honest, I expected my experience with Pastor Daugherty to be much the same. I should learn not to make such assumptions, because he proved to be one of the most down to earth, welcoming, and personable leaders I have ever met. Pastor Daugherty assumed leadership of this church when it had only 300 people attending. God has developed a man with a vision and a passion for relationships with God and with man. Visionaries like Pastor Daugherty possess a few common traits.

Visionaries shepherd their flocks.

The biblical word picture used most often by the Bible for leading God's people is shepherding. Paul instructed the elders at Ephesus, "Keep watch over yourselves and all the flock of which the Holy Spirit has made you overseers. Be shepherds of the church of God, which he bought with his own blood" (Acts: 20:28).

Sadly, many pastors have not allowed God to cultivate a shepherd's heart in them. Some pastors adopt the cell group vision because they want to make their churches grow larger. Others pressure their cell group leaders to grow their groups so they can meet certain goals. Still others are not looking to give up their lives for the sheep as much as they are looking for fame, a book contract, or even a job at a larger church down the road. Such things quench the Spirit's work of shepherding God's people.

When I met Pastor Daugherty, I was impressed by his warmth and hospitality. But the nature of his pastor's heart was recognized when I met some of the other pastors on his staff. Victory's key cell group champions, Jerry and Lynn Popenhagen, along with the other cell pastors, exhibit the same spirit. The thing that made Pastor Daugherty and his staff attractive to me was the fact that they knew how to serve as shepherds of the flock. God had cultivated the heart of a shepherd in Pastor Daugherty and he had passed it to others around him.

A pastor of a traditional church that has developed cell groups confessed that the cell groups have put him in touch with his people. He has to deal with the hard issues that people face, such as a man dying of cancer who doesn't yet know the Lord.

Some people have argued that a pastor cannot serve as a visionary and as a shepherd, because they have identified a shepherd as one who pastors a small church that is going nowhere. Such people have advocated a shift away from a shepherding model to a CEO model of pastoring. They argue that pastors are poor leaders and do not have the skills to manage the church and advance its cause. These writers do have a point, because most pastors lack basic leadership and managerial skills, but gaining such skills does not require a total abandonment of the shepherd model. Good shepherds are visionaries who see where God wants to lead the sheep. Good shepherds develop good leadership skills so that they can lead the sheep according to the vision. Good leaders are not necessarily good shepherds. Glenn Wagner in his book *Escape from Church, Inc.* says, "Good shepherds must be leaders, but leadership is not the whole package."[9]

Visionaries work from solid foundations.

I heard a speaker at one cell conference say, "If you want to be a pastor, don't study theology; study business management. Theology won't give you the skills to lead a church." I was flabbergasted. If pastors are not theologically grounded, then how do they know their vision is God's vision? I know a lot of good leaders from the business world that I do not want leading any churches.

At the same time, I can see the speaker's point. Theology has been divorced from the practical issues of leading a church to the point that theological discussions are rendered useless. As a result, pastors often find their shelves full of church growth books that seem disconnected from the systematic theologies and the Bible commentaries.

This divide between theology and practical ministry has led many pastors to focus on the cell group structure and miss the theological heart that forms the foundation for the structure. This often results in pastors preaching and promoting the new cell group structure from the pulpit without any clear understanding of the biblical values that are required to make cell groups work. The pastors who have made cell groups work the best are the ones who have built their groups on strong theological foundations, not just because groups grow churches.

It is not enough for pastors to know the answers to the "how" questions. The "why" questions reveal the foundation for cell groups that ultimately make them work. Colonial Hills Baptist Church in Southaven, Mississippi is a perfect example of this. Its pastor was an early adopter of the cell group strategy, but he did not focus the church's values upon the cell group structure; he set his sights on the biblical value of community. As a result, when church members found that the structure was not quite working, the pastoral staff was able to adapt it to enhance the biblical value of community development. Answers to the "why" questions give a visionary leader the creativity to adjust the structure to the unique needs of his church and culture. Answers to the "why" questions provide a wealth of knowledge to train people in the biblical values that will prepare people for effective group life.

Visionaries cultivate a life in God.

David Yonggi Cho of Yoido Full Gospel Church spends three hours each day in prayer. Pastors often confess that they are so busy with ministry that they don't have time to pray. Pastor Cho's response to such pastors is, "The more work you have to do the more you need to pray." He believes that "ministry unto the Lord must come ahead of ministry unto the people."

If the visionary is not living in intimacy before God, neither will the people. What he receives from God is what he will pass down to others. One pastor shared, "Now that we have developed cell groups, my counseling load is almost zero. Problems are taken care of before they get so big that they need me." Pastors like this have time to seek the Lord and hear His vision for the church.

Visionaries set models for others.

I asked Dennis Wadley, pastor of Community Covenant Church in Santa Barbara, California, how leading a cell group church is different from leading a traditional church. He responded, "My role is to model the life of a healthy believer, not to be so busy that I burn out. I am to be a full cup that has something to share." Wadley and other effective visionary pastors have realized that their first calling is to be the kind of person that they want the people of their churches to be. To be a good model, there are a couple of shifts that some pastors should consider making.

First, some pastors need to learn to listen. Pastors are trained to tell people what to think because they know more about the Bible than church members. Yet when this approach is imported into cell group leadership, cell members are not allowed to process their thoughts in community. Many pastors turn cell lessons into mini-sermons. They arrive halfway through a cell meeting and assume leadership, even though the cell leader was leading well before they walked in. Such a model communicates to people that they cannot become cell group leaders until they are able to expound like the pastor can. The skills of facilitation and listening do not come easily to those who know the right answers, but they are crucial to establishing a model that others can follow.

Second, pastors need to develop trust so that they can be transparent. Most pastors do not trust the people in their churches well enough to share their lives with them. For many, this lack of trust is justified. Pastors have been fired because they took a stand for a godly value like fighting against racism. Elders have used secrets shared by the pastor to control him or even to get him fired. As a result, pastors often refrain from being transparent so that others will have less ammunition to use against them. Pastors feel trapped between the expectations of perfection and the realities of their struggles.

The experience of cell groups without transparency is like a sandwich with no lunchmeat. Cell group leaders and members will follow the model set by their pastors. My father-in-law is my pastor. Many times he has stood before us and shared his struggles. He has shared past failures. He knows how to laugh at himself. Because of this, hurting people know that they do not need to be perfect. They discover that they can share their struggles in their cell groups and there receive healing.

Note to pastors: There are some things that will cause harm when they are shared with a congregation, because the people are not mature enough to handle the issues their pastor is struggling with. Doug Dorman, a pastor in Savannah, Georgia learned this the hard way. While he was learning about transparency, he began to share honestly with his congregation. He discovered that some of the things a pastor deals with are overwhelming to those he serves. Therefore he has learned to "share up" with other pastors or elders who have the maturity to handle the issues he encounters as a leader.

Third, pastors set the model for an ordered home. If the pastor's marriage is suffering because he is consumed with his work at church, he cannot expect the members of his church to walk in marital health. When churches enter into cell group life, they enter into spiritual warfare. If pastors ignore their families for the sake of the ministry, the enemy will see the weaknesses and try to pull the rug out from under what they are doing.

Visionaries adjust as the cell groups expand.

When starting cell groups, the visionary will most likely perform all four leadership roles: vision and direction, cell pastoring, cell coaching, and cell implementation. As the church develops more and more groups, the senior pastor will shift from being the person who is carrying the vision and doing almost everything else to training and releasing others to carry out the vision. The first-hand experience in the various roles will prove invaluable, because the senior pastor can say with integrity, "I've been there."

Even though others assume the roles below vision and direction, the senior pastor should not step back from cell groups and let the system run itself. The best way to keep the focus on cell groups is for the senior visionary to continue leading an open cell group even after the groups are up and going. If the senior pastor is not willing to lead, or at least participate in, a cell group, church members will realize that cell groups are not a long-term priority.

Cell Pastor's Role

Few people have sought to understand the role of a cell pastor or staff pastor the way Karen Hurston has. She has been fascinated by the stark differences she observed between the job of a staff pastor at Yoido Full Gospel Church and the job of most staff pastors in American churches. Because she grew up as a member of YFGC in Korea, where her father served as a missionary and early mentor to Pastor Yonggi Cho, Karen has a unique understanding of how this church operates.

Karen states that the cell groups are effective at YFGC because the cell group members and cell group leaders receive direct, hands-on personal support, prayer, and ministry from staff pastors. This ministry comes in the form of proactive, daily prayer visits in the homes and in the businesses of cell leaders and cell members. The staff pastors are constantly recruiting and mentoring new leaders by modeling ministry to those leaders who go with them on these prayer visits. Their ministry is aggressive, intentional, and planned. Above all, it is rooted in prayer. Pastor Cho requires his staff pastors to spend three hours each day praying. Karen interviewed one YFGC staff pastor to attain a detailed schedule of what a typical cell pastor does. This schedule illustrates what she found:[10]

	Monday	Tuesday	Wednesday	Thursday	Friday	Saturday	Sunday
	Listening Room	Listening Room	Listening Room	Listening Room	Listening Room	Listening Room	Listening Room
8:30 / 9:00		Pastoral Staff Prayer	Pastoral Staff Prayer	Pastoral Staff Prayer	Pastoral Staff Prayer	Pastoral Staff Prayer	
10:00		Visit Reports	Visit Reports	Visit Reports	Visit Reports	Visit Reports	
11:00							
12:00			Ministry Visits to Homes and Businesses				Serves in his office from 7am to 9pm the span of worship services to pray and counsel with people. He will participate in one worship service
1:00	Day off Family Day	Ministry Visits to Homes and Businesses		Ministry Visits to Homes and Businesses	Ministry Visits to Homes and Businesses	Ministry Visits to Homes and Businesses	
2:00							
3:00							
4:00			Available in office during worship services for counseling	Lead Monthly Sectional Meetings with Cell Leaders			
5:00							
Evening		Home prayer visits			All night prayer service		

Fig 7.7 Yoido Full Gospel Church Cell Pastor's Schedule

In contrast, the typical church staff pastor spends his or her time in the church offices, administrating programs, teaching in classrooms, and waiting for people to come to him for counseling. While the YFGC pastors focus on ministering to people by making five to seven visits per day, the typical American staff pastor is focused on organizing tasks, sitting in meetings, and enlisting people to do other tasks.

Most staff cell pastors cannot make the radical shift to the schedule of a YFGC staff pastor. They have worked for years to refine their system. In addition, YFGC staff pastors do not have to deal with the tasks of organizing worship services, managing budgets, and all of the other tasks that staff members of smaller churches must deal with. Even so, the contrast between the weekly activities of a YFGC staff pastor and the typical staff pastor illustrate that the cell group system requires a different set of habits than those practiced by most pastors today.

Getting out of the office. When visiting the Faith Community Baptist Church in Singapore, I noticed two distinct traits of their offices. First, cell pastors did not have private offices; they had cubicles. The senior pastor clearly did not want his pastors to be comfortable in their office spaces. Second, very few pastors were even in their offices. They were out doing ministry. Bethany World Prayer Center and other major cell group churches around the world practice these same habits. The more cell pastors get out of the office and personally minister to leaders and members, the more effective the cell groups are.

Ministering in the homes and businesses of the people. When staff pastors are out of the office, they are with the people. They make home visits to pray for needs and encourage people in their walks with God. They visit businesses to pray God's blessings over the work done there. They eat breakfast and lunch with people to speak life into cell members and minister to needs. Some might argue that this has been a practice of the traditional church for years, but the difference lies in the fact that the staff pastor does not wait until there is a crisis, an extended absence from church attendance, or a request on the part of a church member. Instead, he takes the proactive or even aggressive approach and sets up appointments to minister to different people during the week.

Mentoring key leaders. The spiritual dynamics of critical mass—prayer, unity, obedience, and order—are transferred from one generation to the next through mentoring. The staff cell pastor must receive this spiritual DNA from his pastor and pass it to those leaders that he oversees. Providing weekly support to these key leaders, usually numbering no more than 12, is a top priority.

Recruiting new leaders. The staff cell pastor is in charge of the future growth of the cell groups under his or her care. Cell leaders need support in the recruitment and training of future cell leaders. Cell pastors should make it a regular practice to sit down over lunch with potential leaders and say, "I see God's hand upon your life. He is raising you up into leadership. Have you ever thought about going through the cell leader training?" When a pastor says this, it carries much more weight than when a cell leader says it.

Based on the experience of the YFGC cell pastors that Karen Hurston observed, combined with the insight provided by effective cell pastors of small churches, I have adapted a schedule to illustrate what a typical week of a cell pastor might look like. While such a schedule might seem impossible, it should be seen as a goal to work toward, not a schedule that must be adopted next week.

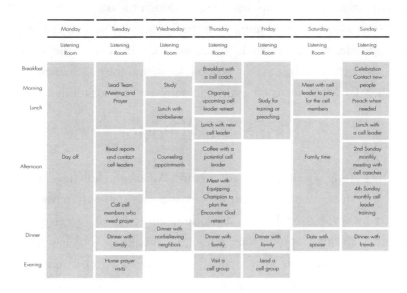

Fig 7.8 Potential American Cell Pastor's Schedule

The weekly schedules outlined in this chapter will seem overwhelming to most pastors. They have too many other responsibilities to make such radical changes. Yet there are three simple ministry tactics that can be adopted that will have huge impacts upon leadership development. The first Carl George calls a "structured debriefing interview." Also called "one-on-ones," they are monthly meetings between a cell pastor and each of his coaches or cell leaders. In these meetings, the pastor aims to discover how the coach or leader is doing personally, receive feedback about his ministry, problem solve, and pray together.

Karen Hurston trains pastors in a second ministry tactic that she calls "leader (or coach) of the day." Each day, the cell pastor will identify a specific leader and pray more intently for that leader. Then he will make a caring phone call, with no discussion of a task unless the leader initiates an issue. Even then, the focus on the phone conversation should lie not on the task or ministry issue but on ministry to the leader. The cell pastor should probe to find areas of concern so that he can pray for the leader and then continue to lift up that person through the day.

Pastors adopt the third ministry tactic by focusing on their cell group responsibilities on one or two days each week. On these days, they devote all their attention to the coaches, group leaders, and the groups, while on the other days, they focus on traditional ministry responsibilities.

Hiring a Cell Pastor

The staffing system most used in North American churches could be called a system of professionalism, because pastoral staff most often consists of professionals. By definition, professionals receive their credentials through a professional school, i.e. medical school, law school, etc. and then maintain their credentials through a series of tests. The process of entering full-time ministry has adopted a similar pattern, with the seminary as the professional school and ordination as a credential.

When seminarians graduate, they look for jobs the same way lawyers seek jobs with upstanding law firms. Church size, position, compensation, benefits, and location all play a part. Seminarians are hired to perform certain job responsibilities and accomplish certain goals. If they do well at their jobs, better positions at other churches will open up. The process repeats itself.

This system creates hirelings, who are committed to the position only as long as they are treated fairly and receive proper compensation. Hirelings work for others; they do not invest personally into their work. Many find such statements harsh. I will be first among those noting that a pastor should follow the call of God when God directs a move to a new ministry setting. I will also be first to lament that often the call of God is ascribed to more human motivations.

Business analysts have reported that the most effective companies promote executives from within the organization. Exceptional companies intentionally develop people within the organization in anticipation of future promotions. Likewise, the most effective churches raise up future pastors from within the volunteer leaders of the church. They are not looking necessarily to seminaries to provide their next leaders.

Why are the best leaders found within the church? There are at least three reasons. First, biblical ministry is relationship-based. Professional ministers who arrive on the scene can do professional things, but it takes time to build the trust required to minister relationally. Some even argue that it takes up to five years to really enter deep trust with the people a pastor is leading. Those who are raised up within the church already have a relationship foundation.

Second, biblical ministry is based upon fruit, not degrees. Fruit should be the test of one's ability to lead as a pastor, not the number or type of degrees on the wall. I am not arguing that degrees are unimportant (my personal history would prove otherwise). My point is this: a person should be given a staff position because he or she is a proven minister, not because of a set of papers. The proving ground for this is in the ministry of the local church.

Third, biblical ministry is learned on the job. Classroom experience prepares people to be teachers, an important function in the church. But relational ministry is learned in the field. The field is the local church, not in a denominational seminary.

Some of the best staff pastors are truck drivers, accountants, fruit pickers, and elementary school teachers. Such people have usually never thought of themselves as having the potential to serve God in a pastoral role because the system does not allow it. They do not see themselves as professional ministers. They might have a calling to love and care for people, but no one has told them that this calling is the true calling of a staff pastor. Therefore, they serve in the system, while their true calling is left untapped.

The issue of hiring a cell pastor is becoming more and more urgent. Weekly, TOUCH receives information about job openings for cell pastors of both large and small churches. These positions are very difficult to fill because few pastors have experience in overseeing life-giving cell groups. Those who have experience feel God calling them to remain in their current oversight positions. In addition, the best training ground for cell pastors is in the local church, but most churches have not developed their cell groups to the point where leaders can be developed from within. If they had a developed cell group system which could raise up cell pastors, they would not be looking to hire one from the outside. But few pastoral training institutions provide a thorough cell group curriculum. Many churches find themselves in a catch-22.

What should a church do? The best option is to fall before God and seek His direction, asking Him to identify a person already in the church who can be trained to oversee cells and possesses the characteristics necessary to learn and be successful.[11] Here are a few traits to look for:

Leadership style. The role of the cell pastor is people-intensive, because the cell pastor focuses on equipping cell leaders and cell members for effective ministry. If the potential pastor's strengths lie in organization and administration, he may find such a role very frustrating. The gifting of this cell pastor should complement the strengths and weaknesses of the senior pastor, especially if the cell pastor is the first addition to the staff.

Devotion to the senior pastor. This potential pastor should walk in humility and submission to leadership. This is not a role for a hotshot pastor who is looking to enter into ministry "greatness." It is a role that requires teamwork, self-sacrifice, and self-demotion. Dr. Neighbour tells the story of Melvin Mak, a man who joined the staff of Faith Community Baptist Church. To do so, he resigned from his job as a stock market trader making lots of money. His former boss did everything possible to keep him, even offering him a new Mercedes Benz. Melvin declined. He once said over lunch, "My job is to make my senior pastor look good." If only more staff pastors had such devotion to their leaders!

Commitment to the vision and philosophy of cells. While the candidate for the cell pastor position might not know a great amount about leading cell groups, he or she must be 100% committed to the vision and to learning about how the groups should work.

Fruitfulness in relational ministry. Even though a potential cell pastor might have little experience with cell groups per se, he or she should be evaluated based on prior experience in relational ministry. Have you observed him mentoring? Does she relate to nonbelievers or searching Christians? Does he deal with conflict in healthy ways? It is quite easy to train such a person in the skills of a cell pastor when he or she already possesses these traits.

Commitment to the long haul. This trait is especially important to evaluate when hiring the first cell pastor. No church needs a pastor who is committed only until a better job opens up. Cell leaders and coaches need relationships with someone who will mentor them into ministry, not someone who sees this job as a step to a better job.

As the church grows, more and more staff pastors will be added. Since the best place to find future staff pastors is within the congregation, some traditional churches must deal with their qualifying requirement of three years in a seminary. Don Tillman experienced the joy of seeing pastors raised up from within the congregation. Douglas Vaughan served first as an associate pastor, later as his co-pastor, and today is senior pastor of the Crosspoint Community Church of Reno, Nevada. Lance Hale, once a newspaper editor and member of the church, is now an associate pastor. Douglas went to seminary; Lance did not. Both are exceptional pastors.

In order to develop pastors from within, senior pastors must realize a few crucial points. First, the process must start years before people are actually needed on staff. Waiting until the need is present before beginning the process will most certainly result in failure. Second, the process is one of recognition rather than seeking out. Church leadership must become adept at recognizing those God is developing and then join God in that work by mentoring and equipping. Such a calling cannot be forced upon people. Third, a pastoral intern should not be appointed until he or she is nearly qualified to be a staff pastor. Someone once said that it is easier to lay hands on than to lay hands off. It is far easier to give more and more to those who prove faithful and then confer the title than to try to remove someone from a position into which he or she was prematurely invited. Finally, raising up pastors from within the congregation should be a natural expansion of the cell member equipping process already in place. Some cell members will be equipped to be disciple-making disciples; some will go on to become cell leaders or coaches; some will go on to serve the congregation at the staff level. Church leaders who take a person-centered approach to discipleship will see their members on a continuum whose end is known only by God. They will help those they shepherd go as far as they are capable and are willing to go.

These staff cell pastors will all have the primary job responsibility of overseeing cell groups, but this does not mean that they all have to do it in the same way. Ephesians 4:11-13 reveals the different ways leaders will lead: some are apostles, some are prophets, some are evangelists, some are pastors, and some are teachers. Some cell pastors will be more expansionary (apostolic) in their leadership, leading their groups into new areas. Some will be more motivational (prophetic). Others will be highly evangelistic in their leadership. Some will be very caring and pastoral, and others will lead with more of teaching element.

Staff cell pastors should have the freedom to specialize in their areas of gifting, in addition to overseeing groups. One pastor might oversee the evangelistic thrust of the church. Another might work with the greeters, ushers, and parking lot attendants. One pastor can coordinate the assimilation effort, while a second oversees the equipping of cell members. All, however, would carry the primary function of overseeing and pastoring cell group leaders and coaches.

Cellularize Administration

Stage 4 addressed the need to create a permission-giving organizational system in order for cell groups to flourish. A church might initiate this process at Stage 4, but by Stage 7, the administrative organization should be changed so that it will support cell group life rather than impede it. The senior pastor should have permission to lead the church, cast vision, and manage the day-to-day affairs. The elder or deacon board should not only support the vision for cell groups, but board members should be actively involved, preferably leading groups themselves. Unnecessary committees should be eliminated so that people are not distracted from doing ministry through the cell groups. To further promote the life of the cell groups, a few steps must be taken to cellularize the administration of the church.

The church must develop a way to track cell group members. When a church has only 20 groups, such a task can easily be accomplished by memory or on paper, but as the groups continue to grow and multiply, keeping up with which groups contain which people will prove increasingly difficult. Such a tracking system should record cell membership, attendance, and the level of equipping each person receives. It is even possible to merge this information with donation records so that all information is integrated. CellTrack[12] and other similar computerized tools have been specifically designed to help cell-based churches develop such a database.

Tracking people will require cell group leaders to submit report forms on a regular basis. Many group leaders resent this mundane administrative task because they see it as a hurdle to jump through with little benefit for the time and effort spent. When they know the information is used to facilitate ministry, cell group leaders will not mind filling out and submitting reports as much. Church leaders should require report forms only if the information contained in them is necessary to enhance the cell group's ministry efforts. One of the most convenient ways to organize such information is through a church web-site.

The church must develop an annual calendar of events. Such calendars should be created and published early on so that people will be able to plan their activities around the vision of the church. This calendar usually includes dates for cell leader training, harvest events, encounter retreats, monthly cell leader meetings, and any other activities planned by the church.

The church budget must be customized to fit the needs of the cell group vision. The budget should address the projected personnel requirements, needed training materials, and a special money pool for supporting cell leaders. This discretionary pool should fund special gifts for cell group leaders, an annual appreciation banquet, and all the materials to train new cell group leaders. Cell group leaders are front-line ministers and the church should support them by blessing them in this way.

What to Do with Sunday School

The Sunday school versus cell group battle has been hard fought. Church members who like Sunday school feel attacked when the new cell group vision is implemented. They often express that they are made to feel like second-class citizens if they don't want to join a cell group. The fact is that belittling Sunday school will not prove helpful in promoting the new vision of cell groups. The road ahead for Sunday school must be presented in a positive way if the people who love their Sunday school classes will support the vision of the church.

One option that many have taken is to allow the Sunday school classes to continue to meet. If Sunday school members want to join a cell group they will, but when they are forced they don't contribute positively. Some churches have even trained Sunday school teachers in the principles of cell leadership and given them the same goals as the cell groups.

A second option is to transition the Sunday school classes into cell groups that meet in the homes. This was one of the transition strategies mentioned in Stages 4 and 5.

Quite a few churches have taken a third route. They transitioned the Sunday school into a training center. They use the Sunday morning time for their cell member equipping, evangelism training, and cell leader training.

The mid-sized group gathering is a fourth option. Four to seven cell groups can gather weekly in groups of approximately 50 people where they can receive training and connect with one another.

For churches with a strong Sunday school heritage, this is a crucial question. It is easy for people to fall in love with what they know and question or resist any change to it. When changing Sunday school, it is important to celebrate what God has done in the past, and then present a way to build upon what God has done.

What To Do with Old Small Groups

Door of Hope Church in Fairbanks, Alaska had 25 small groups when the church leaders caught the vision for cell groups. These small groups were accomplishing good things, but they did not live out the values of Upward, Inward, Outward, Forward. With the new emphasis on cell groups, they had to determine what to do with the old small groups. They knew that they could not invest in the old small groups and the cell groups equally. At the same time they could not force people into cell groups by shutting down the small groups. Therefore they determined to support the small groups, but nurture the life of the cell groups.

Some of the small groups elected to transform into cell groups. Other groups continued and then stopped when the normal life cycle of the group played out. Many of the small group members became members of the cell groups.

Church leadership need not shut down the old small groups. They should instead focus on developing momentum in the cell groups, thereby increasing the benefit of joining a group. The old small groups will either adopt UIOF values or conclude at the end of their life cycles.

SECTION 7.3 Establish a Cell Group System Including Children

In cell group leader seminars across the country, participants never fail to express anxiety over how to minister to children in cell groups. They state that the children interfere with the group ministry rather than enhance it. Cell group leaders become overwhelmed with the responsibility of not only caring for the parents but also organizing something for the children. And most cell groups with children seem to have lots of them, because parents often become friends with other parents and want to be in the same cell group.

Some churches, like Pantego Bible Church, base their entire cell group system on intergenerational cell groups. Others base their groups around homogeneous networks, like Bethany World Prayer Center, which includes a network for children. One of these homogeneous networks could also include family groups. Either way, churches must develop a clear strategy to include children in cell groups or the cells will stall.

Daphne Kirk, an expert in the field of children and cell groups, states that "most of the problems experienced with children, probably 95% of them, are [a result of] the mismanagement of the cell, or the lack of the vision and the values of the cell church, [not due to the fact that] children are present."[13] Such a statement, while probably true, is very hard for pastors in the middle of the cell group fray to swallow. Pastors need practical ways to manage cell activities so that children can be included. Even more importantly, they must lead the people in dealing with the vision and values that hinder a cell group's ability to incorporate the children into group life.

Paradigm Shifts about Children

I have been a member in cell groups that included children, and I have led groups with children. One time, I led a group with 12 kids. At times it was frustrating, but the adults knew a few secrets about children and ministry. The group had shifted its paradigms so that the adults could love the children instead of viewing them as nuisances. Before cell groups can develop strategies to incorporate children, they must begin to shift their views regarding ministry and children. If these views do not change, the new strategies will prove frustrating.

Multiple visions must become one vision. Church leaders have recognized that there are multiple generations in the church. The church's strategy for ministering to the multiple generations is to compartmentalize them by developing multiple visions: a children's vision, a youth vision, and an adult vision. Of course, the "real" vision is the one that the pastor has for the adults. The children's minister and the youth minister each develop a pastor-approved, but less significant, vision for the other two areas of the church. (If your church does not do this anymore, please ignore this point.)

Such a pattern is difficult to find in the ministry patterns expressed in the Bible. The vision for Israel was for all of Israel, not just for the adults. Jesus' vision for the Kingdom of God was for everyone, not just the adults. In fact, he rebuked the adults for discrediting the ability of the children to enter into the vision of the Kingdom. This means that the visionary role of the church cannot be limited to the adults. The senior pastor is called to lead the entire people of God and bring the children and youth into unity with the adults.

One of Daphne Kirk's biggest complaints as she trains church leaders on intergenerational ministry is that the senior pastors express little desire to learn about including the children. Pastors send their children's workers to her seminars, but these workers return home frustrated. They have a new vision, but now they must explain it to the senior pastor and see if he is in agreement with it.

Children are part of cell group life, not an impediment to it. The cell group leaders who confess that the children have been an interference to cell group meetings are being honest. Children are children and they don't always understand that adults want their meetings to be orderly. A baby cries when someone begins to share a deep need. A toddler spills juice on the carpet, disrupting the post-meeting conversation. Someone has to make plans every week for the Kids' Slot time.

Children interfere only if the group expects to have a dignified and uneventful cell meeting experience every week. But such expectations are divorced from the realities of life. The cell group meeting is not like a Sunday celebration service, nor is it like a board meeting. It deals with real life, and children are a part of that real life. Children should not be entertained so that the adults can have a sterile experience without any interference.

True learning focuses on values, not just knowledge. Much of children's ministry focuses on teaching cognitive facts about the Bible. Children need more than information; they need a place to copy or imitate others who are living for God. If children are left to learn about Jesus from age-graded curriculum, they will be deprived from the privilege of learning from adult models. When they have adult models, "children have the benefit and privilege of an extended 'family,' of seeing others who have strengths that their parents do not have. They can copy whatever they see going on, because their parents are doing it and because they see others too!"[14] Daphne Kirk has observed that children learn from models by watching others, questioning the things that trouble them, receiving instruction, and laughing with others.

Children are ministers of the present, not just ministers of the future. Most adults assume that God is preparing the children for use when they become adults. While this is partially true, it does not relegate children to a secondary role of ministry in the church. The Holy Spirit wants to move through every member of the church today. The prophet Joel said, "Your sons and daughters will prophesy." This does not mean that they have to wait until they are 21 to do so. The best people to reach out to elementary-aged students are elementary-aged Christians. They see each other every day at recess, at lunch, and in the classroom. The church doesn't equip the children to minister because it has limited its children's ministry to ministering to the children, rather than showing them how to minister.

Children's Champion

It is the job of the senior pastor to unify each generation under one vision from God. But it is not his responsibility to develop and implement a strategy for each generation. The children need a champion who sits as a part of the pastoral oversight team and asks, "What about the children?" This person is set apart to focus on developing a strategy for guiding the children into dynamic cell group life and oversee its implementation.

An Intergenerational Cell Group

Lorna Jenkins, one of the pioneers in ministering to children in cell groups, defines an intergenerational cell group as,

> …a cell group that welcomes children as full members. It does not set up any age barriers. Although the children may have a separate subgroup during the evening, they belong to the whole cell group and they can bless and minister to the adults as well as be blessed by the adults. Such cell groups include the children in all their activities: prayer, praise, spiritual growth, and evangelism. Families and singles mix together to form a wider family of Christ.[15]

In an intergenerational cell group meeting, the children are expected to participate as much as the adults do. They are not spectators of the real ministry. They are part of the cell family. To help facilitate this participation, cell groups usually assign a time where children have their own discussion and ministry, called a Kids' Slot. Such a time usually occurs after an icebreaker and worship.

The Kids' Slot lasts about 30-45 minutes, when the children go into another room to have a separate time for discussion of a lesson, ministry to one another, and praying for non-believing friends. Cell group members rotate leading the Kids' Slot. Sometimes the children stay for the entire meeting with the adults. Play is often a part of the Kids' Slot time. Playing with the kids is crucial to relationship building and should not be thought of as unspiritual.

To facilitate the cells' ministry to children, each intergenerational cell group should appoint a Child Link, someone who helps the cell leader coordinate the Kids' Slot schedule and the further involvement of children in the cell group.

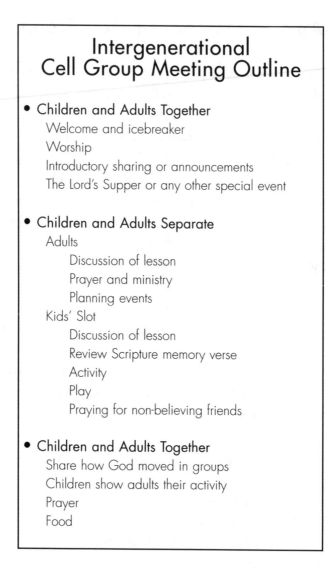

Intergenerational Cell Group Meeting Outline

- **Children and Adults Together**
  Welcome and icebreaker
  Worship
  Introductory sharing or announcements
  The Lord's Supper or any other special event

- **Children and Adults Separate**
  Adults
      Discussion of lesson
      Prayer and ministry
      Planning events
  Kids' Slot
      Discussion of lesson
      Review Scripture memory verse
      Activity
      Play
      Praying for non-believing friends

- **Children and Adults Together**
  Share how God moved in groups
  Children show adults their activity
  Prayer
  Food

Intergenerational cell groups have proven very rewarding for both children and adults alike. Even so, a church still cannot jump into them without much time and preparation. Following are some basic steps for developing intergenerational cells:

Stages of Transition[16]

Step 1: Outline the vision for intergenerational groups.

Step 2: Start a pilot group to learn how to run an intergenerational group on a small scale.

Step 3: Communicate the vision. Parents need to hear how they fit into this new vision. Children's workers need to discover their new roles. Old cell group leaders need to learn how they can expand their ministry.

Step 4: Mentor old cell groups who want to become intergenerational through a four-week process. The Children's Champion will probably provide this mentoring.[17]

> **Week 1**: The Mentor leads the cell group through the icebreaker, worship and the Kids' Slot. The Child Link and one other person (Member A) observe the Kids' Slot.
>
> **Week 2**: The cell group leader leads the worship and icebreaker. The Child Link leads the Kids' Slot with another member (Member B) observing. The Mentor also observes and provides feedback.
>
> **Week 3**: The cell group leader arranges the worship and icebreaker. The Mentor may help with suggestions. Member A leads the Kids' Slot and Member B observes with the Mentor.
>
> **Week 4**: The cell group leader arranges the worship and icebreaker. He may ask someone else to lead them. Member B leads the Kids' Slot. Member C observes with the Mentor.

Step 5: Train new cell group leaders in intergenerational ministry.

Step 6: Support the intergenerational groups with further training and resources.

Children's Cell Groups

Many churches are not ready to take on the challenge of developing intergenerational cell groups. Just learning how to enter basic Christian community as adults often proves challenging enough. Other churches feel called to develop only homogeneous cell groups. Their strategy will focus on cell groups for children.

One strategy for children's cell groups is to transition the current Sunday school classes into cell groups. Each group of 6-10 children will meet in the same room. The groups will gather in a "U" shape so that every child can see the front of the room.

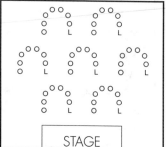

Each will have a leader, most likely an adult, but it could be a child with an adult or with adult support. A coordinating leader is required to facilitate the Word portion of the meeting. These groups consist of children of various ages so that the older children could serve as apprentices and eventually enter into leadership. Daphne Kirk has developed a simple meeting format which proves quite effective:[18]

- Begin with an icebreaker in the cells.
- All groups will worship together, led centrally.
- The coordination leader will provide a short teaching.
- The children discuss and apply the Word in their cell groups.
- The groups will share about personal evangelism in the cells.
- The group members will pray for and minister to each other in their groups.

Another approach to children's cell groups is to equip adults to lead groups in neighborhoods, at schools, or in apartment complexes. Victory Christian Center in Tulsa, Oklahoma has used this strategy to develop one of the most evangelistic children's ministries in the nation. Such a strategy might begin by promoting a three-day Bible Club in a certain area. The leaders would use this club to get to know the kids, share Jesus, and begin a weekly group.[19]

The group meetings consist of:

• Sharing an icebreaker.
• Presenting a short Bible message.
• A puppet show.
• Praying for each other.

Children love cell groups because they love relationships. They love to be loved. Children are changed by this love. Even more, I believe adults are changed when they love children in cell group relationships. There are few things that can touch your heart like a child, except a child who is in love with the Father because of your influence.

Levers

Develop a pattern for accomplishing ministry tasks in the church (nursery, grounds keeping, worship team, etc.) in a way that does not compete with, but instead enhances, cell group life.

Focus the energy of the pastoral staff on mentoring, spiritual mothering and fathering. This will require some restructuring of job descriptions.
Key Resource:
—*Spiritual Mothering and Fathering* by Larry Kreider

Develop a strategy for raising up a new cell pastor from within the current cell group system.

Restructure the pastoral oversight system to facilitate cell group development.
Key Resources:
—*Groups of 12* by Joel Comiskey
—*From 12 to 3* by Joel Comiskey
—*Reap the Harvest* by Joel Comiskey

Restructure the administration to support the life of the cell groups.

Fully incorporate children into cell group life.
Key Resources:
—*Heirs Together* by Daphne Kirk
—*What Shall We Do with the Children* by Daphne Kirk

Vision Team Discussion

1. What is critical mass?
2. Evaluate the critical mass conviction of the church.
3. Evaluate the critical mass spirituality of the church.
4. Evaluate the development of these sub-systems on a scale of one to ten:

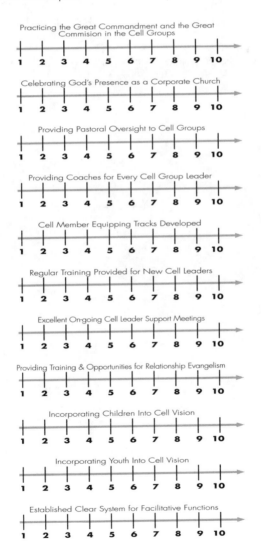

5. Which of the above is the Lord leading the team to develop as a priority at this time?
6. How does the role of a traditional staff pastor differ from the role of an effective cell pastor? Is such care being provided to the cell leaders and members at this time?
7. Has the church developed a strategy for raising up cell pastors through the cell groups?
8. What administrative tasks need to be adjusted to support the cell groups?
9. How do children fit into the cell vision?

STAGE 8
Expand
the Cell Groups
to Reach the Unreached

Every day the lookout stands at the highest point of a ship hoping to yell out "Land ho!" The entire crew anticipates the day that they will come out on the deck to see the port of destination. Churches destined for making cell groups work also long to cry "Land ho!"

At this stage of the journey, it is time to ask, "How do we mobilize groups to reach people?" Stage 8 is the point when cell group life becomes exciting, when groups have embraced the values of the Great Commandment and the Great Commission, and the support system have been established. Now the groups can focus their energies on reaching out to nonbelievers.

After observing the growth of many cell group churches, I noticed that some have hit plateaus while others have taken off. The plateaued churches still have good groups and they have made groups a priority in their structure, but they do not see the conversion growth they had hoped. I asked Dr. Ralph Neighbour, "Why do you think this is the case?" He responded, "They did not develop intentional strategies to penetrate the world of the unreached." The focus of evangelism to this point has been relationship evangelism. In Stage 8, cell groups must develop ways to penetrate nonbelievers' circles.

The focus then must shift to cell group expansion. Groups must take the life of basic Christian community to the unreached and not just sit around, waiting for nonbelievers to come to the groups. This stage will help you:

• "Expand to Re-Anchor the Culture" (Section 8.1). Many churches have not completed the last leg of the journey because the people did not embrace a culture of expansion. Leaders must help people process through cultural anchors that might hold them back and then re-anchor the church in the new ways of expansion.

• "Expansion Strategies" (Section 8.2). Different strategies have been adopted successfully to move a church into expansion. This section suggests some of the best strategies, which should act as a springboard for church leaders to develop even more.

SECTION 8.1 Expand to Re-anchor the Culture

A church of 80 members in rural Kentucky works hard to develop cell groups. In three years, they have seven groups and 95% of Sunday worshippers also attend cell groups. In the last year, five people have received Christ and more church members are actively involved in ministry than ever before.

A church of 150 people in Philadelphia has 12 groups. The groups have brought more life to the church than it has seen in its 15-year history. Their leadership training is in place and the church has established a great cell member discipleship strategy.

A suburban southern California church of 400 has 25 groups with about 60% of church members participating. The groups they have are experiencing the joy of basic Christian community, they are reaching their friends, and more cell members are being discipled.

In all three of the scenarios, the cell groups are strong, the people are committed to the vision, and the pastors are focused. But they have not yet completed the journey. Many churches fail to continue the journey with God because they are satisfied with having a large percentage of the church in working groups. This is like a ship's captain getting frustrated with the journey and pulling into a port that is not the final one he set on his charts. It gives the crew a feeling that they have accomplished something, but they have not yet made the last leg of the journey.

In order to complete the journey, leadership must navigate the church through the stage of expansion. When cell groups expand, the real power of basic Christian community comes to life.

A Culture of Expansion

At this point of the cell group journey, cell groups have started to reap the fruit of their labor. Groups are exciting. People are maturing. New leaders are in training. Many churches face the temptation to savor these benefits and hold on to them rather than risking the final navigational steps of entering the port. One change consultant puts it this way: "Life seems so successful and positive during the early days of Fruition that it is easy for people in the organization to want to prolong the good feelings."[1] Churches do not want to continue pressing on because they are afraid they will lose what they have. They settle for an intermediate destination. Pastors might assume that they have traveled far enough along the cell group journey.

Cell group expansion includes cell group multiplication, but it is more than that. Cell groups must expand by targeting ministry needs in the community, spreading out to every segment of the church, participating in mission activities, starting new churches, training new pastors, and starting focus groups for nonbelievers. All of these activities develop a culture of expansion.

Culture refers to norms of behavior and shared values among a group of people. Norms of behavior are common or pervasive ways of acting that are found in a group and that persist because group members tend to behave in ways that teach these practices to new members, rewarding those who fit in and sanctioning those who do not. Shared values are important concerns and goals shared by most of the people in a group that tend to shape group behavior and that often persist over time even when group membership changes.[2]

The behaviors that are rewarded and reinforced and the values that people practice when no one is telling them what to do reveal the culture of a church. For instance, in many traditional churches, the culture rewards attendance, committee service, and busyness at the church building. Even when no pastors are present to lead the church, the people place value on things like church activities centered around the building, and meetings that are required to maintain those building-centered activities, whether or not these activities actually reach people.

When cell groups have embraced a culture of expansion, people are coming to Christ, cell members are being discipled, new groups are starting, new churches are spawned, and people are involved in mission work. A culture of expansion calls the people out to touch those who need Jesus and prepares a way for it. When a church embraces this new culture, the people will focus on expansion even when top leaders are not directly involved.

The timing of this expansion is crucial. Many churches wait until after the momentum has waned before trying to expand. They wait until the benefits of cell ministry slow down. They wait until the seed is overly mature and begins to lose its fertility to produce fruit, Point B. When a church waits until this point to expand, the cell group has lost the energy that they had at Point A.

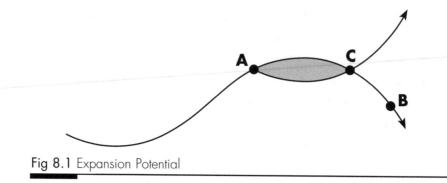

Fig 8.1 Expansion Potential

The best point for expansion is when the energy is on an upswing, Point A. Point C is the latest point for successfully implementing expansion. In between A and C, the cell groups have the most energy to penetrate new areas and expand basic Christian community to those who do not have it.

Resistance to Cultural Change

John Kotter has developed his findings on cultural change by observing people in the business world. He writes:

> Culture is not something that you manipulate easily. Attempts to grab it and twist it into shape never work because you can't grab it. Culture changes only after you have successfully altered people's actions, after the new behavior produces some group benefit for a period of time, and after people see the connection between the new actions and the performance improvement.[3]

Changing the culture of a church can prove to be even more eventful than in the business world. I see at least four reasons that this is true. First, the church has centuries of practice with a culture that has ignored life in basic Christian community. While there have been pockets of those who have had this experience, the norms of behavior and the shared values of the church do not involve basic Christian community. M. Scott Peck states, "Currently the Church is not only not the Body of Christ, it is not even a body, a community. It must become a community before it can serve as the body of Christ."[4] Most churches have much to learn when it comes to life in community.

The second reason can prove especially troublesome. Methods and structures are given theological status in the church. When a specific ministry proves fruitful, people naturally begin to equate the form of ministry with the Spirit that produced the ministry. As a result, people often assume that their way of doing ministry is the biblical way of doing ministry and messing with it is messing with the Bible.

The third reason changing a church culture can be very hard is the religious hypocrisy that is part of most church cultures. The primary impediments to the Kingdom of God that Jesus inaugurated are those steeped in religion. Few churches today are without those people who are encumbered by religious values. They are not interested in participating in transparency. They do not like opening up their homes to people. They like to hide behind religious answers and biblical knowledge. Cell groups are invasive, and those who have a religious spirit do not want their hearts exposed. I have seen pastors write and teach about the importance of transparency and vulnerability in the cell groups, yet never confess a need or ask for prayer. They were so mired in the religious expectations that everyone else puts upon "pastors" that they were not free to be human.

The fourth reason comes in the form of time limitations in the church. Business leaders have 40 hours a week to guide their employees through the process of change. Pastors feel lucky if they get two hours on Sunday. Changing behavioral norms and shared values is impossible when commitment is sporadic and limited. This is the reason why cell group life that exists outside the official cell meetings is so crucial to cultural change.

Culture change does not happen at Stages 1 through 7 but at Stage 8. Cell groups might work structurally at Stage 6 and 7, but the unspoken, unknown, hidden behavioral norms and shared values have not made the shift. It is impossible for people to change until they have participated in cell groups, until they see the power of cell groups, until they begin to contribute to cell groups. After an extended experience of effective cell group life, they will find it difficult to return to the old way. But those who taste the goodness for only a short while often return very easily because they still have the taste of the old in their mouths.

Quitting Before the Culture Changes

Change research provides some insight into why people fail to navigate the final leg of the journey into the harbor. The reasons relate not to the logic of the process but to the emotional journey that people have taken.

Emotions rise and fall over time as a church changes to life in cell groups. At the inception of the idea, some people may be skeptical, but most will be positive. After this, people feel a growing enthusiasm because everything is new. Then those 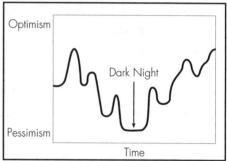 involved discover that the journey is a little longer than they expected and there are more questions about the process than they realized. Results do not come easily and discouragement sets in. When people do not see the expected results immediately, the leaders enter a period called the "Dark Night of the Innovator."[5] This graph illustrates the emotions experienced in the change process.

The change process depends upon this Dark Night experience, especially in God's order of things. It is often a God-ordained period that causes the leaders of the change to die to their own thoughts, ideas, and culture. They discover that cell groups do not work as easily as the books say they do. They leave behind old ideas and instead seek God for His ways.

As people become dependent upon the Spirit, God starts to reveal new ways of doing cell groups in that specific church, cell group momentum is generated, and critical mass is achieved. The church leaders and the people at large see the cell group destination rising on the horizon, and excitement grows. Yet before arriving at expanding cell groups, they experience a downturn.

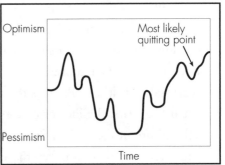

This final downturn in emotional energy is the time when people go through the final change of embracing the new culture of expansion. Yet this final downturn is also the place where people are the most likely to quit. They feel that they will never see the end and they do not want to experience the Dark Night again. Therefore they pull up and never enter expansion.

Cultural Anchors

Navigating a church into a culture of expansion means that the church must fully let go of cultural anchors that hinder sailing the final leg of the journey. Cultural anchors will allow a church to go so far into cell group life, even giving the appearance of developing a system that is working well. But unless cultural anchors are cut away, the ship will sail around in the ocean of mediocrity. Mediocre cell groups that are controlled by old cultural anchors will eventually return the church to the old styles of ministry.

Cultural anchors can be illustrated with a simple rubber band being stretched between two forefingers. The right forefinger represents life in cell groups; the left represents the old way of doing church. In the first seven steps, the right finger has been stretching the rubber band away from the left, but as long as the left finger remains anchored, the two fingers will remain in tension. This is because the old ways of doing church are rooted in an established culture, while the new way has not existed long enough to dig its own cultural roots. Here are a few crucial anchors that must be removed:

Pastoral transitions. Because the average tenure of a senior pastor is less than five years, the idea of pastors changing their jobs is part of the church culture in the United States. Churches do not expect pastors to remain over the long run. Yet the churches that have changed their culture are led by pastors who feel called to make those churches their home. They are not looking for something new.

A few years ago, I worked with a large denominational church. The pastoral team completely embraced the cell group vision. They invested in training, brought in consultants, visited other churches, and were moving into cell groups with great success. I knew the church was "getting it" because, after teaching a seminar, I overheard a cell member share with her cell leader how she had been praying and talking with a nonbeliever who wanted to come to their group. Recently, the two primary leaders of this church felt God calling them to other ministry positions. While waiting for a new pastor, the cell groups tried to move forward, but they wandered aimlessly. The new pastor has a slightly different vision, even though the church is still focused on small groups.

Pastoral professionalism. Cell groups are designed to grow and multiply. As these groups grow, more and more leaders are required, which creates the need for more and more pastoral support and oversight. If a church requires seminary credentials before a person can minister as a staff pastor, the church will find it difficult to find enough pastors to oversee the growing groups. Cell group churches that grow raise up new pastors from within the church. They do not depend upon seminaries to produce their future leaders.

New-building focus. Contrary to what some have argued, buildings are not the bane of the church. Every growing cell group church that I have seen uses buildings of various kinds. Yet buildings have been the cultural focus of the church for centuries; when a church needs a new building, it is very easy for the pastoral staff to focus its energy on the construction of buildings. Staff members must choose how they spend their energy, and they must realize that when this energy is not spent upon the mentoring and supporting of coaches and cell group leaders, the groups will inevitably struggle. One church has decided not to build until it could also afford to hire an administrative pastor capable of overseeing the project. In that manner, the construction needs can be met without sacrificing the people-to-people ministry.

Maintenance satisfaction. Some churches are satisfied with cell groups that contain 80% or more of the people who attend the church worship services. The energy of the cell group change has been spent upon getting those who already attend church into groups. While this is a noble effort, getting churched people into cell groups is not the destination God set for the church. Cell groups are Great Commission platoons who mobilize people for ministry. If people are sitting stagnant in cell groups like they have been sitting stagnant in church, it matters little how many groups a church has.

Trying to keep everyone happy. A pastor is often anchored by the desire to make sure everyone feels good about the church and his leadership. The new cell group leaders need his support and mentoring. The new infrastructure needs his strategy and wisdom. The new vision needs his teaching and communication. Yet the old church members want their programs. They want their pastor to be a sheep-herder. They want the church to provide training for Sunday school or choir or the children's program. The pastor cannot invest his time and energy into both the old ways and the new way of being the church. If the church is going to move forward, he must choose to invest his time in those things that will carry the ship to port. To state it bluntly, pastors must be willing to let some people go. Cell group ministry will not work for everyone. If a pastor attempts to keep everyone, he will inevitably compromise the vision.

Removing Anchors

Leaders need to do two things in order to navigate the final leg of the journey. First, the pastoral leaders must propel the church forward by challenging the church and the cell groups to focus on expansion by providing practical strategies for penetrating new areas of ministry. Second, the pastoral leaders must address those anchors that hinder the advancement into the final stage of the journey.

Researchers in organizational change have found that it is easier and more important to remove the hindering forces to change than to increase the propelling forces. Out of these findings, Kurt Lewin developed a planning and implementation tool called force-field analysis. The goal of force-field analysis is to remove or minimize the hindering forces (the anchors) to change and maximize the propelling forces. Here is the process for performing a force-field analysis:[6]

- After picking an issue that you want to improve, take a blank piece of paper and place it horizontally.
- Draw a line down the middle of the page to signify the current location of the church.
- Draw a line down the right edge of the page to represent where you want to be.
- Draw arrows to the right of the center line pointing away from it to represent each force helping to move you toward your goal.

- Place arrows to the left of the center line pointing away from it to signify each force hindering your movement toward your goal.
- Make the length of the lines proportional to the strength of the helping and hindering forces.
- Develop a clear and simple strategy for removing or minimizing the hindering forces.

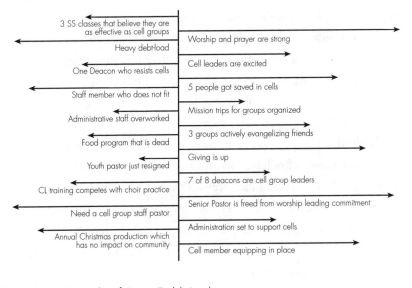

Fig 8.2 An Example of Force-Field Analysis

The method for dealing with these anchors will vary from problem to problem. The answers to some of these problems will only come through prayer. For others, the Lord will reveal specific steps to take.

Re-Anchor

As these anchors are cut away, there is no time to waste; the new culture must be re-anchored immediately. New behavioral norms and shared values must be reinforced and rewarded. Here are a few practical strategies to re-anchor the culture.

Expand. Expand groups, expand ministers, expand churches. God will reveal many ways he wants to lead the church into expansion.

Concentrate. Contrary to the practices of many churches, this is time to re-emphasize and concentrate on cell groups more than ever. The pastors and vision team cannot succumb to the temptation to focus on something else because the cells seem to be working so well.

Communicate. Church leaders must communicate the cell group vision regularly. This communication should come in written and public forms, but the most important form of communication is interpersonal. Cell pastors and coaches must re-emphasize the cell group vision and the important role their cell leaders play.

Celebrate. The pastoral team must provide specific ways to celebrate and reward those who have made the shift into cell group life. Ideas include a cell group banquet, rewarding cell group leaders for their service, and public praise that reveals how the cell groups have advanced.

Refine. At this point, the church leaders should refine materials and methods that they have copied from other churches. Writing training materials is especially important.

The next section deals with specific ways to re-anchor the church through expansion, ways that have proven effective in many different churches.

SECTION 8.2 Expansion Strategies

Dietrich Bonhoeffer wrote, "The Church is the Church only when it exists for others."[7] Jesus as the incarnate Son of God came in a physical body to redeem the world. The church, the Body of Christ through the work of the Spirit, is now the body that God breathes life into to redeem the world.

Cell groups are cells within this body. Cell groups are only truly cell groups in His Church when they exist for others. They must give life to receive it. Without this giving, cells grow static and stale. The flesh seeks to withhold the power of the Spirit from others and keep basic Christian community to itself. The flesh resists expansion. Yet expansion is the way of the Spirit. The Holy Spirit never allows the church to contain His presence. He is only experienced as the church moves out in an ever-expanding way. "But you will receive power when the Holy Spirit comes on you; and you will be my witnesses in Jerusalem, and in all Judea and Samaria, and to the ends of the earth" (Acts 1:8). The Holy Spirit is on the mission of expansion. The mission of cell groups is to join Him.

Four Questions that Stimulate Expansion

People will make time for cell groups when they like what they experience. If cell groups help them, they will come back. If they don't, then they won't. There are four basic questions that people ask which cell groups are uniquely qualified to answer. If the cell groups and all the other expansion strategies developed answer these questions, people will come back. If they fail to address them, they will look for answers elsewhere.

"Who am I?"

The identity of human beings has been a core question for hundreds of years. The philosopher Descartes determined that the essence of man is thinking. Freud concluded that the center of identity lies in the subconscious. The economist Adam Smith found the key in competition. America's founding fathers determined that the pursuit of happiness is the key to identity.

In the past, people banked their identities on family or heritage. They knew who they were because they knew their fathers. But this is no longer the case. Some call this generation "fatherless." The normal family now has divorce somewhere in its history. The normal child is the one whose father lives in a different state or whose name is unknown. Even for those who live with their fathers, the relationships are often so strained that children question their ability to do anything in this world. Today, life is characterized by a loss of identity.

People are silently screaming, "Who am I?" They are waiting for someone who can tell them. The cell group on mission has an answer to this question, an answer that does not come in the form of words alone but in the form of action. Cell groups on mission have the ability to surround people with the truth of who they are and show them their names: Son of God, Daughter of the Most High, Loved of

God, Beautifully and Wonderfully Made. This is the kind of truth that no book can communicate. This is the kind of reality that requires impartation from one life to another. People answer the question "Who am I?" when they are surrounded by other people who love them and edify them with God's Word, revealing their identity in Christ.

"Where do I belong?"

The average family moves every 11 years. Most people will change their careers four to five times before they retire. The beginning of the 21st century is a transient age. This unstable state of life causes people to protect themselves. They do not trust people they do not know and people are not around long enough to get to know them. The only option is to hide behind alcohol, television, work, activity, even religion. As a result, people's lives are full of acquaintances but few friends. Relationships are shallow.

People need a place to call home. Cell groups have the miraculous ability to provide this home to the homeless. A man named Terry visited my church. He lived in a house, but he had no home. He was lonely and had no friends. Then he arrived at church, and shortly thereafter, he joined a men's group. He never misses a meeting. He shares freely about his former struggles and the men pray for him. Terry has finally found a place to belong.

"What do I do?"

I grew up on a farm. As a result, I was able to spend a lot of time with my father. At first, I would watch what he did on the farm, asking him why he did things the way he did. With anticipation, I waited for the day that he would allow me to hammer a nail, drive the tractor, or put out hay for the cattle. I knew that if I had something to do, I would grow closer to my father.

The same is true in church. At first, people might like being entertained. But deep down they want to contribute something. One Chicago church has enlisted a "techie" to run the sound and video even though he is still on the journey to Christ. One man in a Houston church played the drums on the worship team even though he and the mother of his child were not yet legally married. Because he felt he could contribute something, he was given the room to work through his questions and his pain. One day, he stood before the entire church and his wife walked down the aisle to officially marry him.

Cell group members also want to contribute to the mission. They want to help organize an outing, lead an icebreaker, host the meeting, make a hospital visit, and reach out to someone outside the group. They want to know what they can do to help.

"What is my destiny?"

Today's life is filled with a lack of hope. Drugs, physical abuse, divorce, and depression all stem from an absence of hope. Cell groups enter God's mission by providing hope for those without it.

Hope is not found by faithfully attending a cell group. It is found as cell group members discover that they have a God-ordained destiny, that they have a purpose that extends beyond the mundane routines of life. God did not create two kinds of people in the church, those with a call to minister and those who will receive ministry. He called everyone to live out their destinies as a part of the body. "Just as each of us has one body with many members, and these members do not all have the same function, so in Christ we who are many form one body, and each member belongs to all the others" (Romans 12:4-5).

Many have concluded that some people have special skills to lead a group, while most are just not the leadership type. Research has found this conclusion false. Cell group leadership is not limited to those with outgoing personalities, more education, or verbal giftings. In fact, research shows that these things have no impact on a person's ability to lead and grow a group. In other words, God has not set some apart to lead and others to follow. If people are willing to allow God to do whatever He wants in their lives, they can be trained to lead a dynamic group. A person's destiny is not limited to watching other people minister.

Equipping People for Their Expansion Calling

Church members have been limited to pew sitting in churches for centuries, waiting for the official ministers to minister to them. Peter calls the church a "royal priesthood." A priest is one who has access to the Father; this is a cornerstone to evangelical theology. But a priest is also a person who connects others to Him as he or she serves as a conduit of the Father's love to those who do not know the Father.

Cell group members often feel that they have been relegated to sitting in cell group meetings. They expect the cell group leader to be the priest who does the ministry. Cell group members must see themselves as more than cell sitters, as "priests" who can operate in the ministry of expansion.

Dr. Ralph Neighbour has developed a three-step process for entering into an expansion calling. First, cell group members discover how the Spirit moves through His priests in spiritual gifts. The presence of Christ in the midst of the cell group stimulates the activity of the gifts of the Spirit and the cell members edify one another in this Spirit. From day one of cell participation, cell members should see the power of God moving through the people in the group.

Second, people begin to serve other group members, family members, and lost people in their lives. They discover the ways the Spirit of God empowers them for this unselfish service and how to give without expecting anything in return. They do this through relational evangelism, through serving as a part of a mission team, or by working with another person as a part of an expansion ministry. This service culminates in leading a cell group.

Third, people discover their calling, their destiny, the dream into which they want to invest the rest of their lives. For some, it is reaching out to youth and establishing youth cell groups. For some, it will be starting children's cell groups in low-income government projects. Others will feel called to develop men's cells or women's cells. Still others will want to minister to the homeless and even raise up homeless cell group leaders. The callings are limitless: single mothers, kids in gangs, under-privileged immigrants, the unemployed, HIV-positive patients. When people feel a passion to reach out to people who are in need, they have reached a place of realizing their destiny, a place of internal motivation that will stimulate expansion through others.

Church leaders must help cell group members and cell group leaders discover their destinies, not to just do cell groups. Cell groups are for reaching people, and it takes people of passion to reach people through those groups.

Expand Cell Group Leaders

Joel Comiskey polled the cell group leaders in the world's most effective cell group-based churches to determine the characteristics of effective group leaders. His findings revealed some interesting conclusions. He reports:[8]

- The leader's gender, social class, age, marital status, or education have no impact upon his or her ability to lead a group effectively.
- The leader's personality type has no impact on his or her ability to lead a group effectively. The shy introvert has just as much potential to lead a strong group as a highly energized extrovert.

- The leader's spiritual gifting has no impact. Some had previously taught that the leader must have the gift of evangelism to lead a growing group, but Joel found that those with a gift of teaching, pastoring, mercy, leadership, or evangelism equally multiply their cell groups.
- The length of time a leader has been a Christian has no impact on his or her ability to lead a group effectively. Some churches have a goal of turning new Christians into cell group leaders in less than a year.

No one is excluded from the potential of doing the things that make an effective cell group leader. All cell group members are on a journey to leadership. The goal is to keep them from stalling out before they reach that level. Cell group leaders and coaches should assess where people are on the journey to leadership. Those who are closest should be mentored, trained, and released.

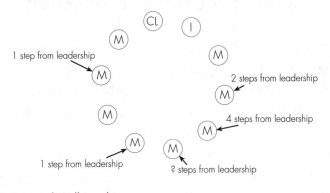

Fig 8.3 Potential Cell Leaders

Those who are one step away from being leaders should be mentored to lead cell groups in the future. Those who are two steps away require a different kind of mentoring. Just because all can be cell group leaders does not mean that all are ready to be trained to do so.

Some churches have chosen to cast the vision of "every member a cell group leader" to the entire church. This works best in churches who are at Stage 8 because the church has already established what cell group participation looks like. They have training in place. And the current leaders know how to mentor future leaders. When a church tries to enforce this principle prematurely, cell group members only feel pressured to do something they do not understand. After the church has established its cell member and cell leader equipping components and the cell leaders have experience in mentoring future leaders, then it is time to cast the vision for "every member a cell group leader." Many churches do this at the first cell member equipping retreat. One pastor shared, "We see men get set free at our retreat, we share the vision for leading a cell group and tell them about the training. Many of them immediately start thinking about people they can reach and how they can get trained to start a new group."

Expand Penetration Evangelism

Relationship evangelism is a cornerstone to the expansion of cell groups (see Stage 6). Every growing cell church equips and encourages cell group members to reach out to their neighbors, family members, and co-workers. Without intentional relationship evangelism, cell members will not develop the compassion needed for expansion. But the churches that fully enter into expansion embrace penetration evangelism.

Dr. Ralph W. Neighbour Jr., has been arguing for group penetration for over 30 years. He discovered as he related to lost people that many would not come to the church or even to a cell group. The groups have to go to them. As he developed penetration methods, he discovered two types of nonbelievers. Type A nonbelievers are those who are open to the message of Christ and have a relationship with a believer. Type B nonbelievers have a relationship with a Christian and are open to this messenger, but are not yet open to hearing about the message. Different types of nonbelievers require different types of ministry.

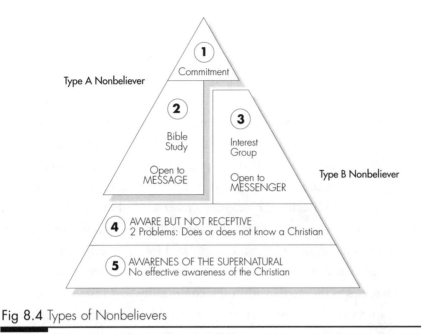

Fig 8.4 Types of Nonbelievers

Type A nonbelievers are ready to wrestle with the message of the Gospel; they only need friends who can discuss it with them. These people are often ready to visit a cell group. The use of a short-term seeker Bible study works well here (see *Introducing Jesus* by Pete Scazzero).[9] A one-on-one Bible study method is also effective (see *Handbook for Successful Living* by Ralph W. Neighbour, Jr.). Many churches are using Alpha effectively in conjunction with their cell group system.[10]

If a church wants to penetrate society, it must move into ministering to the Type B nonbelievers. These people range from Level 5—No Awareness of the Gospel, to Level 4—Aware but not receptive, to Level 3—Open to the messenger. There is a growing number of people who fall into these categories because they are having supernatural experiences in other religions and they have had less than supernatural exposure to the church. The job of the cell group members is to meet these people at a point of need and take them one step closer to Christ. This can happen in many ways.

Interest Groups. Cell group members can start groups with nonbelievers around shared interests like books, fishing, golfing, hiking, cooking, quilting, volleyball, or even Monday night football. The group gathers at least once per month and relates to each other in between the outings. The leader's goal is to see each group member take one step closer to Christ during a four-month period.[11] Celebration Church in New Orleans has adapted this concept to create Focus Groups. Every Family Cell is encouraged to start at least two Focus Groups that should meet weekly or biweekly. These groups meet around the normal routines of life to build relationships with unchurched individuals so that they can be won to Christ, discipled, and assimilated into a Family Cell.

Target Groups. These groups are very similar to Interest Groups, but they target specific needs within the community. For instance, a church can start an English class for internationals. Dr. Neighbour has started a free course for those who have lost their jobs to help them get back on their feet. A cell group member could start a support group for those who are HIV positive. The ideas are as endless as the needs.

Share Groups. Dr. Neighbour developed this strategy. He states, "Three or four mature members of a Shepherd (Cell) Group become the Body of Christ as a Share Group team is formed. As group members reach out, the group grows—numerically and spiritually. Unbelievers become interested in the Gospel, leading to in-depth Bible study to explain the plan of salvation to them at a later time."[12] *The Opening Hearts Trilogy* walks this team through a process of developing relationships with lost friends, starting a group, and then building further relationships with the networks of the group members.

Expand with Harvest Events

Harvesting involves a coordinated effort to reap the harvest God provides from among new and cultivated friends. At harvest events

Christians create a welcoming environment where nonbelievers can hear the message of the Gospel. Harvest events can be created on three levels: church-wide, for specific congregational networks, or for individual cell groups.

Church-wide harvest events include Christmas or Easter presentations, special dramas, and special speakers for crusades. These harvest events should be held at least annually. About four months before the harvest event, the church should emphasize evangelism training. Cell leader training should be held immediately before the event to prepare leaders for the groups created to enfold the people who receive the Lord at the event.

One church taught its members to ask the question, "So what did you think…?" following a church-wide harvest event. "What did you think about what pastor had to say Sunday morning?" or "What did you think about what you saw in the film Saturday night?" These individuals receive training to lead searching people through a conversation that allowed them to share their impressions and ask questions. Church members are prepared to lead people to Christ.

Congregational networks can develop harvest events like picnics, parties, game nights, etc. to invite their lost friends. The youth might hold a special concert that would target their school friends. Cell groups located close to one another might throw a block party to get to know their neighbors. Some churches have created regular men's, women's, and youth meetings that serve as places to invite the unchurched. For instance, a monthly women's network meeting on Saturday morning might prove an excellent front door for some nonbelievers.

Individual cell group harvest events might include birthday parties, barbeques, or watching the *Jesus Video*, an evangelism tool developed by Campus Crusade for Christ. One cell group decided to hold a yard sale where they could only sell good items. When a neighbor started to haggle on the price, a cell member would respond, "You can have it if you will let me share about the love of Jesus." Three families were added to the group through this event.

Practical Tips
for Conducting Harvest Events

- Conduct at least one significant church-wide harvest event per year.
- Conduct numerous cell-based harvest events per year.
- Plan your church's annual calendar around harvest events.
- Precede each harvest event with cultivation activities.
- Precede each harvest event with needed training events:
    - –personal evangelism training
    - –mentor training
    - –cell leader training
- Precede or follow harvest event with cell multiplications.
- Have New Believers material available to give those who receive Christ.

Expand with Assimilation

Research shows that newcomers to worship services will not remain unless they develop six significant relationships within six months. The church needs to develop a clear track for connecting visitors with a cell group. Such an assimilation system usually requires a "point person" to oversee the process, one that might look like this:

- Visitors fill out a card when they attend the service.
- The assimilation "point person" gathers the cards.
- This person makes copies of these cards and places the copy in the box of an appropriate cell group. He will seek to match the person with a group that is either close geographically or shares a point of interest.
- This person also provides a follow-up packet along with some kind of gift (some give fresh bread).

- The cell leader makes a short visit to the home of the visitor within 48 hours of the visit. The leader intentionally limits the visit to conversation at the door and invites the person(s) to the cell group.

After cell groups are established, the church should make it very easy for visitors to find a cell group. They should receive a packet that includes information on the benefits of participating in a cell group. Some hold a monthly newcomers lunch to share about the vision of the church and how the cell groups work. One idea that works very well is to create a board on a wall near the entrance to the church with pictures of all the cell group leaders. Beneath each picture should be some cards that visitors can take home that would include information about each cell group.

Expand the Number of Groups

As new people are added to groups, new groups must be launched. During the time of expansion, cell group leader training should be provided two or three times per year. Even if only three or four people are ready to take the training, training them will increase the leadership by three or four people. Through this training, the number of cell group interns/apprentices will increase as well as the number of new leaders.

Expand the Types of Groups

After the church gains experience in the practices of basic Christian community and people understand how to operate a UIOF group, cell group leaders can be more creative in the types of groups they start. Someone might start a college cell group. Women's cells that meet in the middle of the day are great for reaching stay-at-home mothers. Workplace cells are very powerful. Expansion of these kinds of groups requires creativity.

Other group types include groups of people that gather as teams within the church. For instance, the worship band might form a cell group. The four sections of the choir might form four different cell groups. Youth sponsors or children's workers might gather as a cell group. The key to making these groups work is not creativity, but recognition of values.

Colonial Hills Baptist Church in Southaven, Mississippi has expanded the types of groups by borrowing some of the concepts from the Free Market Cell Model. They allow leaders to gather groups around an interest like cooking, but they clearly state that every group, no matter how creative, must include the same components as a regular cell group. They define these components with the acronym HEALTH.

> **H**eart to serve others
> **E**arnest Prayer
> **A**ssociate with the lost
> **L**earning God's Word
> **T**ouching other's needs
> **H**arvest events

Therefore if someone starts a group that plays volleyball together, the group must also meet to minister to one another and reach out to the unchurched.

Long Reach Church of God in Maryland has adopted a slightly different approach. They have recognized three different kinds of groups. First is the basic cell group, and the goal is to get everyone into one of these groups. But not everyone is ready for such a group. Therefore they have common interest groups which focus on evangelism and ministry groups for those who minister together, i.e. the dance team or worship team.

Diversification of cell group types like this is not wise until the people have embraced the values that make cell groups work. The churches that have been able to diversify their types of groups like this did not do so until about five years after starting their first groups. Troy Palermo of Colonial Hills states that they had to develop the values in a more simple structure first before they could become creative. If the values of basic Christian community are not in place, these groups will become task teams, missing the key elements of edification and evangelism.

Expand with Ministries

As people experience life in cell groups, they will discover their gifts and callings. The creativity of the Holy Spirit will stir normal people to start unique ministries to reach out to hurting people. Faith Community Baptist Church developed TOUCH Community Services, which includes ministries like a day care center, which was open to the community. Such ministries are created to build bridges to the community to develop relationships with the unchurched.

Such ministries grow out of the values of cell group life. This allows them to grow organically, rather than programically. Door of Hope Church has seen cell members and leaders catch a vision for developing unique ministries. For instance, a single mother reached through the ministry of a cell group felt compelled to reach out to other single mothers. She started with one interest group. From there, she now oversees several groups and has started a non-profit organization to minister to the needs of single mothers.

The ideas for such ministries are endless. But the leadership of the church need not make these ministries happen. They only need to cultivate the cell group life, which allows the Holy Spirit to speak to people and then watch what He develops through those people.

Expand Trained Pastors

Future expansion of the church requires the development of future pastoral leaders. In order to be an effective pastor, a person must develop his or her values through the affective domain and skills through the psychomotor domain. This learning component is best developed through mentoring by an experienced staff pastor and through discussion groups.

At the same time, there are cognitive components that seminaries have addressed for years. Topics such as basic doctrine, an overview of Christian theology, surveys of the Old and New Testaments, Bible study methods, pastoral care, communication skills, etc., provide a needed foundation for effective pastoral ministry.

A model for such training marries classroom experience with expert teachers, a pastoral mentor, a specific ministry assignment, and small group discussions. The classroom element can be addressed many different ways, including video training, local seminaries, seminars, and distance education. A church does not need to develop mediocre courses when there is so much rich teaching available. The students should be matched with pastoral mentors who will show them how to minister. The mentor's aim is to multiply himself in the student. This is very different than a seminary internship program where students intern with a church during the last semester or year of their studies. This mentoring process begins as students enter the training.

Attached to the program should be a specific ministry responsibility. The basic element of this is leading a cell group, but he or she should also be involved in some kind of target ministry, like youth outreach, street ministry, children's outreach, etc.

The final element is that of small group discussions. This element is crucial to the learning experience. Most academic curriculum focuses on individual processing, but research reveals that learning best occurs when students are allowed to process topics with peers in a small group. On a weekly basis, students should gather to discuss what they are learning.

Expand New Congregations

As new pastors are developed, new congregations can be started. I am using "congregations" to refer to groupings within the church, usually of 50 cell groups or fewer. Congregations might include a men's network, a women's network, a youth network, a college network, a specific ethnic network, or a geographic network. As a volunteer leader grows as a cell group leader and coach, more and more cell groups will develop under him or her.

Expand with New Churches

Some have made the cell-based church synonymous with a mega-church, but this need not be the case. Many cell-based churches have a vision for starting new churches by transplanting a mature group of people with an equipped leader. While some church starts can begin with the solo approach long used in the church, a new church will produce fruit much more quickly when a larger group of 70-120 people are sent together to start the new church. Bill Beckham states: "The larger and healthier the church planting team, the stronger the new church will be and the sooner it will produce fruit."[13]

New Life Church in urban Chicago was not very large when it began cell groups in 1991. Since then the church has not only developed cell groups but also has planted six new churches and three other troubled churches have joined its network. The pastors of these churches work with Mark Jobe, the senior pastor of New Life, and they operate under the same vision and strategy.

Cypress Creek Church in rural Texas has a similar vision. Senior Pastor Rob Campbell works with pastors in surrounding counties who want to network with him. Since 1993, it has planted three churches in the church's home county and has planted one church in the UK, one church in Yugoslavia, and two churches in Zimbabwe.

Levers

Key Resource:
   —*Redefining Revival* by William A. Beckham

Identify and address cultural issues that are holding back the cell groups and preventing the church from expanding.

Begin to cast the vision of "every member a potential cell group leader."

Develop a strategy for penetration evangelism.
   Key Resource:
      —The *Opening Hearts Trilogy* by Ralph W. Neighbour, Jr.

Develop harvest events.

Develop the assimilation system.

Develop new congregations of cells.

Establish a training system to raise up new pastors.

Plant new churches.

Vision Team Questions

1. What is the difference between changing cultures and changing structures?
2. What does it mean to have a culture of expansion?
3. What are some old cultural anchors that are holding back the cell groups from entering expansion?
4. Prayerfully develop some creative ways to lead the groups into expansion.

CONCLUSION

In his book *Knowing God*, J.I. Packer compares two kinds of Christians: balconeers and travelers. Balconeers sit on balconies, watching travelers go by. They may chat with the travelers as they pass, criticize the way the travelers walk, or discuss where the path the travelers are taking might lead. The one thing they do not do is travel. Travelers, on the other hand, actually move down the path. They go beyond discussing and theorizing and become personally involved.

There are two types of churches in the world today: balconeer churches and traveler churches. Balconeer churches are trying to maintain their status as a "church." They practice the arts of self-preservation, self-sustenance, and self-promotion. These churches have found a comfortable place and are trying their best to protect themselves from anything that would disrupt their comfort. The people in these churches find themselves commenting on what they see God doing in other places, even critiquing what other churches are doing, but they would never attempt to become one of those churches they are discussing.

Traveler churches, on the other hand, are churches that are actually going somewhere. These churches listen to God not to maintain what they have but to find out what is next; they step outside comfortable boundaries and aim to transform their world for the sake of Christ. These churches have a vision to fulfill God's mission in the world.

The ultimate destination of your church is to know Christ by joining him in His mission. Your journey does not end when your church arrives at the port of expanding cell groups. In reality, the journey has only just begun. At that point, your church members are equipped to walk with God, showing His redeeming life to the powers and the principalities of this world. Cell groups are a means of entering into God's mission and participating with Him as He seeks to reconcile the world to Himself. Avery Willis and Henry Blackaby write, "It is His mission, not ours. But He has determined to accomplish His mission through His people. He is actively working to involve His people with all the peoples of the world so they may know Him and worship Him."[1]

Elton Trueblood, an early 20th century advocate for small group life in the church wrote, "The nature of the church is such that it must always be engaged in finding new ways to transcend itself."[2] Life in expanding cell groups will launch your church on new journeys with Him. The port of call becomes the starting point of your next journey. Watch and see the new ways in which your church will transcend itself.

NOTES

INTRODUCTION

[1] George Barna and Mark Hatch, *Boiling Point: Monitoring Cultural Shifts in the 21st Century* (Ventura, CA: Regal Books, 2001), 248.

[2] Christian Schwarz, *Natural Church Development* (Carol Stream, IL: ChurchSmart Resources, 1996), 33.

[3] George Gallup.

[4] George Barna and Mark Hatch, *Boiling Point: Monitoring Cultural Shifts in the 21st Century* (Ventura, CA: Regal Books, 2001), 228.

[5] Charles Colson, *Kingdoms in Conflict* (Grand Rapids, MI: Zondervan, 1987), n.p.

[6] J. I. Packer, "The Church in Christian Thought" (Department of Theology, Regent University, 1996, photocopy), 3.

[7] Howard Snyder, *The Problem of Wineskins Revisited* (Houston, TX: TOUCH Publications, 1996), 91.

[8] Deitrich Bonhoeffer, *Life Together* (New York: Harper & Row, 1954), 20.

[9] Jim Egli, *Alternative Models of Mennonite Pastoral Formation*, Occasional Papers vol. 15 (Elkhart, IN: Institute of Mennonite Studies, 1992), 43.

[10] Ralph W. Neighbour, Jr., *Where Do We Go From Here?* (Houston: TOUCH Publications, 1990), 36.

[11] Adapted from Michael Green, *Asian Tigers for Christ: The Dynamic Growth of the Church in South East Asia* (London: SPCK, 2001), 44-45.

[12] Peter M. Senge, *The Fifth Discipline* (New York: Doubleday, 1990), 63-64.

NAVIGATIONAL HAZARDS

[1] Ralph W. Neighbour, Jr., *Where Do We Go From Here?* (Houston, TX: TOUCH Publications, 1989), 92.

[2] Larry Stockstill, *The Cell Church* (Ventura, CA: Regal Publishing, 1998), 16.

[3] These eight hazards point toward eight stages in the transition to an effective and expanding cell group system. These eight stages have been developed through a series of interviews with North American pastors of churches who have been developing cell groups for more than three years.

STAGE 1

[1] Karen Hurston first recognized six different models: Cho, 5x5, G-12, Meta, Free Market, and Mixed. While my categories are similar, the approach taken here is slightly different. Although the Cho and 5x5 models are not synonymous, I have combined them into one category, called Cho/Neighbour. I have chosen this approach because most churches have equated the principles of Cho's teaching with that of Neighbour's teaching on the 5x5. In my analysis, I include four cell group models and two small group models.

[2] *Church Growth and The Home Cell System,* Revised (Seoul, Korea: Church Growth International, n.d.), 35.

[3] Randy Frazee, *The Connecting Church* (Grand Rapids: Zondervan, 2001), 99-100.

[4] Ibid, 98.

[5] Ted Haggard, *Dog Training, Fly Fishing, and Sharing Christ in the 21st Century: Empowering Your Church to Build Community through Shared Interests* (Nashville: Thomas Nelson), 28.

[6] Karen Hurston, "Six Group Models," appendix to lecture notes presented at a cell church conference, April 2002.

[7] Ibid., 65.

[8] Peter Senge, et. al., *The Fifth Discipline Fieldbook: Strategies and Tools for Building a Learning Organization* (New York: Currency Doubleday, 1994), 90.

[9] Peter Senge, *The Fifth Discipline: The Art & Practice of the Learning Organization* (New York: Currency Doubleday, 1990), 68.

[10] Christian Schwarz, *Natural Church Development* (Carol Stream, IL: ChurchSmart Resources, 1996), 32.

[11] Joel Comiskey, *Reap the Harvest* (Houston, TOUCH Publications, 1999), 51.

[12] Clinton Stockwell, "Cathedrals of Power: Engaging the Powers in Urban North America," in *Confident Witness—Changing World: Rediscovering the Gospel in North America,* ed. Craig Van Gelder (Grand Rapids: Eerdmans, 1999), 80.

[13] For a thorough understanding of the end of Christendom see Douglas John Hall, *The End of Christendom and the Future of Christianity* (Harrisburg, PA: Trinity Press, 1997).

[14] Stanley Hauerwas and William H. Willimon, *Resident Aliens* (Nashville: Abingdon, 1989), 22.

[15] Ibid., 17.

[16] R. Paul Stevens, *The Other Six Days: Vocation, Work, and Ministry in Biblical Perspective* (Grand Rapids: Eerdmans, 1999), 197.

[17] Brian McLaren, *The Church on the Other Side* (Grand Rapids, MI: Zondervan, 2000).

[18] Leonard Sweet, *SoulTsunami* (Grand Rapids, MI: Zondervan, 1999), 34.

[19] Douglas John Hall, *The End of Christendom and the Future of Christianity* (Harrisburg, PA: Trinity International Press, 1997), 7.

[20] David Bosch, *Transforming Mission: Paradigm Shifts in Theology of Mission* (Maryknoll, NY: Orbis, 1991), 390.

[21] Ibid., 390.

[22] Howard Snyder, *Liberating the Church: The Ecology of Church & Kingdom* (Downers Grove, IL: InterVarsity Press, 1983), 11.

[23] Ralph W. Neighbour Jr., *The Seven Last Words of the Church: "We Never Tried It That Way Before"* (Nashville, TN: Broadman, 1973).

[24] Brain D. McLaren, The Church on the Other Side (Grand Rapids: Zondervan, 2000), 25.

[25] Adapted from The Pricewaterhouse Change Team, *Better Change: Best Practices for Transforming Your Organization* (Chicago: Irwin Professional Publishing, 1995).

[26] Paul Heibert, *Anthropological Insights for Missionaries* (Grand Rapids, MI: Baker House, 1985), 30.

[27] Ralph W. Neighbour, Jr. is currently writing about on this subject entitled *Don't Ask a Fish What Water Is Like.*

[28] Elaine Dickson, *Say No, Say Yes to Change* (Nashville: Baptist Sunday School Board, 1982), 26.

[29] Joel Barker, *Tactics of Innovation*, prod. James Bright, 22 minutes, Star Thrower, 1998, videocassette.

[30] Kennon Callahan, *Effective Church Leadership* (San Francisco: Jossey-Bass, 1990), 66.

[31] Kent Hunter, *Move Your Church to Action* (Nashville, TN: Abingdon, 2000), n.p.

[32] Leonard Sweet, *AquaChurch* (Loveland, CO: Group Publishing,, 1999), 257.

[33] Ibid., 73.

STAGE 2

[1] Howard A. Snyder, *Radical Renewal: The Problem of Wineskins Today* (Houston: TOUCH Publications, 1996), 76.

[2] "An Interview with George Hunter," in *Next 2*, no. 2, p. e: in reference to *Church for the Unchurched* (Nashville: Abingdon, 1996), quoted in Brain McLaren, *The Church on the Other Side* (Grand Rapids, MI: Zondervan, 2000),113.

[3] George Barna, *The Power of Team Leadership* (Colorado Springs: Waterbook Press, 2001), 101-106

[4] This list was adapted from John Kotter, *Leading Change* (Boston: Harvard Business Press, 1996), 57.

[5] Everett M. Rogers, *Diffusion of Innovations*, 4th ed. (New York: Free Press, 1995), 398.

[6] Peter M. Senge, *The Fifth Discipline* (New York: Currency Doubleday, 1990), 247.

[7] Ibid., 241.

[8] Adapted from John Kotter, *Leading Change* (Boston: Harvard Business Press, 1996), 81.

[9] Jeannie Daniel Duck, *The Change Monster* (New York: Crown Business, 2001), 102.

[10] *Church Growth and The Home Cell System*, Revised (Seoul, Korea: Church Growth International, n.d.), 157.

[11] Bill Beckham, *The Second Reformation* (Houston, TX: TOUCH Publications, 1995), 142.

[12] Bill Beckham has developed another way of communicating the values of the cell group using an image of the hand:

The value priority [the palm] is Christ. The group meets around the presence of Christ. They do not meet around volleyball, book reading, hiking, or any other common interest. They do not meet around a task, an evangelism outreach, or leadership responsibilities. They meet around Christ. From Christ, we move to the thumb. All of the other fingers act in relationship with the thumb. Likewise, community life coordinates the other four priorities of equipping, accountability, leadership, and evangelism. The little finger represents equipping of baby Christians. Baby Christians need spiritual parents (coming in the form of cell group leaders and interns), and older brothers and sisters (coming in the form of cell group members), to show them how to live, to listen to their struggles, and to help them process what they are learning. The cell group provides this context. The ring finger is the place where married couples wear the symbol of commitment to one another; therefore this finger represents accountability. Cell group members need someone else from the group to be a close brother or sister who will take care of them. The middle finger is the largest finger, representing leadership. Just as Jesus led the disciples through small group experiences to discover life in the Kingdom of God, so must cell group leaders cut a path for the cell members to follow into life in basic Christian community. The forefinger represents evangelism because life in community points unbelievers to Christ.

[13] Jim Egli, *Upward, Inward, Outward, Forward* (Houston, TX: TOUCH Publications, 2000).

[14] There is some biblical merit to this as is argued in Gereth Icenogle, *Biblical Foundations for Small Group Ministry* (Downer's Grove, IL: InterVarsity Press, 1994).

[15] This is the approach of the pure Groups of 12 system that was developed by International Charismatic Mission in Bogota, Colombia.

STAGE 3

[1] Peter Senge, *The Fifth Discipline* (New York: Currency Doubleday, 1990), 155.

[2] David A. Nadler, Robert B. Shaw, and A. Elise Walton, *Discontinuous Change: Leading Organizational Transformation* (San Francisco: Jossey-Bass, 1995), 84.

[3] Larry Stockstill, "6 Powerful Reasons to Base Your Cells on Prayer," *CellChurch Magazine*, Fall 1994, 19.

[4] William A. Beckham, *Redefining Revival* (Houston: TOUCH Publications, 2000), 191.

[5] Bob Logan and Jeannette Buller, *Cell Church Planter's Guide* (Houston, TX: TOUCH Publications, 2001), 2-15:2-20.

[6] These conclusions were drawn from Robert Wuthnow's extensive research. He reported in 1994 that 40% of the population of the United States participates in some kind of faith-based small group and 29% of those involved in small groups are members of Sunday school classes. Wuthnow did conclude that Sunday school classes are more satisfying when they focus on more than discussing a lesson: "The activities that contribute significantly to both satisfaction and high composite evaluations in Sunday school classes are: singing together, eating together, doing things for the community, meditating, and speaking in tongues. This list suggests that Sunday school classes work better when they involve members in a wide range of activities, rather than simply meeting together to discuss the Bible or some other lesson" Robert Wuthnow, *Sharing the Journey* (New York: Free Press, 1994), 145.

7 Ken Hemphill, *Revitalizing the Sunday Morning Dinosaur: A Sunday School Growth Strategy for the 21st Century* (Nashville, TN: Broadman & Holman, 1996), 4

8 Carl George, *Prepare Your Church for the Future* (Grand Rapids, MI: Fleming H. Revell, 1992).

9 Bill Donahue and Russ Robinson, *Building a Church of Small Groups: A Place Where No One Stands Alone* (Grand Rapids, Zondervan, 2001), 77.

10 Ibid., 183.

11 John Kotter, *Leading Change* (Boston: Harvard Business Press, 1996), 40.

12 These categories of change are adapted from Everett M. Rogers, *Diffusion of Innovations*, 4th ed. (New York: Free Press, 1995).

STAGE 4

1 The concept of three types of change is developed in Dean Anderson and Linda Ackerman Anderson, *Beyond Change Management: Advanced Strategies for Today's Transformational Leaders* (San Fransisco, Jossey-Bass, 2001), 31-50.

2 For details on Bethany World Prayer Center's journey into cell group life, see Billy Hornsby, *The Cell-Driven Church: Bringing in the Harvest* (Mansfield, PA: Kingdom Publishing, 2000).

3 Dean Anderson and Linda Ackerman Anderson, *Beyond Change Management: Advanced Strategies for Today's Transformational Leaders* (San Fransisco, Jossey-Bass, 2001), 37.

4 Ibid., 39.

5 George Barna and Mark Hatch, *Boiling Point: Monitoring Cultural Shifts in the 21st Century* (Ventura, CA: Regal Books, 2001), 89.

6 Ibid., 91.

7 Jeannie Daniel Duck, *The Change Monster* (New York: Crown Business, 2001), 101-2.

8 Miraslov Volf, *Exclusion and Embrace: A Theological Exploration of Identity, Otherness, and Reconciliation* (Nashville, TN: Abingdon Press, 1996), 116.

9 Randy Frazee, *The Comeback Congregation: New Life for a Troubled Ministry* (Nashville: Abingdon, 1995), 38.

10 Ibid., 94.

11 Ibid., 97.

12 The presence of God as the key to the need for new containers is also illustrated in the history of Israel. Isaiah repeatedly refers to God as the Holy One of Israel, a unique title given only by Isaiah. He is not just the high and exalted one, separated from all creation, he is the one who is for his chosen people Israel. Walter Bruggeman makes this conclusion: "As a consequence of this articulation, the One who might dwell in splendid, guarded isolation is the One who is with Israel, and therefore is or can be mobilized to act on behalf of Israel in order to save and deliver." (Bruggeman, *Theology of the Old Testament* (Minneapolis, MN: Fortress Press, 1997), 289). The presence of God is the key to life in Israel. He is not just the Holy One, but the Holy One present in Israel. Again, Bruggeman, "Clearly, the withdrawal of the Holy One is an ominous possibility to Israel, for the life of Israel depends on that Presence." (Ibid., 288).

13 Robert Quinn, *Deep Change: Discovering the Leader Within* (San Fransisco: Jossey-Bass, 1996), 24.

14 Robert Coleman, *The Master Plan of Evangelism*, 30th Anniversary Edition (Grand Rapids, MI: Revel, 1993), 35.

[15] Neal Anderson and Charles Mylander, *Setting Your Church Free* (Ventura, CA: Regal Books, 1994).

[16] *Intercession as a Lifestyle* Video Series, Distributed by Marilyn Neubauer, P.O. Box 302, Vista California. (760) 730-1808.

[17] Visit <www.alphacourse.org> for more information.

[18] To order the Serendipity *Small Group Plus* Series, call 1-800-525-9563 or visit <www.serendipityhouse.com>.

[19] Carl George, *Prepare Your Church for the Future* (Grand Rapids, MI: Revel, 1992), 101.

[20] Randy Frazee, *The Comeback Congregation: New Life for a Troubled Ministry* (Nashville: Abingdon, 1995), 41.

[21] William Easum, *Leadership on the Other Side* (Nashville, TN: Abingdon, 2000), 35.

[22] Ibid.

[23] William Easum, *Dancing with Dinosaurs* (Nashville: Abingdon, 1993), 67

[24] Peter M. Senge, *The Fifth Discipline*, 4th ed. (New York: Currency Doubleday, 1990), 94.

[25] Jeannie Daniel Duck, *The Change Monster* (New York: Crown Business, 2001), 24.

[26] Rick Warren, *The Purpose-Driven Church* (Grand Rapids: Zondervan, ?), ?.

[27] Joel Comiskey, *Reap the Harvest* (Houston, TX: TOUCH Outreach, 1999), 62.

[28] Larry Stockstill, "6 Powerful Reasons to Base Your Cells on Prayer," *CellChurch Magazine*, Fall (1994): 19.

[29] David Yonggi Cho, "Praying Heaven Open," *CellChurch Magazine*, Fall (1994): 24.

STAGE 5

[1] Some churches do this because their church tradition does not allow women to lead a cell group; therefore women's groups are not an option.

[2] Robert Quinn, *Deep Change* (San Francisco: Jossey-Bass, 1996),148.

[3] *Advanced Cell Training* (Houston, TX: TOUCH Conferences, 1998).

[4] Dean Anderson and Linda Ackerman Anderson, *Beyond Change Management: Advanced Strategies for Today's Transformational Leaders* (San Fransisco, Jossey-Bass, 2001), 56.

[5] The goals are adapted from Laurence Singlehurst, *Loving the Lost: The Principles and Practice of Cell Church* (Eastbourne, England: Kingsway, 2001), 210-211.

STAGE 6

[1] John Kotter, *Leading Change* (Boston: Harvard Business School Press, 1996), 119.

[2] Ibid., 120.

[3] The Pricewaterhouse Change Team, *Better Change: Best Practices for Transforming Your Organization* (Chicago: Irwin Professional Publishing, 1995),17.

[4] Jim Egli, "Successful Small Groups: Critical Factors in Small Group Growth" (Ph. D. diss., Regent University, 2002), 93.

[5] Larry Crabb, *The Safest Place on Earth* (Nashville, TN: Word Publishing, 1999), 22.

[6] Ibid., 53-56

[7] David Watson, *I Believe in the Church* (Grand Rapids: Eerdmans, 1978), 248-250.

[8] Gene Getz, *Sharpening the Focus of the Church* (Chicago: Moody Press, 1974), 65-66.

[9] This information is taken from an unpublished manuscript by Cecilia Belvin.

[10] These include: C. Peter Wagner, *Churches that Pray* (Ventura, CA: Regal Books, 1993) and Elmer Towns, *Fasting for Spiritual Breakthrough* (Ventura, CA: Regal Books, 1996).

[11] Jim Cymbala, *Fresh Power* (Grand Rapids, MI: Zondervan, 1991), 14.

[12] George Gallup in Randy Frazee, *The Connecting Church* (Grand Rapids, MI: Zondervan, 2001), 24.

[13] Robert Wuthnow, *Sharing the Journey* (New York: Free Press, 1994), n.p.

[14] Randy Frazee, *The Connecting Church* (Grand Rapids, MI: Zondervan, 2001),193.

[15] Neil Cole, *Cultivating a Life for God* (Carol Stream, IL: ChurchSmart, 1999), 90.

[16] Jay Firebaugh, *The Key is the Coach* (Houston, TX: TOUCH Publications, 1999).

[17] George Hunter III, *Church for the Unchurched* (Nashville, TN: Abingdon, 1996),115.

[18] Howard Snyder, *Liberating the Church: The Ecology of Church and Kingdom* (Downer's Grove, IL; InterVarsity Press, 1983), 154.

[19] George Barna, *Evangelism that Works* (Ventura, CA: Regal Books, 1995), 90.

[20] Wayne McDill, *Making Friends for Christ* (Nashville: Broadman Press, 1979), 6.

[21] Rick Richardson, *Evangelism Outside the Box* (Downer's Grove, IL: Intervarsity Press, 2000), 100.

[22] Darrell Guder, *Missional Church* (Grand Rapids, MI: Eerdmans, 1998), 206.

[23] Ralph W. Neighbour, Jr., *Where Do We Go From Here?* (Houston, TX: TOUCH Publications, 1990), 332-333.

[24] Order toll-free from TOUCH Outreach Ministries 1-800-735-5865 or order online at <www.touchusa.org>.

[25] Cell Group Assessment available from Missions International at <www.missions.com>.

[26] Jim Egli, "Successful Small Groups: Critical Factors in Small Group Growth" (Ph. D. diss., Regent University, 2002), 92.

[27] Jay Firebaugh, *The Key is the Coach* (Houston, TX: TOUCH Publications, 1999), 9.

[28] Mike Shepherd, *A Small Group Coaching Strategy that is Working*, Small Group Network accessed on 5/8/02. <http://smallgroups.com>

[29] Len Woods, *Successful Coaching*, Small Group Network accessed on 5/8/02 <http://smallgroups.com>

STAGE 7

[1] Bill Beckham, *The Second Reformation* (Houston, TX: TOUCH Publications, 1995), 214.

[2] Paul Taffinder, *Big Change: A Route-map for Corporate Transformation* (Chichester, England: John Wiley & Sons, 1998), 71.

[3] Ibid., 70.

[4] Paul M. Zehr and Jim Egli, *Alternative Models of Mennonite Pastoral Formation* (Elkhart, IN: Institute of Mennonite Studies, 1992), 46.

[5] Robert Coleman, *The Master Plan of Evangelism* (Grand Rapids, MI: Fleming, H. Revell, 1993),109.

[6] Gordon Fee, *The First Epistle to the Corinthians* (Grand Rapids: Eerdmans, 1987), 185.

[7] Gary McIntosh, *Staff Your Church for Growth* (Grand Rapids, MI: Baker Books, 2000), 36.

[8] Bill Beckham, Redefining Revival (Houston, TX: TOUCH Publications, 2001), 110.

[9] E. Glenn Wagner, *Escape from the Church, Inc.* (Grand Rapids, MI: Zondervan, 1999),145.

[10] Adapted from Karen Hurston, "A Day in the Life of a Staff Pastor: A Study in Contrasts," <www.hurstonministries.org/art_c_of.htm>.

[11] These traits are adapted from Peter Wagner, *Leading Your Church to Grow* (Ventura, CA: Regal Books, date), 213-214.

[12] CellTrack available from TOUCH Outreach Ministries, 1-800-735-5865 or <www.touchusa.org>

[13] Daphne Kirk, *Heirs Together* (Suffolk, England: Kevin Mayhew, 1998), 23.

[14] Ibid., 43.

[15] Lorna Jenkins, *Feed My Lambs: A Handbook for Intergenerational Cell Groups* (Singapore: TOUCH Ministries International, 1995), 22.

[16] Adapted from Lorna Jenkins, *Shouting in the Temple: A Radical Look at Children's Ministry* (Singapore: TOUCH Ministries International, 1999), 98-108.

[17] Adapted from Lorna Jenkins, *Feed My Lambs* (Singapore: TOUCH Ministries International, 1995), 71.

[18] Daphne Kirk, *What Shall We Do With the Children?* (Suffolk, England, Kevin Mayhew, 2000), 156.

[19] For more information contact, Rod Baker at Victory Christian Center, 918-491-7845.

STAGE 8

[1] Jeannie Daniel Duck, *The Change Monster* (New York: Crown Business, 2001), 262.

[2] John Kotter, *Leading Change* (Boston: Harvard Business, 1996), 148.

[3] Ibid.,156.

[4] M. Scott Peck, *The Different Drum* (New York: Simon and Schuster, 1987), 300.

[5] Source unknown.

[6] Source unknown.

[7] Dietrich Bonhoeffer, *Letters and Papers from Prison* (New York: Macmillan, 1953), 203.

[8] Joel Comiskey, *Home Cell Group Explosion* (Houston: TOUCH Publications, 1997), 26.

[9] See Pete Scazzero, *Introducing Jesus* (Downers Grove, IL: InterVarsity Press, 1991).

[10] Go to <www.alpha.org> for more information on this excellent Type-A evangelism tool.

[11] Dr. Neighbour developed this idea in the mid-1990s. Senior Pastor Ted Haggard of the New Life Church has developed his own spin on this idea, which he calls Free-Market Cell Groups. These groups aim to lead nonbeliever one step closer to a commitment to Christ. The steps are based on the Engel Scale. The Christians are not participating in basic Christian community cell groups. Their focus is on evangelistic small groups. See Ted Haggard, *Dog Training, Fly Fishing and Sharing Christ in the 21st Century* (Nashville,TN: Oliver Nelson, 2002).

[12] Ralph W. Neighbour, Jr., *Where Do We Go From Here?: A Guidebook for the Cell Group Church*, revised edition (Houston, TX: TOUCH Publications, 2000), 294.

[13] William A. Beckham, *Redefining Revival* (Houston, TX: TOUCH Publications, 2000), 189.

CONCLUSION

[1] Avery Willis and Henry Blackaby, *On Mission with God: Living God's Purpose for His Glory* (Nashville, TN: Broadman & Holmann, 2002), 8.

[2] Elton Trueblood, *The Company of the Committed* (New York: Harper & Row, 1961), n.p.

INDEX

5x5 Structure, 20, 41, 46, 50-51, 62, 341-342, 344, 412

Administration, 114, 224, 314, 324, 332, 357, 359, 372
Alpha, 206, 250, 298, 397, 418
Anderson, Neal, 204, 416
Assessment, 28, 50, 148-149, 155, 170, 175-177, 180-181, 309-310, 321, 417
Assimilation, 62, 359, 400, 407

Barker, Joel, 90, 413
Barna, George, 14, 110, 178, 192-193, 290, 411, 413, 415, 417
Basic Christian Community, 10, 25, 58, 106, 116, 129-131, 133, 136, 138, 141, 163, 165, 289, 369, 376-378, 380-381, 389, 401, 403, 414, 418
Bethany World Prayer Center, 18, 40-41, 55, 97-98, 102, 150-151, 153, 190-191, 205-206, 228, 239, 352, 363, 415

Blackaby, Henry, 179, 203, 410, 418
Bonhoeffer, Deitrich, 15, 389, 411, 418
Bosch, David, 79-80, 413
Buller, Jeannette, 154-155, 180, 414

Callahan, Kennon, 94, 413
Cell Group Champion, 113-115, 125, 142-143, 261, 294, 366, 369
Cell Group Leaders, 2, 20, 44, 47-48, 52, 59, 88, 133, 137, 139-140, 191, 205, 238, 242-244, 246, 252-253, 255-257, 261, 267, 273-274, 278, 282, 288, 294-296, 298-299, 302, 304-305, 307, 312-317, 320, 329, 344, 348, 353, 360-361, 363, 367, 369, 384, 393, 395-396, 399, 401, 405, 407, 423
Cell Pastor, 2, 23, 33, 55, 121, 192, 270, 311, 318, 324, 341-342, 344, 350-354, 356-357, 372, 374
Change, 7, 22-23, 25, 30-31, 35, 38, 51, 53, 56, 63-64, 74, 83-93, 95-101, 103-104, 111-112, 116-

117, 124, 127, 131, 149, 151-
152, 168, 170-175, 177, 181,
185-189, 191-195, 197, 207,
210, 216-217, 220, 222-226,
228-229, 231, 238, 249-252,
258, 266, 268, 271, 290, 300,
308, 313, 326, 333, 361, 364,
378, 380-383, 385-386, 391,
413-418
Child Link, 367, 369
Children, 8, 16, 21, 34, 49, 52, 80, 134,
139, 153, 159, 173, 187, 220,
244-245, 283, 295, 301-302,
324, 329-331, 336, 340, 363-
372, 374, 385, 390, 394, 402,
404, 418
Cho, Yonggi, 17, 27, 46, 59, 112, 218,
229, 236, 312, 341, 347-348,
350-351, 412, 416
Christendom, 69-72, 75-76, 412-413
Church Health, 14, 57, 146, 176, 180-181
Church Health Assessment, 176, 180-181
Church on Mission, 73-75, 102
Church Planting, 154-155, 180, 206, 405,
414
Church Polity, 220-221, 223, 230-231
Cell Coach, 44, 51, 239, 261, 299, 316,
318, 321-322, 341-344, 350
Coaching, 2, 8, 34, 44, 51, 59, 94, 96, 124,
239, 242-243, 264, 298-299,
305, 311-319, 321-322, 329,
341-344, 350, 354, 405, 417
Coleman, Robert, 200, 335, 415, 417
Comiskey, Joel, 1, 48, 59, 102, 142, 227,
256, 299, 320-321, 344, 372,
394, 412, 416, 418, 423
Committee, 87, 109, 151, 215, 220, 223-
226, 230, 283, 379
Community, 8, 10, 12-13, 16-19, 24-25,
27-28, 40, 46, 50-51, 58-59, 67,
75, 81, 97, 106, 108-109, 113,
115-116, 123, 128-133, 135-
136, 138, 141, 147-149, 154,
163, 165, 178, 195, 202, 204,
238, 254, 264-265, 267, 269-
277, 279, 281, 283, 285-287,
289-291, 293, 297-298, 306,

314-315, 317, 322, 330, 347-
348, 352, 357-358, 369, 376-
378, 380-381, 389, 398, 401,
403, 412, 414, 418
Complacency, 171-173, 177
Corporate Gathering, 18, 20, 42, 56, 58-
60, 62-63, 88, 140, 154, 159,
196, 203, 329-330, 332, 365,
398
Crabb, Larry, 270-271, 273, 320, 416
Critical Mass, 8, 324-329, 331-335, 337,
352, 373, 383
Culture, 8, 68-69, 73, 83, 86-88, 102,
104, 146, 159, 172, 191, 194,
347, 376-385, 387-388, 408

Dialogue, 120-121, 125, 143, 170, 220,
262
Donahue, Bill, 51-52, 163, 415

Earley, Dave, 312, 315, 320-321, 423
Egli, Jim, 1, 11, 13, 115, 134, 207, 211,
250, 268, 293-294, 298, 309,
311, 317-318, 320, 334, 411,
414, 416-417
Elim Church, 17, 41, 128
Equipping, 44, 47-51, 53, 74, 94-95, 223,
254, 261, 296-305, 320, 322,
329, 356, 358-361, 393, 396,
414
Evangelism, 43, 45, 52, 93, 113, 124, 154,
160, 177, 200, 206, 254-255,
257, 277, 289-294, 302-303,
320, 322, 329-330, 333, 335,
361, 367, 370, 376, 393, 395-
396, 399-400, 402-403, 407,
414-415, 417-418

Faith Community Baptist Church
(FCBC), 17, 40, 59, 97, 128,
352, 357, 403
Forward, 23, 34, 36, 122, 134-137, 148,
169, 171, 202-204, 207, 219,
234, 250, 252, 257, 259, 264,
270-271, 275-276, 278, 283, 294,
303, 307, 309, 320, 326-328,
333, 362, 384, 386, 414, 423

Frazee, Randy, 1, 50, 194, 215-216, 286, 320, 412, 415-417
Free Market Model, 42

Galloway, Dale, 27, 65, 236
Gallup, George, 14, 411, 417
George, Carl, 42, 52, 162, 208, 354, 415-416
Group Multiplication, 14, 50, 58, 132, 136, 138, 140, 265, 306-307, 325, 378
Groups of Twelve (G-12), 20, 41, 47-49, 62, 64, 342, 344, 412

Haggard, Ted, 52-53, 412, 418
Harvest Events, 399-400
Hauerwas, Stanley, 71, 412
Heterogeneous, 138, 244-245, 268
Homogeneous, 46, 138, 245, 363, 370
House Church, 163-164, 313
Hunter, George III, 108, 289, 413, 417
Hunter, Kent, 95, 413
Hurston, Karen, 1, 11, 41, 47, 49, 350-351, 353-354, 412, 417

Intergenerational Cell Group, 50, 138, 244-245, 268, 363, 365, 367-369, 418
International Charismatic Mission (ICM), 17, 40-41, 48, 55, 97, 228, 259, 414
Inward, 45, 99, 134-137, 202-203, 207, 234, 250, 252, 257, 275-277, 294, 320, 322, 328, 333, 362, 414, 423

Kid's Slot, 365, 367-369
Kotter, John, 25, 103, 122, 266, 380, 413, 415-416, 418
Kreider, Larry, 2, 336, 372

Life Transformation Groups, 288
Logan, Bob, 154, 180, 414

Mentoring, 31, 33, 44, 47, 56, 61-62, 75, 95, 137, 201, 208, 210, 221,

241, 243, 258, 278, 287-288, 298-299, 303-305, 322, 324, 351-352, 357-358, 369, 372, 385, 395-396, 404, 423
Meta-church, 41-42, 51-52, 55, 412
Mission, 16-17, 25, 35, 40-41, 48, 55, 57, 73-76, 78-81, 92-94, 97, 102, 104, 108, 117, 121-123, 128, 130, 135, 157, 169-170, 172, 195, 228, 259, 304, 378-379, 389-390, 392, 394, 410, 413-414, 418
Mylander, Charles, 204, 416

Neighbour, Ralph Jr., 10, 16-17, 27-28, 41, 45-47, 51, 55, 83, 96, 102, 140, 142, 185, 203, 218, 246, 288, 290, 293, 298, 301, 303, 320, 341, 357, 376, 393, 396-398, 407, 411-413, 417-418
Neighbour, Randall, 282
Network, 76-77, 154, 185, 245, 324, 345, 363, 399, 405-406, 417
New Life Church, 42, 405, 418

Outward, 45, 89, 134-137, 202-203, 207, 234, 250, 252, 257, 275-277, 294, 320, 322, 328, 333, 362, 414, 423

Packer, J.I., 15, 409, 411
Pantego Bible Church, 1, 18, 42, 123, 194, 363
Prayer, 15, 18, 40-41, 52, 55, 97-98, 102, 112, 128, 136-137, 141, 150-154, 157, 179, 187, 190, 193, 202-206, 208, 214, 219, 227-231, 237, 239, 246, 249-251, 253-254, 260, 276-278, 284-285, 291-292, 299, 312-313, 320, 322, 330, 333-334, 337, 347, 350-352, 363, 367-368, 381, 387, 402, 414-416, 423
Prototype, 13, 98, 154, 235, 243, 251-258, 261

Relational Evangelism, 113, 255, 257, 277, 289-292, 302, 320, 322, 329, 376, 393, 396
Repentance, 32, 92, 184, 193, 196-197, 199, 201, 204, 206, 215, 231, 273, 275
Robinson, Russ, 51-52, 163, 415

Saddleback Church, 42, 294
Schwarz, Christian, 14, 57, 176, 180, 411-412
Senior Pastor, 13, 29-30, 34, 39-40, 43, 46, 62-63, 91-93, 95, 106, 110-116, 122, 142-143, 162, 167, 191, 203, 210, 217, 220-225, 227, 230-231, 241, 254-255, 284, 287, 290, 311, 317, 324, 344, 350, 352, 357-359, 365-366, 384, 405-406, 418
Snyder, Howard, 15, 81, 107, 289, 411, 413, 417
Staff Pastor, 48, 162, 221, 341, 344, 350-352, 356, 358, 374, 384, 404, 417
Sub-system, 62
Sweet, Leonard, 77, 98-99, 412-413

TOUCH Outreach Ministries, 1, 5-6, 11, 13-14, 16, 20-22, 25, 28, 42, 60, 63, 75, 87, 103, 139, 149, 153-154, 159, 191, 210, 285, 289, 292, 303, 346, 356, 371, 379, 403, 411-414, 416-418
Transformational Change, 2, 5, 8, 24, 32, 38, 68, 183-187, 189-193, 195-199, 201, 205-206, 215-216, 218, 231, 288, 414, 417
Transition, 1, 29, 32, 78, 96, 117, 185-186, 188, 190, 198, 250, 258, 361, 370, 412
Transitional Change, 187-188, 197, 231
Trueblood, Elton, 410, 418

Upward, 134-136, 202-203, 207, 234, 250, 252, 257, 275-276, 294, 320, 322, 328, 333, 362, 414, 423

Urgency, 7, 40, 124, 146, 167-171, 173-181, 327, 333

Victory Christian Center, 18, 41, 49, 59, 98, 151, 287, 345, 370, 418
Vision, 1, 6-7, 13-16, 21-22, 24, 27, 29-35, 37, 39, 46, 49-50, 59, 61-65, 73, 76-77, 80, 84, 87-88, 90-91, 93-96, 102-107, 109-117, 119-125, 127-129, 138-140, 142-143, 146, 148-149, 151-155, 161-162, 165, 168-171, 173-175, 179, 184, 190-191, 193, 199, 202-207, 210-211, 213-216, 218-221, 223-227, 230-231, 234, 237, 240-242, 244-246, 252, 255-256, 259-260, 262, 265-269, 276, 283, 290-291, 294, 306-307, 309, 311, 313, 315, 317-319, 322, 324, 326-329, 333, 339, 343-348, 350, 357, 359-362, 364-366, 369, 373-374, 377, 384-386, 388, 395-396, 401, 403, 405-408, 410
Vision Team, 7, 104, 106-107, 109-113, 115, 117, 119, 121-123, 125, 127-129, 138, 140, 142-143, 155, 184, 199, 210-211, 221, 225-226, 231, 234, 246, 260, 262, 307, 309, 311, 322, 373, 388, 408

Wagner, Peter, 94, 416-417
Willis, Avery, 410, 418
Willow Creek, 42, 51, 55, 163
Wong, Ben, 59, 287
Works and Mission Baptist Church, 17, 40

Yoido Full Gospel Church (YFGC), 17, 27, 41, 45, 55, 97, 128, 228-229, 347, 350-353
Youth, 21, 34, 46, 68, 88, 162, 214, 220-221, 245, 251, 259-261, 329, 340, 364-365, 394, 399, 402, 404-405

CELL GROUP RESOURCES

MAKING CELL GROUPS WORK: NAVIGATION GUIDE:

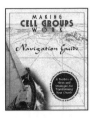

by M.Scott Boren,Bill Beckham, Joel Comiskey, Ralph W. Neighbour, Jr., and Randall G. Neighbour

These five authors have trained pastors for years. Now in this Navigation Guide, pastors will have the wisdom of these five cell group church experts, along with others, at their fingertips. Following the eight-stage pattern found in *Making Cell Groups Work*, this guide compiles evaluational instruments, instructional chapters, planning sheets, sample forms, process charts, and other practical tools. This comprehensive toolbox is full of ideas and strategies that will show you how to put cell groups into action.

CELL GROUP LEADER TRAINING:

Leadership Foundations for Groups that Work,

by Scott Boren and Don Tillman

The Trainer's Guide and Participant's Manual parallel the teaching of Comiskey's *How to Lead a Great Cell Group Meeting*. This eight-session training will prepare people for cell group leadership like no other tool. The Trainer's Guide provides teaching outlines for all eight sessions and options for organizing the training, including different weekly options and retreat options. The Trainer's Guide also has bonus sections, including teaching outlines for the *Upward, Inward, Outward, Forward* Seminar and detailed interview discussion guides for *The Journey Guide for Cell Group Leaders.*

HOW TO LEAD A GREAT CELL GROUP MEETING

by Joel Comiskey

Joel Comiskey takes you beyond theory and into the "practical tips of the trade" that will make your cell group gathering vibrant! This hands-on guide covers all you need to know, from basic how-to's of getting the conversation started to practical strategies for dynamic ministry times. If you're looking to find out what really makes a cell group meeting great…this book has the answers! 144 pgs.

8 HABITS OF EFFECTIVE SMALL GROUP LEADERS,

by Dave Earley

Are your cell leaders truly effective in changing lives? They can be! After years of leading and overseeing growing small groups, Pastor Dave Earley has identified 8 core habits of effective leaders. When adopted, these habits will transform your leadership too. The habits include: Dreaming • Prayer • Invitations • Contact Preparation • Mentoring • Fellowship • Growth. When your leaders adopt and practice these habits, your groups will move from once-a-week meetings to an exciting lifestyle of ministry to one another and the lost! 144 pgs.

Make Cell Groups Work Online!

Our website was designed for pastors just like you!

Free articles from
CellChurch Magazine &
CellGroup Journal.

Fast and secure online
resource purchases.

Watch a streaming video on
the cell movement.

Discover other churches
with cell groups in your area
or denomination.

Post your resume or search
for a new staff member in
our cell-based classifieds
area.

Free downloads of leader's
guides, presentations, and
software to track cell
growth.

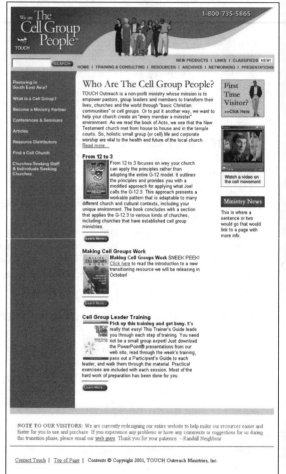

What are you waiting for?

Grab a cup of coffee and visit us now...

www.cellgrouppeople.com